MICROSOFT®

WORD 6.0
for WINDOWS™
by PICTORIAL

PicTorial Series

Dennis P. Curtin, Series Editor

Microsoft® Word 6.0 for Windows™ by PicTorial
WordPerfect® 6.0 for Windows™ by PicTorial
Microsoft® Excel 5.0 by PicTorial
Microsoft Access® 2.0 by PicTorial
Windows™ 3.1 by PicTorial
Essentials of Windows™ 3.1 by PicTorial

MICROSOFT®

WORD 6.0
for WINDOWS™
by PICTORIAL

Dennis P. Curtin

Donna M. Matherly
Tallahassee Community College

Prentice Hall
Englewood Cliffs, New Jersey 07632

Library of Congress Cataloging-in-Publication Data

Curtin, Dennis P.
    Microsoft Word 6.0 for Windows by PicTorial / Dennis P. Curtin,
Donna M. Matherly.
        p.   cm.
    Includes index.
    ISBN 0-13-121898-0
    1. Microsoft Word for Windows. 2. Word processing. I. Matherly,
Donna M. S. (Donna May Schopmeyer). II. Title.
Z52.5.M523C87 1995
652.5'536—dc20

94-44232
CIP

Microsoft is a registered trademark,
and Windows and Wingdings are trademarks, of Microsoft Corporation.

Acquisitions editor: Carolyn Henderson
Development editor: Cecil Yarbrough
Marketing manager: Nancy Evans
Director of production and manufacturing: Joanne Jay
Managing editor: Joyce Turner
Production services manager: Lorraine Patsco
Electronic composition: Christy Mahon and John A. Nestor
Illustrations: Warren Fischbach and Freddy Flake
Screen shots: Cathleen Morin
Design director: Linda Fiordilino
Cover art: © David Bishop/Phototake NYC
Manufacturing buyer: Paul Smolenski
Editorial assistant: Jane Avery
Production assistant: Renée Pelletier

© 1995 by Prentice-Hall, Inc.
A Division of Simon & Schuster
Englewood Cliffs, NJ 07632

ISBN 0-13-121898-0

Prentice-Hall International (UK) Limited, *London*
Prentice-Hall of Australia Pty. Limited, *Sydney*
Prentice-Hall of Canada Inc., *Toronto*
Prentice-Hall Hispanoamericana, S.A., *Mexico*
Prentice-Hall of India Private Limited, *New Delhi*
Prentice-Hall of Japan, Inc., *Tokyo*
Simon & Schuster Asia Ptd. Ltd., *Singapore*
Editora Prentice-Hall do Brasil, Ltda., *Rio de Janeiro*

CONTENTS

PicTorial 1

Jump-Starting Word   **1**

    1-1. Starting Word for Windows   2
    1-2. Exploring the Word Application Window   3
    1-3. Opening and Closing Documents   6
    1-4. Entering a Document   11
    1-5. Saving a Document   12
    1-6. Getting Around a Document with the Mouse   15
    1-7. Getting Around a Document with the Keyboard   18
    1-8. Editing a Document   19
    1-9. Exploring the Toolbar   22
    1-10. Using On-Line Help   26
    1-11. Exiting Word   29
    Review Questions   **30**
    Lab Activities   **32**
    Computer-Based Tutorials   32
    Skill-Building Exercises   33
        1-1. Loading Word on Your Own System   33
        1-2. Describing the Anatomy of the Word for Windows Display   34
        1-3. Exploring Word's Dialog Boxes   34
        1-4. Getting Around a Document with a Mouse   35
        1-5. Getting Around a Document with the Keyboard   36
        1-6. Using On-Line Help   37
        1-7. Exploring the Standard Toolbar   37
        1-8. Exploring the Formatting Toolbar   38
        1-9. Opening and Closing Documents   38
        1-10. Saving and Opening Documents on Your Own System   39
        1-11. Entering Text and Saving Documents   39

PicTorial 2

Mastering the Essentials   **41**

    2-1. Entering Text   41
    2-2. Editing Text   45
    2-3. Checking Spelling   50
    2-4. Previewing and Printing Documents   52
    2-5. Selecting Text   55
    2-6. Copying and Moving Text with the Clipboard   59
    2-7. Copying and Moving Text by Dragging and Dropping It   64
    2-8. Finding Text   67
    2-9. Replacing Text   69
    2-10. Looking Up Synonyms and Antonyms in the Thesaurus   70
    Review Questions   **72**
    Lab Activities   **75**
    Computer-Based Tutorials   75
    QuickStep Drills   76
        2-1. Entering Text   76
        2-2. Editing Text   77
        2-3. Checking Spelling   78
        2-4. Previewing and Printing Documents   78
        2-5. Selecting Text   78
        2-6. Copying and Moving Text with the Clipboard   79
        2-7. Copying and Moving Text by Dragging and Dropping It   80
        2-8. Finding Text   80

2-9A. Replacing Text 80
2-9B. Replacing Text 81
2-10. Looking Up Synonyms and Antonyms in the Thesaurus 81
Skill-Building Exercises 82
2-1. Entering and Editing a Memo on Training 82
2-2. Entering and Editing a Memo on Punctuation Marks 82
2-3. Entering and Editing a Business Letter on Training 84
2-4. Entering and Editing an Announcement 85
2-5. Writing and Editing a Personal Letter Home for Money 87
2-6. Editing and Printing the Job-Guide Document 88
2-7. Editing the Careers Document 89
2-8. Editing the Rights Document 90
2-9. Editing the Desktop Publishing Document 90
Real-World Projects 91
2-1. The Job-Search Kit—The Cover Letter 91
2-2. The Job-Search Kit—The Followup Letter 92

PicTorial 3
Basic Formatting

.... 95

3-1. Types of Formats 95
3-2. Changing Fonts, Font Styles, and Font Sizes 101
3-3. Aligning Text 106
3-4. Changing Line and Paragraph Spacing 107
3-5. Controlling Page Breaks 111
3-6. Using and Setting Tab Stops 114
3-7. Indenting Paragraphs 119
3-8. Automatically Numbering and Bulleting Lists 123
Review Questions **125**
Lab Activities **127**
Computer-Based Tutorials 127
QuickStep Drills 128
3-1. Types of Formats 128
3-2A. Changing Font Faces, Styles, and Sizes 129
3-2B. Changing Font Faces, Styles, and Sizes 129
3-2C. Changing Font Faces, Styles, and Sizes 130
3-2D. Changing Font Faces, Styles, and Sizes 130
3-2E. Changing Font Faces, Styles, and Sizes 130
3-2F. Changing the Font for the Entire Document 131
3-3. Aligning Text 131
3-4. Changing Line and Paragraph Spacing 131
3-5. Controlling Page Breaks 132
3-6. Using and Setting Tab Stops 132
3-7. Indenting Paragraphs 133
3-8A. Automatically Numbering and Bulleting Lists 133
3-8B. Automatically Numbering and Bulleting Lists 134
Skill-Building Exercises 134
3-1. Formatting a Description of Memo Formats 134
3-2. Formatting a Description of Block-Style Letter Formats 13
3-3. Formatting the Job-Guide Document 135
3-4. Formatting the Careers Document 136
3-5. Formatting the Bill of Rights Document 138
3-6. Formatting the Newsletter Document 138
3-7. Formatting the Desktop Publishing Document 139
3-8. Formatting the Menu from Alyce's Restaurant 140
Real-World Projects 141
3-1. The Research Paper 141
3-2. The Flier's Rights Booklet 143

PicTorial 4
Advanced Formatting

	145
4-1. Formatting from the Ruler	145
4-2. Copying Formats	151
4-3. Finding and Replacing Formats	153
4-4. Adding Headers and Footers	155
4-5. Adding and Removing Page Numbers	158
4-6. Entering Footnotes and Endnotes	161
4-7. Changing Page Setup	165
4-8. Entering Section Breaks	168
4-9. Sorting Documents	173
Review Questions	**176**
Lab Activities	**178**
Computer-Based Tutorials	178
QuickStep Drills	179
4.1. Formatting from the Ruler	179
4-2. Copying Formats	179
4-3. Finding and Replacing Formats	180
4-4. Adding Headers and Footers	181
4-5. Adding and Removing Page Numbers	181
4-6. Entering Footnotes and Endnotes	182
4-7A. Changing Page Setup	182
4-7B. Changing Margins	183
4-8. Entering Section Breaks	183
4-9. Sorting Documents	184
Skill-Building Exercises	184
4-1. Formatting the Job-Guide Document	184
4-2. Formatting the Careers Document	185
4-3. Formatting the Bill of Rights Document	186
4-4. Formatting the Newsletter Document	186
4-5. Formatting the Desktop Publishing Document	186
Real-World Projects	187
4-1. The Research Paper—Continued	187
4-2. The Flier's Rights Booklet—Continued	188

PicTorial 5
Automating Procedures

	189
5-1. Introduction to Mail Merge	189
5-2. Mail-Merging Form Letters	196
5-3. Mail-Merging Labels	203
5-4. Selecting Specific Records to Merge	205
5-5. Automating with Macros	208
5-6. Using AutoText	212
5-7. Using AutoCorrect	213
Review Questions	**215**
Lab Activities	**217**
Computer-Based Tutorials	217
QuickStep Drills	218
5-1. Introduction to Mail Merge	218
5-2A. Mail-Merging Form Letters	218
5-2B. Using Operator Input	219
5-3. Mail-Merging Labels	220
5-4. Selecting Specific Records to Merge	221
5-5. Automating with Macros	221
5-6. Using AutoText	222
5-7. Using AutoCorrect	222
Skill-Building Exercises	223
5-1. Merge-Printing a Form Letter to Computer Companies	223

5-2. Merge-Printing Mailing Labels to Computer Companies 224
5-3. Keyboarding Data into the Letter to Computer Companies 225
5-4. Creating Macros to Enter Fractions 226
Real-World Projects 226
5-1. Mail-Merging the Cover Letter 226

PicTorial 6
Desktop Publishing 227

6-1. Adding Paragraph Borders and Shading 227
6-2. Generating a Table of Contents 230
6-3. Formatting in Columns 233
6-4. Inserting Pictures 236
6-5. Creating Tables 239
6-6. Formatting and Editing Tables 241
Review Questions **246**
Lab Activities **248**
Computer-Based Tutorials 248
QuickStep Drills 249
6-1. Adding Borders Around Paragraphs 249
6-2. Generating a Table of Contents 249
6-3. Formatting in Columns 250
6-4. Inserting Pictures 250
6-5. Creating Tables 251
6-6. Editing and Formatting Tables 251
Skill-Building Exercises 251
6-1. Formatting the Job-Guide Document 251
6-2. Formatting the Bill of Rights 252
6-3. Formatting the Newsletter Document 252
6-4. Adding Tables to the Sexism Guidelines Document 253
Real-World Projects 254
6-1. Desktop-Publishing a Booklet 254

Index 255

Appendix
Introducing Windows 3.1 A-1

A-1. Loading Windows A-2
A-2. Exploring the Windows Screen A-4
A-3. Exploring Program Manager A-6
A-4. Exploring Your Mouse A-6
A-5. Clicking, Double-Clicking, and Dragging A-8
A-6. Minimizing, Maximizing, and Restoring Windows A-10
A-7. Using Control Menus A-12
A-8. Exiting Windows A-14

PREFACE

This text is an introduction to Microsoft Word 6.0 for Windows, one of the leading word processing programs. Word processing is probably the most common application of computers. The ease with which you can draft and revise memos, letters, reports, and other documents with a word processing program like Word increases both the speed and quality of your writing. You can enter, edit, change, reorganize, format, and print text without having to retype all of it each time you make a change. This ease of use encourages you to revise and reorganize your material more frequently so that you can express your ideas more clearly and prepare more professional-looking documents.

The applications of programs such as Word are almost endless, ranging from the same tasks that can be done on a typewriter, such as writing memos, letters, and reports, to entirely new kinds of tasks that aren't possible without the power of the computer. For example, you can prepare a form letter that you can then use over and over again, with just a name or phrase changed here and there. Contracts, sales letters, and collection notices are typical form documents. You can even desktop-publish documents because Word can change fonts, print in columns, and print graphics along with text. These features open up a new world of opportunities since you can now inexpensively desktop-publish catalogs, advertising circulars, reports, articles, and even books.

This text assumes only limited prior computing experience. Everything you need to know to become a proficient Word for Windows user is presented here. You needn't bring anything else to your learning experience except a willingness to explore a new and exciting way to compute.

CONTENT AND APPROACH

Many people are intimidated by application programs because they seem so complicated. Despite any preconceptions you might have, application programs are easy to learn and use. What makes them seem complicated is the vast number of things they can do. For example, Word for Windows can automatically generate a table of contents for a long report or can automate many of the procedures that you use repeatedly. However, you don't start learning Word with these kinds of applications. You start by using it to write memos or letters—and this part is easy. One way to look at learning any application program is to divide its features into four levels: core procedures, performance-enhancing procedures, productivity-enhancing procedures, and task-specific procedures. To learn a new program, you normally master each level before moving on to the next. In this respect it is much like climbing the stairs one step at a time. It is around this step-by-step approach that this text is structured.

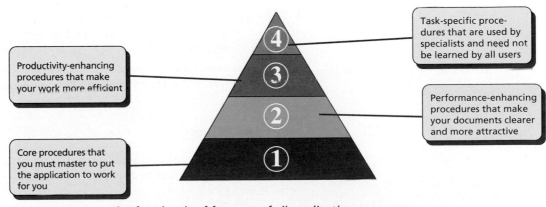

The four levels of features of all application programs

Core procedures are those procedures that you absolutely need to master to make an application useful. These core procedures include opening and saving files, getting around the program, entering and editing data, and making printouts. To master this level of procedures in a program takes a few days at most.

Performance-enhancing features are those that allow you to prepare more sophisticated documents. For example, you can use a variety of fonts, add illustrations, or put text in shaded boxes.

Productivity-enhancing features are those features that speed up your work and make you more efficient. For example, you can customize the application so it works better for you or automate tasks that you perform frequently. You can also use a procedure called Mail Merge to automatically print hundreds or even thousands of letters or labels, with each being customized with its own information.

Task-specific procedures are those that you learn only as the need arises. For example, Word has features especially designed for use with languages other than English and for people who prepare papers or reports by extracting data from other programs. Almost no one today knows how to use all of these features of their programs. Some have limited value for most users and are aimed at small segments of the overall user group. These types of procedures are beyond the scope of this text.

■ ORGANIZATION AND COMPUTER ACTIVITIES

This text is organized into pictorial tutorials called *PicTorials*. Each PicTorial begins with objectives and then proceeds step by step through a series of related procedures. The concept behind each procedure is first discussed, and then a *tutorial* guides you in exploring the concept on the computer. At the end of each PicTorial are review questions and a large number of lab exercises that you complete at the computer.

Many textbooks use a projects approach, having you work on a limited set of documents as you progress through the text. The problem with this approach is its limitations. How many procedures are required for even a complex document, and how many times need they be repeated? Without practicing procedures, and doing so repeatedly, you don't master them. This text uses a more structured approach that incorporates the following classes of documents:

▶ *Tutorial Documents* are used in the tutorials in the text. In many cases these are typical business-type documents such as memos and letters. In other cases they are documents designed to specifically illustrate a point that is being discussed.

▶ *Procedure Mastery Documents*, used in the QuickStep Drills, are designed to reinforce a single procedure though repetitive use. This narrow focus and use of repetition makes you much more familiar with a procedure than a typical document where you might use a number of procedures but use each only once.

▶ *Skill-Building Exercise Documents* require more than a single procedure for completion. Many are threaded through the text from the beginning to the end so as you master new procedures, you revise and refine these documents.

▶ *Project Documents* are like Exercise Documents but are more complex so they require a more thorough understanding of how procedures interact with each other.

■ KEY FEATURES

Windows is a visually oriented program, so this text uses a visual approach. It features PicTorials in addition to a number of other features designed to make it a better learning tool.

▸ *PicTorials* are heavily illustrated tutorials. The visuals serve two purposes. First, they help explain concepts. Second, they tell you when you are on course as you follow the steps in the tutorials.

▸ *QuickSteps boxes* summarize the steps you use for each procedure. These highlighted boxes are easy to find in each concepts section and make the text an ideal reference manual as well as a teaching tool.

▸ *Pausing for Practice boxes* appear periodically in tutorials when essential procedures have been introduced. They encourage you to stop at key points and practice these procedures until they become second nature.

▸ *Common Wrong Turns boxes* alert you to where many people make mistakes and show you how to avoid them.

▸ *Tips boxes* point out shortcuts and other interesting features about many procedures.

▸ *Looking Back boxes* are used whenever a procedure that has been discussed earlier is essential to completing a new task. These summaries are intended to remind you how to perform a task without your having to refer back in the text for the information.

▸ *Looking Ahead boxes* are used whenever a procedure is unavoidably referred to before it has been discussed in detail. Although this text has been written to make that situation occur infrequently, these boxes should help you avoid confusion by providing a brief description and an assurance that a more detailed discussion will follow.

▸ At the end of each PicTorial you will find a wide variety of true-false, multiple choice, and fill-in-the-blank questions to test how well you have understood the material.

▸ Exercises and Projects at the end of the PicTorials give you the opportunity to practice the procedures you have learned in that chapter and demonstrate that you have mastered them.

▸ The documents used for lab activities are real-world applications. For example, at various times you work on memos, letters, research papers, and résumés. You also work on articles, papers, and reports discussing such topics as careers in the computer field, your rights to the software you use, and desktop publishing. The depth and variety of these documents is one of the major strengths of this text.

▸ An appendix, "Introducing Windows 3.1," explains important Windows procedures for students who are new to the Windows environment.

■ SUPPLEMENTS

A *Word Student Resource Disk* and a *Word Instructor's Manual with Tests*, the latter prepared by this book's co-author, Donna M. Matherly of Tallahassee Community College, are available. The manual contains suggested course outlines for a variety of course lengths and formats, teaching tips and a list of competencies to be attained for each PicTorial, solutions and answers to quizzes and all computer activities, and a complete test bank of over 200 questions.

■ NOTE TO INSTRUCTORS

Most of the lab activities in this text have a step telling the student to print the document. In most cases, these printouts are for your use, not theirs. To reduce paper consumption in your classroom, tell your students to ignore all printing steps unless you ask them specifically to make them or when they have a problem they want to show you.

■ NOTE ON THE STUDENT RESOURCE DISK

The *Word Student Resource Disk* is provided to instructors for dissemination to their classes in whatever form best suits their laboratory needs. The disk includes all the documents needed to complete the lab activities in this text. The text assumes that each student will have the documents, which are intended to be copied onto two high-density floppy disks in order to leave room for students to do their own work. Files used in the tutorials and drills are placed on the *Word Student Resource Disk (Part 1)*, while those used in exercises and projects are placed on the *Word Student Resource Disk (Part 2)*.

To make the documents easy to use as class exercises to be turned in, most of them include a placeholder for the student's name and have the date entered as a field. Word automatically updates date fields whenever a document is repaginated, as it is when it is printed; so the date on which students print their documents will appear automatically.

Two other aspects of date fields deserve mention:

▶ Clicking in a date field and pressing F9 updates it, and students are prompted to do this as a step in the lab exercises.

▶ If you save a document that contains a date field and then print it before closing it, Word will ask whether you want to save your changes—because it updated the date field when you printed it. Because saving Word files on floppies can be slow, time is saved by answering "No."

■ NOTE TO STUDENTS AND INSTRUCTORS

We are always happy to hear from users or potential users of the PicTorial Series; it's through such exchanges that improvements are made. If you have any comments or questions, send them to Dennis Curtin by e-mail on the Internet at P00359@PSILINK.COM. (You can use this address when sending e-mail from CompuServe, America Online, or any of the popular commercial services and it will get to him.)

■ ACKNOWLEDGMENTS

We would like to thank all of those people who have worked hard to make this the best possible text.

On the academic end have been the following reviewers:

▶ Kathleen. T. Camarena, Heald Business College

▶ Stephen P. Leach, Florida State University

▶ Sally L. Kurz, Coastline Community College

▶ Mike Michaelson, Palomar College

At the publisher's end Carolyn Henderson and Jane Avery have smoothed the way for the authors' efforts. And thanks to the people in design and production who turned a manuscript into the final four-color book: they include Linda Fiordilino, Warren Fischbach, Joanne Jay, Christy Mahon, John A. Nestor, Lorraine Patsco, and Joyce Turner. And finally, thanks to Cathy Morin, who did the screen illustrations in the book and tested the materials over and over.

All of these people, each and every one, took a personal interest in this text;

and that interest shows in the work you are now holding. Any shortcomings are of course the responsibility of the authors and in no way reflect on the professionalism and talent of this fine group.

DEDICATION, BY DENNIS CURTIN

This book is dedicated to Cecil Yarbrough, the editor who has worked on all of my books for the past three years. Under a flood of manuscripts and the demands of an unrelenting calendar, Cecil has managed at all times to remain calm and courtly—something I cannot say about myself. He has not only brought greater accuracy and a higher quality to my texts; he has been a pleasure to work with and learn from. I hope we'll have the chance to work together on a lot more books over the coming years.

About the Authors

Dennis Curtin's 25-plus years' business experience in educational publishing provide a rich and unique perspective for his computer applications texts. He has served in executive positions at several companies, including Prentice Hall, where he has been a textbook sales representative, an acquisitions editor, editorial director of the engineering, vocational, and technical division, and editor in chief of the international division. For the past decade he has been primarily a writer of college textbooks on end-user computer applications.

He has been involved with microcomputers since the introduction of the original Apple II and was one of only nine alpha testers of the first version of Lotus 1-2-3, when Lotus Corporation had only a few employees squeezed into a small Kendall Square office. In the years since, he has taught in adult education and corporate training programs, but he readily acknowledges that he has learned most of what he knows about textbooks by working with instructors as an editor and during the writing, reviewing, and revising of his own books.

The primary author and series editor of the COMPASS Series and author of several popular microcomputer concepts texts, he is now spearheading and developing an exciting new series of highly visual Windows applications text called the PicTorial Series, of which this book is a part.

Donna Matherly combines extensive professional experience in computer-related instruction with a strong academic background. Currently an instructor in and coordinator of the Introduction to Computer Literacy course at Tallahassee Community College, Dr. Matherly has previously taught at Indiana University as well as at the secondary level and is active as a trainer and consultant. She is the author of numerous articles related to computer issues, office automation, and business education and has developed instructor-related materials and more than a dozen instructor's manuals for Prentice Hall.

PicTorial 1

Jump-Starting Word

After completing this PicTorial, you will be able to:

▶ Start Word and describe the parts of the Word screen

▶ Open, save, and close documents

▶ Describe the parts of the Word screen display

▶ Move around documents on the screen

▶ Use Word's on-line Help system to get help on procedures

▶ Exit Word at the end of a session

The programs you use on a computer to do your work are called application programs. Different kinds of application programs do different kinds of tasks. For example, you use spreadsheet application programs to work with numbers and word processing application programs, such as Word for Windows, to work with text.

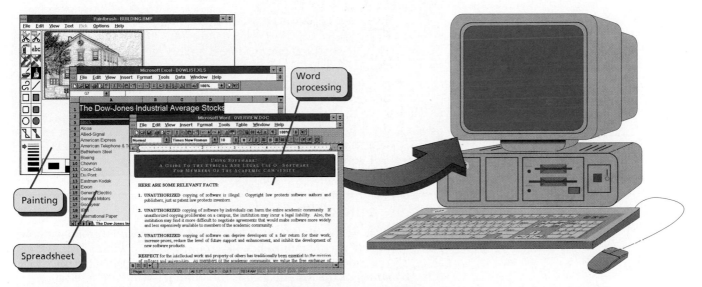

Learning how to use a new application program is much like learning how to drive. To drive well, you have to learn the rules of the road and how the car should be maintained for safety and reliability, but you can't wait to get behind the wheel. Once you have taken at least a spin around the block, you have a feel for driving that makes you want to learn more. In this PicTorial, you take Word for Windows for a spin around the block. Just as an experienced driver sat next to you and told you everything to do on your first drive, we'll sit beside you and guide you through your first drive around the block with Word for Windows. The goal here is to master some of Word's most basic features—starting and exiting Word; opening, saving, and closing documents; getting around a document; and using Help. You should relax as you explore these procedures and just get a feeling for the program.

1-1. STARTING WORD FOR WINDOWS

To load the Word for Windows application, you must first load Windows and display Program Manager as a window. When Program Manager is displayed as a window, it usually contains other windows known as group windows because they contain groups of related application icons. However, some or all of these group windows may be displayed as icons—called group icons—as shown in the margin illustration. To open a group icon into a window so you can see its contents, you double-click it.

It is easy to customize Windows, so group windows and icons vary widely from system to system. However, your system should have a group window for Word for Windows named *Word for Windows 6.0* or *Microsoft Office*. Inside this group window are icons called application icons because they start Word application programs. Once you can see an application icon, you can double-click it to start the application.

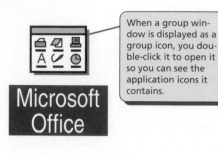

When a group window is displayed as a group icon, you double-click it to open it so you can see the application icons it contains.

TIP: QUICKSTEPS BOXES

QuickSteps boxes, identified with the [icon], summarize the steps you follow to complete a Word procedure. These boxes can be found throughout this text and serve two purposes:

▶ On your first pass through a section, they give you an advance look at the steps you must follow to complete the tutorial. Don't actually execute the commands this time around. If you do so, you may not know how to recover from any mistakes you might make.

▶ Later on, when you want to refresh your memory about a procedure, they make it easy to find and review the steps you must follow. At this stage, you can use them as a quick reference guide.

QUICKSTEPS: STARTING WORD

1. If the *Word for Windows 6.0* or *Microsoft Office* group window isn't open, double-click its group icon to open it. In the open window you should be able to see an icon labeled *Microsoft Word.* This is the icon that starts the Word for Windows application.

2. Double-click the application icon labeled *Microsoft Word.* If your system is set up to display a Tip of the Day window when you start Word, read the tip and then click the **OK** command button to close the Tip window.

TIP: TIP OF THE DAY

When the Tip of the Day window is displayed, you can click the **Show Tips at Startup** check box to turn this feature off. If the tip isn't displayed at startup and you want it to be, pull down the **Help** menu and click the **Tip of the Day** command to display it, then click the **Show Tips at Startup** check box to turn it on (☒).

TUTORIAL

In this tutorial, you locate the group window in which the Word application icon is stored and then use that icon to open Word.

Opening the Group Window

1. With Windows running and Program Manager displayed as a window, open the *Word for Windows 6.0* or *Microsoft Office* group window if it isn't already open. To open it, double-click its group icon.

Starting Word

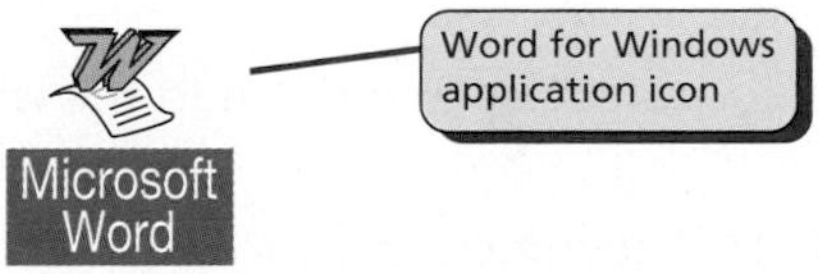

2. Double-click the application icon labeled *Microsoft Word* (see the margin illustration) to open Word and display its application window, as shown with its parts labeled at the bottom of this page. On some systems a Tip of the Day window may be displayed. Read the tip, then click the **OK** button in the Tip window to close it.

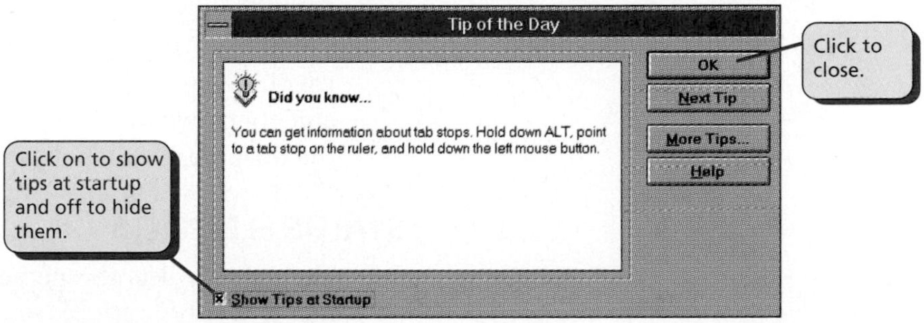

1-2. EXPLORING THE WORD APPLICATION WINDOW

The Word screen, called the *workplace*, actually contains two windows: an application window and a document window. When you first start Word, the application window is maximized so it fills the screen, and the document window is maximized so it fills the application window. Each window can be independently maximized by clicking ▲, minimized by clicking ▼, and restored by clicking ⇕. The application window displays a number of elements that make the program fast and efficient to work with. You should become familiar with the names of these elements.

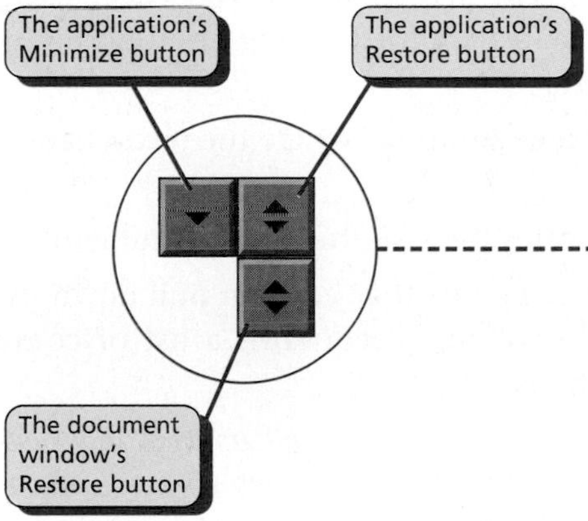

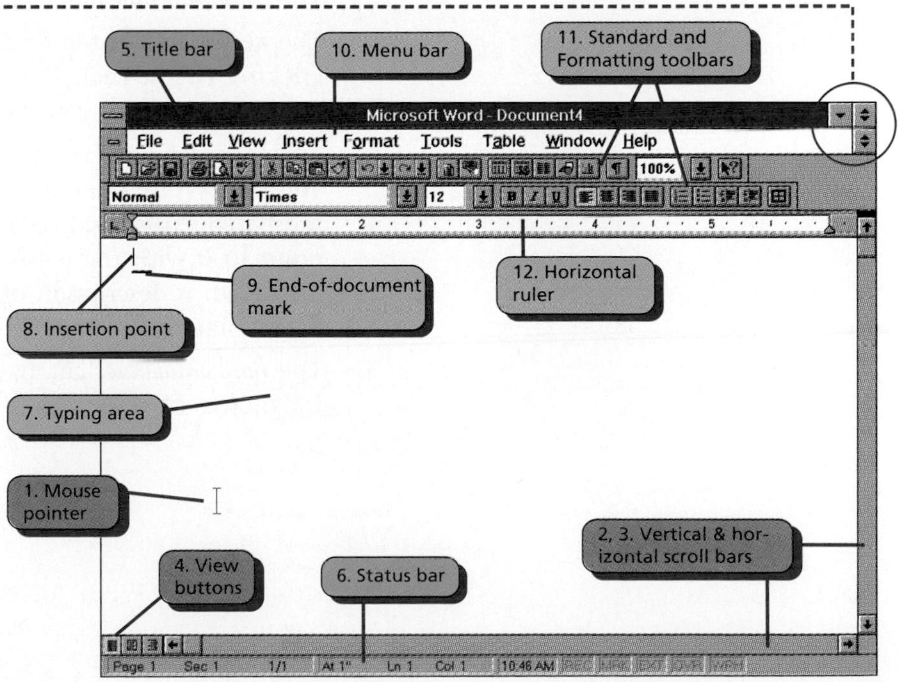

NAVIGATION AND DISPLAY ELEMENTS

1. The *mouse pointer* moves when you move the mouse so you can point to things on the screen and click to select them. It changes shape when you move it about the screen. In the text area it takes the shape of an I-beam (I) so you can position it correctly between letters or words. On the menu or toolbar it's shaped like an arrow (↖) so you can click on commands.

2. The *vertical scroll bar* scrolls the document up and down in the window.

3. The *horizontal scroll bar* scrolls the document side to side in the window.

4. Three *View buttons* display the document in Normal View, Page Layout View, or Outline View. You usually work in Normal View and then switch to Page Layout View when you want to see how the document will look when printed.

STATUS ELEMENTS

5. The *title bar* lists the name of the application and any open document.

6. The *status bar* displays information about your document and the program. The first section indicates which page is displayed on the screen and the second section indicates the position of the insertion point in the document.

EDITING AND FORMATTING ELEMENTS

7. The *typing area* is the area of the screen where you enter text. Initially the only things in this area are the flashing insertion point and the end-of-document mark.

8. The *insertion point* in the text area indicates where the next character you type will appear.

9. The *end-of-document mark* indicates the last line in the document.

10. The *menu bar* lists the names of menus that you can pull down by clicking them. Each pulled-down menu contains a list of commands from which you can choose.

11. The *Standard* (upper) and *Formatting* (lower) *toolbars* appear when you start Word. They contain buttons you can click to execute the most frequently used commands. To see the name of any button, point to it with the mouse pointer, and a box called a ToolTip is displayed. A description of the button's function is also displayed on the status bar.

12. The *horizontal ruler* changes indents, margins, and tab stops using the mouse. (A vertical ruler is also displayed in Page Layout view.)

UNDERSTANDING THE STATUS BAR

The status bar describes highlighted commands or buttons you point to, prompts you for the information it needs you to enter to complete a command, and informs you of the progress of some commands. Here is a brief description of the things you see displayed on this bar.

Col indicates the number of characters, including spaces and tabs, between the left margin and the insertion point.

Time displays the time of your system's clock.

REC, when not dimmed, indicates the macro recorder is active.

MRK, when not dimmed, indicates that revision marking is on.

Page tells you the page that is displayed on the screen. (*Sec* tells you the section that is displayed.)

1/1 indicates the page that is displayed on the screen and the total number of pages in the document.

At indicates the distance from the line with the insertion point to the top of the page.

Ln indicates the number of lines from the line with the insertion point to the top of the text page.

EXT, when not dimmed, indicates that you have pressed F8 (the Extend Selection key). Press F8 again to turn it off.

OVR, when not dimmed, indicates that overtype is on. Text you type in existing text types over the original text. Press Ins to turn overtype off.

WPH, when not dimmed, indicates that help for WordPerfect users is active.

TIP: YOUR SCREEN DOESN'T MATCH OURS

If you screen doesn't match the one shown here, some settings have been changed on your system. However, you can easily reset it to match.

▸ If the toolbars are not displayed correctly, pull down the **View** menu and click the **Toolbars** command to display the Toolbars dialog box. If either the Standard or Formatting check box is off (☐), click it to turn it on (☒). Click any other check box that has an X to turn it off. Then click the **OK** command button.

▸ If the horizontal ruler is not displayed below the Formatting toolbar, pull down the **View** menu and click the **Ruler** command to put a check mark (✔) in front of it.

▸ If the status bar at the bottom of the window or scroll bars are not displayed, pull down the **Tools** menu and click the **Options** command to display the Options dialog box. Click the *View* tab in the dialog box to display that set of options, and turn on the **Status Bar**, **Horizontal Scroll Bar**, and **Vertical Scroll Bar** commands in the *Window* section. (Those with X's in the box are on (☒)). Click the **OK** command button to return to the document.

TUTORIAL

In this tutorial you explore the Word application window to familiarize yourself with some of its elements.

Exploring the Mouse Pointer

1. Move the mouse pointer around the screen to see how it takes on one of three shapes, as shown in the margin illustration.

   ▸ It is shaped like an I-beam (I) when inside the typing area or in one of the text boxes on the toolbar.

   ▸ It is normally shaped like a left-pointing arrow (🡤) when outside of the typing area.

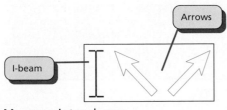

Mouse pointer shapes

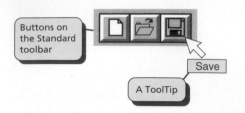

Buttons on the Standard toolbar

Save

A ToolTip

> It is shaped like a right-pointing diagonal arrow when in the left margin or to the left of any centered text.

Exploring the Toolbar

2. Point to any button on the Standard toolbar (just below the menu bar), and a small yellow box—called a ToolTip—appears with the name of the button. You'll also see a brief description of the button's function displayed on the status bar at the bottom of the screen.

3. Move the mouse pointer along the row of buttons on the toolbar, and you will see the names and descriptions change.

Exploring the Status Bar

4. Press [Ins] to see the *OVR* indicator on the status bar become undimmed. Press [Ins] again to dim it. When dimmed it's off so text moves aside when you type into existing text.

1-3. OPENING AND CLOSING DOCUMENTS

To use Word or any other Windows application program you must know how to open and close documents.

OPENING NEW DOCUMENTS

When you start Word, it opens a new document automatically. But if you are already working in Word and want to create another new document, you will need to open it. The title bar of each new document that you open reads *Documentx*, where x stands for the number of new documents you have opened in the current session. This automatically assigned name is replaced with the name you give to the document when you save it.

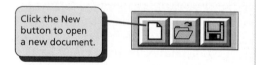

Click the New button to open a new document.

QUICKSTEPS: OPENING NEW DOCUMENTS

To open a new document, do one of the following:

> Click the **New** button on the Standard toolbar.

> Pull down the **File** menu, click the **New** command, and then click the **OK** button on the New dialog box.

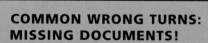

COMMON WRONG TURNS: MISSING DOCUMENTS!

You can open as many documents as your system's memory allows and have them all on the screen at one time so you can edit, format, or print them. If you open a new document without closing the original one, the new document covers up the original document so you can't see it. To see what documents are open at any time, pull down the **Window** menu and click the name of a document to move it to the top of the pile. From the **Window** menu you can also click the **Arrange All** command to see all documents. Then click in the document you want to work on to make it active and click its Maximize button (▲) to enlarge it.

OPENING EXISTING DOCUMENTS

To open an existing document that was previously saved onto a disk, you use the Open dialog box to specify the drive it's on, the directory it's in, and its filename.

QUICKSTEPS: OPENING EXISTING DOCUMENTS

1. Click the **Open** button on the Standard toolbar, or pull down the **File** menu and click the **Open** command to display the Open dialog box.

2. Click the **Drives** box's drop-down arrow () to display a drop-down list of the drives on your system. Click the letter of the drive on which the document is stored to select the drive and list it the **Drives** box.

3. Double-click the file's directory in the **Directories** list to select it and list the files that it contains in the **File Name** list. (You may have to double-click the root directory, *c:*, to see other directories.)

4. Use the scroll bar in the **File Name** list to scroll the desired document's name into view. Then click it to select it and display its name in the **File Name** text box.

5. Click the **OK** command button to open the document.

Click the Open button to open an existing document.

CLOSING DOCUMENTS

Once you have saved a document, you can close it. This clears the document from the screen and removes it from the computer's memory. If you want to work on the document again, you open it from the disk on which you saved it.

Normally you save a document before you close it, but there are occasions when you do not want to save it. For example, if you make a serious mistake, you may not want to overwrite the document on the disk with the one on the screen. In cases like this, you close the document without saving it. This removes it from the screen and the computer's memory, and it is lost.

QUICKSTEPS: CLOSING DOCUMENTS

To close a document do one of the following:

▶ Double-click the document window's Control-Menu box (⊟). (See the box "Understanding Control-Menu Boxes.")

▶ Pull down Word's **File** menu and click the **Close** command.

COMMON WRONG TURNS: DOCUMENT NOT SAVED

Keep in mind that if you close a document without first saving it, the document is gone forever. Any data that you have entered is lost. If you try to close a document without first having saved any changes, a dialog box is displayed.

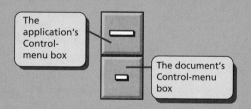

▶ Click the **Yes** command button to save the document and then close it.

▶ Click the **No** command button to abandon the document and close it.

▶ Click the **Cancel** command button to return to where you were.

UNDERSTANDING CONTROL-MENU BOXES

Every window, including application windows, document windows, dialog boxes, and Help windows, has a Control-menu box (⊟) in the upper-left corner of its screen. The most frequent use of these Control-menu boxes is to quickly close document or application windows. To do so, you just double-click the correct Control-menu box. If you look carefully at the Control-menu boxes on the screen, you'll see that the one for an application (⊟) is different from one for a document (⊟). When the document window is maximized, its Control-menu box appears directly under the application's, so it's easy to click the wrong one.

The application's Control-menu box

The document's Control-menu box

▶ An application's or Help window's Control-menu box contains a longer dash representing the spacebar (⊟) because you can pull down its Control menu by pressing Alt +Spacebar.

▶ A document's Control-menu box contains a character that represents a hyphen (⊟) because you can pull down its Control menu by pressing Alt + - .

UNDERSTANDING DIALOG BOXES

When you execute some Word commands, a dialog box is displayed. The elements in the dialog boxes vary but include those shown and described here.

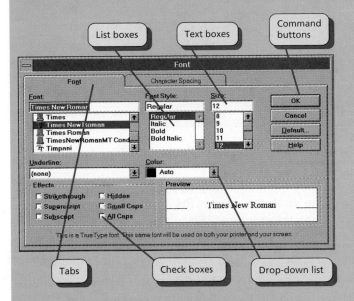

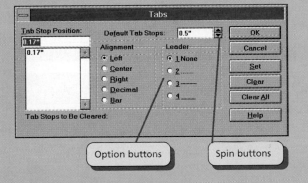

Tabs are found on many dialog boxes and look much like a card index file where related settings are grouped together on their own card. When you click one of the tabs, it becomes active and moves to the front of the pile.

Text boxes contain space for typing new data or changing data that is already in them:

▶ When a text box is empty, you click anywhere in it to move the insertion point into the box. As you then type characters, the insertion point moves to indicate where the next character you type will appear.

▶ When a text box already contains an entry when you open a dialog box, that entry may be selected (highlighted). To replace the selected entry, type a new entry, and the first character you type deletes the original entry. (If the entry isn't selected, you can double-click it to select it.) To edit a selected entry, press ← or → to remove the highlight and position the insertion point, and then insert or delete characters just as you would in normal text.

List boxes display a list from which you can choose an item by clicking it. Lists too long to be displayed in full can be scrolled with the box's scroll bar.

A *drop-down list box* is displayed as a rectangular box listing only the current selection. To display other choices, click the down arrow (↧) to the right of the box.

Command buttons such as [Cancel] or [OK] execute commands when you click them. If a button is dimmed, it cannot be chosen from where you are in a procedure.

Option buttons offer mutually exclusive options (only one can be selected at a time). The one that is on contains a black dot (●). If you click a button that is off (○), any other related button that is on automatically turns off.

Check boxes offer nonexclusive options (one or more of them can be on at the same time). To turn an option on, click it to display an X in its box (☒). To turn the option off, click the box to remove the X (☐). If the name of one of the check boxes is dimmed, it can't be chosen from where you are in a procedure.

Spin buttons (⬍) let you increase or decrease a number by clicking the up or down arrow. If you point to one of the arrows and hold down the mouse button, the number will "spin" up or down.

TUTORIAL

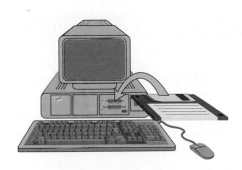

In this tutorial you open an existing document supplied to you on the *Word Student Resource Disk* designed to be used with this text. (If you do not have a copy of this disk, ask your instructor how you can obtain one.) This disk contains all of the documents on which you work while completing the lab activities in this text. The document you open is a memo containing only a heading. You will enter the document's body paragraphs.

Getting Ready

1. Insert your *Word Student Resource Disk (Part 1)* into the floppy disk drive you use to open and save documents.

Opening a Document Using the Menu

2. Pull down the **File** menu bar and click the **Open** command to display the Open dialog box.

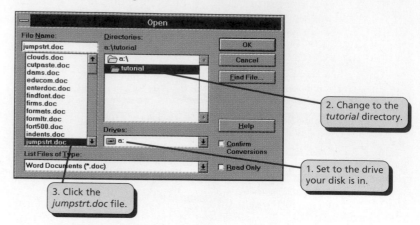

▶ Click the **Drives** box's down arrow (⬇) to display a drop-down list of the drives on your system. Click the letter of the drive you put the disk in to select it and list it in the **Drives** box.

▶ Double-click the *tutorial* directory listed in the **Directories** list to select it and list the files that it contains in the **File Name** list.

▶ Click the *jumpstrt.doc* filename to select it and display its name in the **File Name** text box. (If necessary, use the scroll bar in the **File Name** list to scroll it into view.)

3. Click the **OK** command button to open the document.

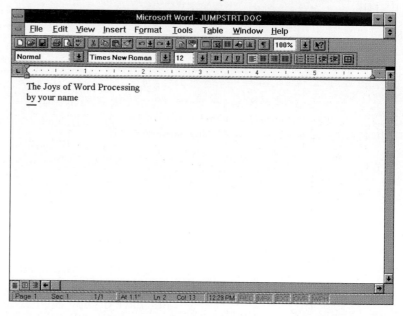

Closing the Document

4. Pull down the **File** menu and click the **Close** command to close the document.

5. Pull down the **File** menu and you will see the name of the document listed at the bottom of the menu (see the margin illustration). Word remembers the last four documents that you opened.

6. Click the name *1 JUMPSTRT.DOC* to open the document.

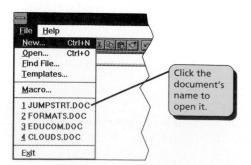

7. Double-click the document window's Control-menu box (be sure to click the lower ⊟, not the upper ⊟) to close the document.

1-4. ENTERING A DOCUMENT

The point of learning Word is to use it to create documents. Without further ado, let's create one.

TUTORIAL

In this tutorial you open a document containing only a memo heading and then enter a few paragraphs to become familiar with entering text.

Getting Ready

1. Open the *jumpstrt.doc* document stored in the *tutorial* directory of the *Word Student Resource Disk (Part 1)*.

2. Click just to the left of the *y* in *your name*, press [Del] nine times to delete the phrase, then type your own name.

Entering a Document

3. Press [Enter ↵] twice to end the line and insert a line of space.

4. Enter the document shown here. As you do so, keep the following points in mind:

   ▶ Notice the blinking vertical line in the upper-left corner of the typing area. This is called the *insertion point*, and it indicates where the next character you type will appear. It will move as you type.

   ▶ Do not press [Enter ↵] at the end of lines. Press [Enter ↵] only where indicated by the [Enter ↵] symbol. Word automatically wraps text that will not fit on a line—that is, moves it to the next line. Except for the headings, your lines will probably end at places other than the ones shown in the figure; don't worry if they do. Where they end depends on your system.

   ▶ Don't worry about mistakes; you'll see how to correct them later. However, If you make typos you want to correct immediately, press [←Bksp] to erase them, and then enter the correct letters.

The Joys of Word Processing [Enter ↵]
by your name [Enter ↵]
[Enter ↵]
The latest word processing applications make typewriters and even earlier word processing programs seem like something Grandma would have used. These programs can turn out finished documents that look as if they had been prepared by a professional publisher. The first things I've noticed about this program are: [Enter ↵]
[Enter ↵]
The document on the screen looks much as I'd expect it to look on the printed page. This feature is WYSIWYG, or "What You See Is What You Get." [Enter ↵]
[Enter ↵]
The application has menus and buttons that I can click to execute commands quickly and easily. [Enter ↵]

Click the Save button to save the document.

Finishing Up

5. Click the **Save** button on the toolbar to save the document. (It is the third button from the left and looks like a floppy disk. Remember that you can find the name of any button by pointing to it to display a ToolTip.)

6. Pull down the **File** menu and click the **Close** command to close the document.

1-5. SAVING A DOCUMENT

You should frequently save the document you are working on. If you turn off the computer, experience a power failure, encounter hardware problems, or make a mistake, you may lose documents that are in the computer's memory. Your documents are not safe from these disasters until you save them onto a disk. You should always save a document:

▶ Before experimenting with unfamiliar commands

▶ Before making major revisions

▶ Before printing it (in case something goes wrong during the process)

▶ Before closing it or exiting Word

On many systems, you save your documents onto a hard disk. On others, especially those you share with other students in a computer lab, you save them onto a floppy disk (usually in drive A or B) so that you can take them with you.

When you save a document the first time, you must assign it a filename (see the margin illustration). Word uses the DOS file-naming conventions. You can assign names to files that have up to eight characters. When you do so, Word automatically adds the three-character identifying extension DOC that is separated from the name by a period. (Think of this as an eight-character first name separated by a period from a three-character last name.)

The characters that you can use in a filename are called *legal characters*. The characters are listed and illustrated in the table "Legal Filename Characters." If you enter any other character when saving a file, a dialog box will appear telling you *This is not a valid filename.*

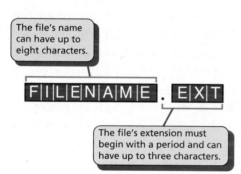

The file's name can have up to eight characters.

The file's extension must begin with a period and can have up to three characters.

Legal Filename Characters			
Character	**Example**	**Character**	**Example**
Letters, uppercase	A–Z	Percent sign	%
Letters, lowercase	a–z	Ampersand	&
Numbers	0–9	Hyphen	-
Underscore	_	Braces	{}
Caret	^	Parentheses	()
Dollar sign	$	At sign	@
Tilde	~	Grave accent	`
Exclamation point	!	Apostrophe	'
Number sign	#		

When you save a document the second and subsequent times, you don't have to specify a name again—the version on the screen overwrites the version with the same name on the disk.

Click the Save button to save the document.

QUICKSTEPS: SAVING DOCUMENTS

1. Click the **Save** button on the toolbar, or pull down the **File** menu and click the **Save** command.

▶ If you have previously saved the document, it is resaved with the same name in the same place.

▶ If this is the first time you've saved the document, the Save As dialog box appears. If this box appears, continue to Step 2.

2. Click the **Drives** box's drop-down arrow (⬛) to display a drop-down list of the drives on your system. Click the letter of the drive on which you want to save the document to select the drive and list it the **Drives** box.

3. Double-click one of the directories listed in the **Directories** list to select it. (You may have to double-click the root directory, *c:*, to see other directories.)

4. Type a filename into the **File Name** text box and click the **OK** command button to save the document.

TIP: SAVING A DOCUMENT UNDER A NEW NAME

There are times when you want to save a document under a new name. You may have made a mistake and don't want to overwrite the version on the disk with the new version until you are certain it's OK to do so. Or you may have opened an existing document that you want to revise into a new and different one. In cases such as this, you can save the document on the screen under a new name by pulling down the **File** menu and clicking the **Save As** command instead of the **Save** command. Then just type a new filename into the **File Name** text box and click the **OK** command button. (If you don't change the name, or if you enter the name of a file already on the disk, and then click **OK**, you are asked *Do you want to replace the existing FILENAME.DOC?*. Click **Yes** to replace it or **No** to cancel the command so you can enter a new name in the **File Name** text box.)

UNDERSTANDING THE SUMMARY INFORMATION DIALOG BOX

When you save a file the first time, a summary information dialog box may appear. Into this box you can enter information about the document that helps you locate or identify it later. We do not use this box in the documents in this text but you can get information on how to use it or turn it on and off in Word's on-line Help by searching for the topic *summary information* and choosing the subtopic *Controlling whether Word prompts for summary information*.

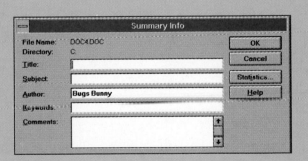

COMMON WRONG TURNS: REMOVING A FLOPPY DISK TOO SOON

When you work on Word documents, Windows creates temporary files on the disk. When saving a document to and opening a document from a floppy disk, do not remove the disk from the drive until you have quit Word. If you do, you may see a message telling you that there is a disk error. If this message appears, reinsert the disk and click the **OK** command button.

COMMON WRONG TURNS: DUPLICATE FILENAMES

If you enter a filename in the Save As dialog box that is the same as a filename already on the disk, a warning dialog box is displayed so you have the option of canceling the command or overwriting the document on the disk with the document on the screen.

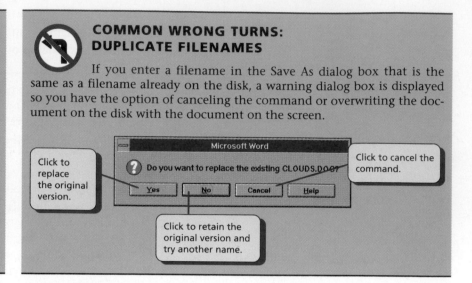

TUTORIAL

In this tutorial you save a document by clicking a button. This saves the document under the same name and in the same directory from which you opened it or in which you previously saved it. You then use the Save As command to save the document under a new name.

Getting Ready

1. Open the *jumpstrt.doc* document stored in the *tutorial* directory of the *Word Student Resource Disk (Part 1)*.

Saving Under the Original Name

2. Click the **Save** button on the toolbar. (If you don't know which it is, you can point to any button to display its name.) As the document is saved, an hourglass (⧗) is displayed, and the status bar keeps you informed of the command's progress.

Saving Under a New Name

3. Pull down the **File** name and click the **Save As** command to display the Save As dialog box. The document's name is highlighted in the **File Name** text box and the drive and directory are set to the same settings you used to open the document.

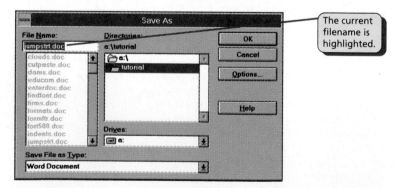

4. Type **newname** into the **File Name** text box (the first character you type deletes the original name) and click the **OK** command button to save the document under that name. You now have two copies

of the same document, one named *jumpstrt.doc* and one named *newname.doc*.

Finishing Up

5. Pull down the **File** menu and click the **Close** command to close the document.

1-6. GETTING AROUND A DOCUMENT WITH THE MOUSE

The fastest way to move the insertion point in the document on the screen is to point to where you want to move it and click. However, if the place you want to move it to isn't displayed on the screen, you have to scroll the document. You can do so using the mouse and scroll bars. A *vertical scroll bar* is located on the right edge of the document window, and a *horizontal scroll bar* is located on the bottom edge of the document window.

The vertical scroll bar contains three basic elements: the *up scroll arrow* (⬆), the *down scroll arrow* (⬇), and the *scroll box* (☐). The horizontal scroll bar contains the same three elements, but its scroll arrows are left (⬅) and right (➡). Below the vertical scroll bar in Page Layout View are two buttons you can click to page up and down through the document (see the margin illustration).

The scroll box (☐) serves a dual function. When you drag it up or down the vertical scroll bar with the mouse, you move quickly to any point in a document or window. The scroll box also indicates where you are in a document. If it is at the top of the scroll bar, you are at the top of the document. If it is at the bottom of the scroll bar, you are at the bottom of the document. If it is halfway between the top and bottom of the scroll bar, you are at the middle of the document.

The insertion point always remains displayed on the screen except when you use the scroll bars to scroll the document. This is because scrolling the screen doesn't move the insertion point. To move it, you have to point with the I-beam-shaped mouse pointer to where you want to move it and then click. If you click in an area that contains no text, the insertion point jumps to the nearest place on the line that does or to the left margin.

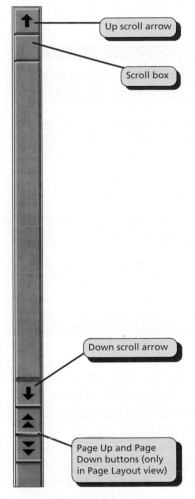

The vertical scroll bar

 QUICKSTEPS: GETTING AROUND A DOCUMENT WITH SCROLL BARS

▶ To scroll the contents of the window a line at a time, click one of the scroll arrows.

▶ To continuously scroll the contents of the window, point to one of the scroll arrows and hold down the mouse button.

▶ To scroll one screen at a time, click the scroll bar above or below the scroll box.

▶ To scroll to a specific place in the document, drag the scroll box to where you want to move, and then release it.

▶ To scroll one page at a time, click the **Page Layout View** button and two buttons are displayed below the vertical scroll bar. Click the top one to page up and the bottom one to page down.

TUTORIAL

In this tutorial you are introduced to many of the basic techniques for getting around the screen with a mouse. To do so, you open a long document that is a guide to your rights when using an application program such as Word.

Getting Ready

1. Open the *overview.doc* document stored in the *tutorial* directory of the *Word Student Resource Disk (Part 1)*.

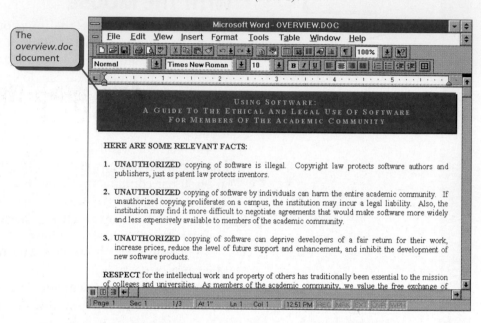

The *overview.doc* document

Scrolling the Document

2. You'll see a vertical scroll bar displayed at the right side of the window. Point to the scroll bar's down scroll arrow (⬇) and hold down the left mouse button until the scroll box reaches the bottom of the scroll bar. This indicates that you are at the end of the document. Click the up scroll arrow (⬆) a few times until you can see some lines of text, then click anywhere in the text to move the insertion point there. Notice the position of the insertion point as indicated on the status bar.

3. Point to the up scroll arrow (⬆) and hold down the left mouse button until the scroll box reaches the top of the scroll bar. This indicates that you are at the beginning of the document. Click anywhere in the text to move the insertion point there. Notice the position of the insertion point as indicated on the status bar.

4. Point to the scroll box (▭), hold down the left mouse button, and drag the scroll box to the bottom of the scroll bar. When you release the mouse button, you move to the end of the document. Click anywhere in the text to move the insertion point there.

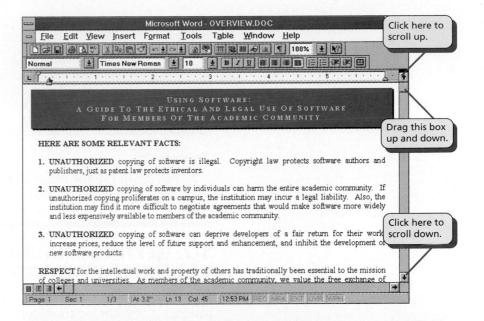

COMMON WRONG TURNS: DRAGGING SCROLL BOX DOESN'T WORK

If you drag the scroll box off the scroll bar when you release the mouse button, the scroll box jumps back to where it was when you started. To be sure the screen scrolls the way you want, release the mouse button only when you can see the outline of the scroll box on the scroll bar.

5. Practice scrolling the window's contents up and down a line at a time by clicking the up (⬆) and down (⬇) scroll arrows.

6. Practice scrolling the window's contents up and down a screen at a time by clicking the scroll bar above and below the scroll box (☐).

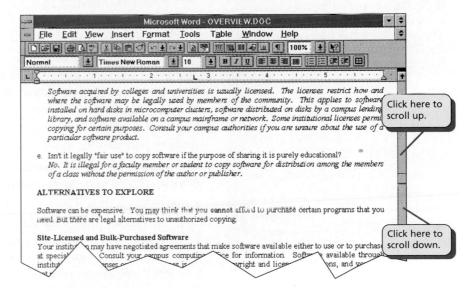

Finishing Up

7. Pull down the **File** menu and click the **Close** command to close the document.

1-7. GETTING AROUND A DOCUMENT WITH THE KEYBOARD

Word provides you with several keyboard commands that move the insertion point through a document. Since you are typing much of the time and your hands are on the keyboard, these commands are frequently faster than reaching for the mouse when moving the insertion point to where you want it.

The four directional arrow keys (←, →, ↑, and ↓) move the insertion point one character or line at a time and repeat if you hold them down.

When moving the insertion point with keyboard commands, you will notice:

▶ When you move the insertion point along a line of text, it moves through the text and does not affect it.

▶ When you move the insertion point past the rightmost character on a line, it jumps down to the beginning of the next line.

▶ When you move the insertion point past the leftmost character on a line of text, it jumps up to the end of the preceding line.

▶ When you move the insertion point up and down through a document, it stays in roughly the same position relative to the left margin unless a line contains no text.

▶ If the document is longer than the number of lines displayed on the screen, it can be scrolled into view by moving the insertion point to the top or bottom of the screen and pressing ↓ or ↑. Instead of moving off the screen, the insertion point stays on the top or bottom row, and the text scrolls into view.

▶ You cannot move the insertion point off the screen (except with the scroll bar), and you cannot move it past the end of the document.

Some commands move you slowly over short distances and some move you quickly over long distances. In that respect, these commands are much like the gas pedal in your car. You may want to crawl down the driveway but you'll want to fly on the freeway. For example, pressing the arrow keys moves the insertion point one character or line at a time. When you hold down Ctrl while pressing the arrow keys, the insertion point moves in larger jumps. These keys are like accelerators. For example, pressing Ctrl+↓ moves the insertion point to the beginning of the next paragraph. Pressing Ctrl+→ moves it to the beginning of the next word.

COMMON WRONG TURNS: PRESSING ARROW KEYS ENTERS NUMBERS

If pressing the arrow keys on the numeric keypad enters numbers instead of moving the insertion point, either press NumLock to turn off the numeric keypad (most keyboards have a light that indicates when it's on or off), or use the other set of arrow keys on the keyboard to move the insertion point.

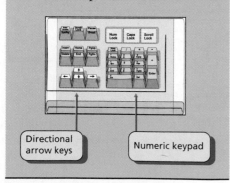

Directional arrow keys   Numeric keypad

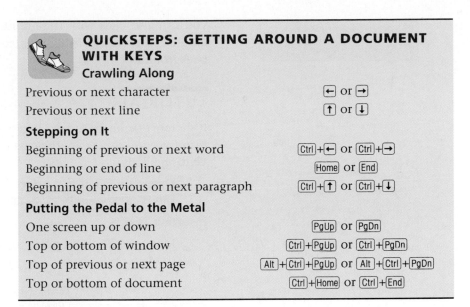

TIP: THE GO TO COMMAND

To jump to a specific page, press F5, or pull down the **Edit** menu and click the **Go To** command to display the Go To dialog box. Type the number of the page you want to jump to into the **Enter Page Number** text box and click the **OK** command button.

TUTORIAL

In this tutorial you are introduced to many of the basic techniques for getting around a document on the screen with keyboard commands.

Getting Ready

1. Open the *overview.doc* document stored in the *tutorial* directory of the *Word Student Resource Disk (Part 1)*.

Getting Around the Document with the Keyboard

2. Practice moving the insertion point around the document using the commands described in the QuickSteps box "Getting Around a Document with Keys." As you do so, watch the second panel of the status bar. The numbers following *At* and *Ln* tells you the insertion point's distance down from the top edge of the page in inches and lines. The number following *Col* indicates the number of characters between the insertion point and the left margin.

Finishing Up

3. Pull down the **File** menu and click the **Close** command to close the document.

1-8. EDITING A DOCUMENT

Any good writer will tell you that the secret to good writing is editing, editing, and more editing. Usually, the more passes you make through a document looking for ways to improve it, the better it will become. Programs such as Word make this process easy to do. To edit a document, you first position the insertion point accurately by clicking the place in the document where you want to move it. You can also press the arrow keys on the keyboard to make final adjustments.

A basic rule of editing is that you first select text and then tell Word what you want to do with it. For example, to delete a word or phrase, you select it and then press Del. To select text, you drag the insertion point over it while holding down the left mouse button(⇨). However, you can also click with the mouse to select words, sentences, and paragraphs. Selected text is highlighted—usually as white text against a black background.

TUTORIAL

It's a rare document indeed that needs no editing. In this tutorial you are introduced to some very basic editing commands.

Getting Ready

1. Open the *jumpstrt.doc* document stored in the *tutorial* directory of the *Word Student Resource Disk (Part 1)*.

Inserting Text

2. Move the insertion point to the immediate left of the word *make* in the first sentence.

> Position the insertion point here.

The latest word processing applications **make** typewriters and even earlier word processing programs seem like something Grandma would have used.

3. Type in the words **such as Word for Windows** and then press Spacebar to insert a space.

The latest word processing applications **such as Word for Windows** make typewriters and even earlier word processing programs seem like something Grandma would have used.

4. Move the insertion point to the immediate left of the word *like* in the first sentence.

The latest word processing applications such as Word for Windows make typewriters and even earlier word processing programs seem **like** something Grandma would have used.

> Position the insertion point here.

5. Type in the words **old fashioned** and then press Spacebar to insert a space.

The latest word processing applications such as Word for Windows make typewriters and even earlier word processing programs seem **old fashioned** like something Grandma would have used.

Deleting Text

6. Double-click the word *like* following the insertion you just made, and hold down the button after the second click. Drag the mouse (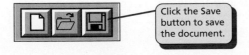) to select the entire phrase *like something Grandma would have used*. Release the mouse button, and the selection remains highlighted.

> The latest word processing applications such as Word for Windows make typewriters and even earlier word processing programs seem old fashioned **like something Grandma would have used**. These programs can turn out finished documents that look as if they had been prepared by a professional publisher. The first things I've noticed about this program are:

7. Press ⌨Delete to delete the selected phrase. Notice how the unselected space following the previous word is automatically deleted. Your edited first sentence should now look like the one shown here.

> The latest word processing applications such as Word for Windows make typewriters and even earlier word processing programs seem old fashioned.

Replacing Existing Text

8. Double-click the word *publisher* in the second sentence of the opening paragraph to select it.

> The latest word processing applications such as Word for Windows make typewriters and even earlier word processing programs seem old fashioned. These programs can turn out finished documents that look as if they had been prepared by a professional **publisher**. The first things I've noticed about this program are:

9. Type **printer** and the new entry automatically deletes the selected text. Your document's edited first paragraph should now look exactly like the one shown here.

> The latest word processing applications such as Word for Windows make typewriters and even earlier word processing programs seem old fashioned. These programs can turn out finished documents that look as if they had been prepared by a professional printer. The first things I've noticed about this program are:

Click the Save button to save the document.

Finishing Up

10. Click the **Save** button on the toolbar.

11. Pull down the **File** menu and click the **Close** command to close the document.

1-9. EXPLORING THE TOOLBAR

The two toolbars just below the menu bar contain buttons, any one of which you can click to execute a command. All of these commands can also be executed using the menus, but the toolbars are faster—one click and the command is executed. The top toolbar is the Standard toolbar and the lower one is the Formatting toolbar. You can also display other toolbars—or even create your own.

The Standard toolbar includes buttons that open new or existing documents, save documents, or print them.

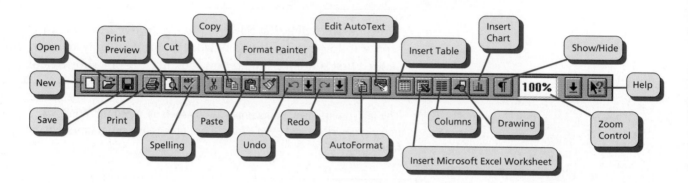

The Formatting toolbar contains buttons and drop-down arrows (⬇) you use to format your text. The text boxes and buttons on the Formatting toolbar indicate the format settings in effect at the insertion point. For example, in a new document you may see that the **Style** is *Normal*, the **Font** is *Times New Roman*, and the **Font Size** is *12*. The alignment button that appears depressed indicates that text is set to **Align Left**

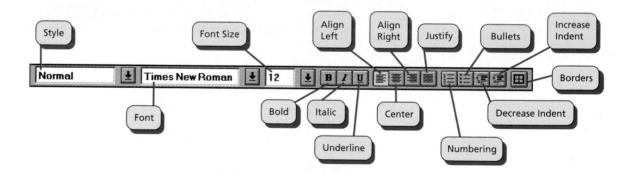

TUTORIAL

The buttons on the toolbar make executing commands fast and easy. In this tutorial you practice executing commands by just clicking buttons. Before beginning, make sure your printer is on, is connected, and has paper in it.

Getting Ready

1. Open the *jumpstrt.doc* document stored in the *tutorial* directory of the *Word Student Resource Disk (Part 1)*.

Formatting Text

2. Point to the left margin next to the second to last paragraph in the document and notice how the mouse pointer turns into an inward-pointing arrow. When it takes this form, clicking the mouse button will select text for you.

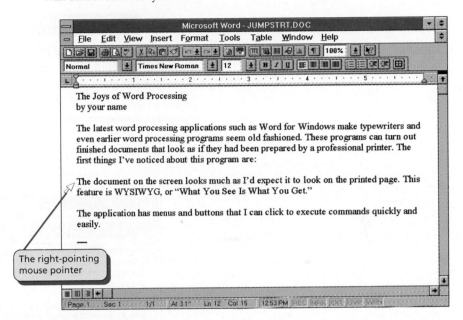

3. Double-click in the left margin next to the second to last paragraph in the document to select it. Don't release the mouse button after the second click.

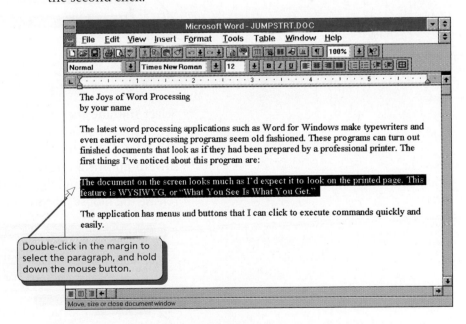

4. Drag the mouse down to select the last paragraph and then release the button. Both paragraphs remain highlighted.

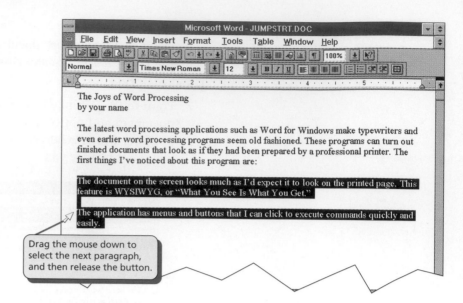

Drag the mouse down to select the next paragraph, and then release the button.

5. Click the **Bullets** button on the Formatting toolbar to add bullets to the two paragraphs.

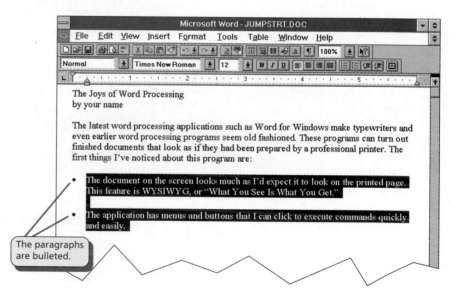

The paragraphs are bulleted.

6. Select the line that reads *The Joys of Word Processing* and the line below it with your name. To do so, point to the left margin just to the left of the first line. The mouse pointer will change to an inward-pointing arrow. Hold down the mouse button, drag the mouse down to highlight both the first and second lines, and then release the mouse button.

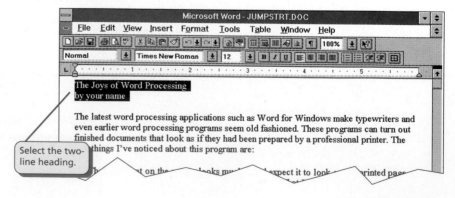

Select the two-line heading.

7. With the two lines still selected, click the **Center** button on the Formatting toolbar, and the lines are centered between the margins and remain highlighted. Notice how the button now looks as if it has been pushed in. A button will look this way whenever the insertion point is positioned in text that the button was used to format.

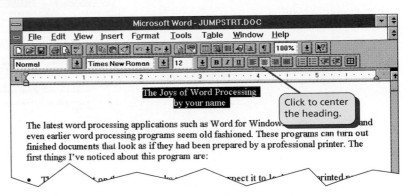

The Bold button

The Italic Button

8. With the two lines still selected, click the **Bold** button on the Formatting toolbar to boldface the lines.

9. Click anywhere to the left of the second line in the heading you just centered to select it. (It's the line with your name on it.)

10. Click the **Italic** button on the Formatting toolbar to italicize the line. Then click the **Bold** button on the same toolbar to turn off boldfacing.

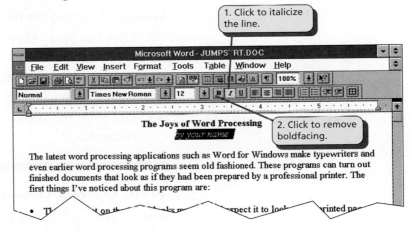

Changing the Document Display

11. Click the **Zoom Control** drop-down arrow (⬇) to display a list of zooms you can use.

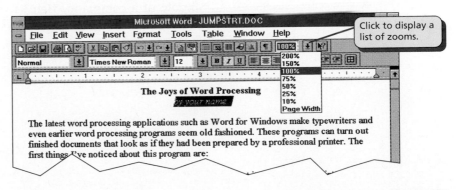

12. Click the **50%** command and the document is reduced in size. The text may be unreadable at this zoom, but you can see the layout. The percentage in the **Zoom Control** text box changes to 50%.

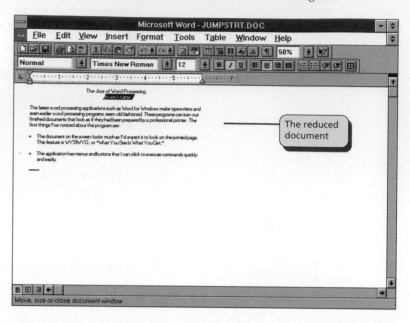

13. Repeat Steps 11 and 12, but this time click the **Page Width** command. The document expands to fill the available space on the screen. On many systems this is the best zoom to use when working on a document.

Saving and Printing the Document

14. Click the **Save** button on the Standard toolbar to save the revised file again.

15. Click the **Print** button on the toolbar to print the document.

Finishing Up

16. Pull down the **File** menu and click the **Close** command to close the document.

1-10. USING ON-LINE HELP

When you are using Word, you can ask for detailed help whenever you want information on a specific procedure. Word has extensive *on-line help* available at all times. Once you are in the Help system, you can navigate through topics by clicking underlined terms or command buttons or by searching for specific topics by name. If you display Help in the middle of a command, Help is *context-sensitive*—it describes the procedure you are using and the options you can choose from.

QUICKSTEPS: USING ON-LINE HELP
Displaying Help

To display Help, do one of the following:

▶ Press F1 at any point in the program.

▶ Pull down the **Help** menu and click any of the listed Help commands.

▶ Double-click the **Help** button on the toolbar to display the Search dialog box described in the "Searching for Help" QuickSteps box.

▶ Click the **Help** button on the toolbar (or press ⇧Shift+F1), and a question mark is added to the mouse pointer. When you then click anywhere on the screen, the element you click on is explained.

▶ Click a **Help** command button in a dialog box.

Closing Help

To close Help, do one of the following:

▶ Pull down the Help window's **File** menu and click the **Exit** command.

▶ Click the Help window's **Close** or **Cancel** command button.

▶ Double-click the Help window's Control-menu box (⊟). (See the box "Understanding Control-Menu Boxes" on page 8.)

QUICKSTEPS: SEARCHING FOR HELP

1. To display the Search dialog box used to search for specific Help topics, do one of the following:

   ▶ Double-click the **Help** button on the toolbar.

   ▶ Click a **Search** command button on a Help window.

   ▶ Pull down the **Help** menu and click the **Search for Help on** command.

2. Type the text you are looking for into the text box. As you do so, the list in the window below scrolls to the first topic that begins with those letters. To scroll though the list, use the scroll bar on the window.

3. Once you find the topic you want help on, click its name on the list to move it into the text box, and then click the **Show Topics** command button to list related topics in the lower window.

4. Click any topic listed in the lower window and then click the **Go To** command button to display it.

TUTORIAL

There are many ways to use Word's on-line Help, and they are essentially the same for all Windows applications. In this tutorial you explore how to find on-line help by clicking items on the screen and using the Help **Search** command.

Identifying Items on the Screen

1. Click the **Help** button on the Standard toolbar to add a question mark to the mouse pointer (see the margin illustration).

2. Click the **Save** button on the toolbar to display Help on saving documents.

Click the Help button on the toolbar or press ⇧Shift+F1 to add this question mark to the mouse pointer.

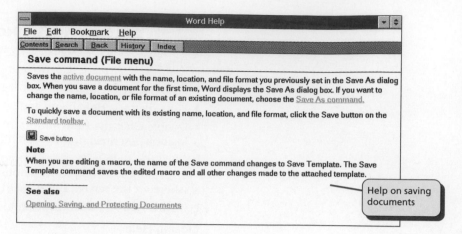

Help on saving documents

3. After reading the information on saving documents, double-click the Help window's Control-menu box (⊟) to close the Help window.

Searching for Help Topics

4. Double-click the **Help** button of the Standard toolbar to display the Search dialog box. The insertion point is flashing in the text box where you enter the topic you want to search for.

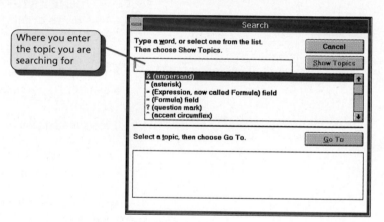

Where you enter the topic you are searching for

5. Type **help** to display any topics that begin with those letters in the window below.

6. Click the topic *Help* in the lower window to select it and move it to the text box. Then click the **Show Topics** command button to list related topics in the lower window.

7. Click *Overview of the Word Workplace* in the lower window to select it and then click the **Go To** command button to display Help on that topic. Click the Help window's Maximize button (▲) to enlarge it, and read the Help text.

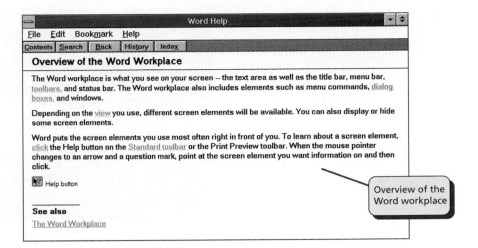

8. Click any term with a dotted underline to display its definition, then click again to close it.

Finishing Up

9. Pull down the Help window's **File** menu and click the **Exit** command to close the Help window.

PAUSING FOR PRACTICE

When working with Word, knowing how to find the information that you need is a very useful skill. Pause here to practice using on-line Help until you feel comfortable navigating the Help system. The Help system is much like a web since you can get to any place from so many others using menu commands, keyboard keys, or toolbar buttons. However, you will always find the same familiar terms such as *Contents, Search,* and *Index* that you can use as guides. If you get lost, click the **Contents** command button to return to a list of contents you can access.

1-11. EXITING WORD

When you are finished with Word, you can exit it. This removes it from the computer's memory and removes its window or icon from the desktop. However, its icon remains in the *Word for Windows 6.0* or *Microsoft Office* group window so you can start it again whenever you want to use it.

It is important to quit Word using the commands designed for this purpose. Although you can exit the program by simply turning off the computer, this is a bad habit to get into, because Word creates temporary files on the disk while you are working, and these are deleted only if you exit correctly. If you quit incorrectly, your document may be left damaged.

QUICKSTEPS: EXITING WORD
To exit windows do one of the following:

▶ Double-click Word's Control-menu box (▭). (See the box "Understanding Control-Menu Boxes" on page 8.)

▶ Pull down the **File** menu and click the **Exit** command.

If you quit Word without saving changes to your document, a dialog box asks if you want to save the current changes. Click the **Yes** command button to save the document or the **No** command button to abandon it. To return to Word instead of quitting it, click the **Cancel** command button.

Click to save the changes.

Click to return to the document.

Microsoft Word

Do you want to save changes to Document4?

Yes   No   Cancel   Help

Click to abandon the changes.

TUTORIAL

When you are finished with Word, you can exit the program as demonstrated in this tutorial.

Exiting Word

1. Pull down the **File** menu and click the **Exit** command to close the Word application.

Finishing Up

2. If you are through for the day, exit Windows and turn off your computer. Be sure to remove your floppy disk from the drive so you don't lose it.

PicTorial 1 Review Questions

True-False

T F **1.** When the OVR indicator is dimmed on the status bar, Word is in the insert mode.

T F **2.** You can open as many documents as your system's memory allows.

T F **3.** You can assign names to files that have up to nine characters.

T F **4.** If you open a new document without closing the original one, the new document erases the original document.

T F **5.** There is more than one way to close a document.

T F **6.** All windows have a Control-menu box.

T F **7.** You should always save a document before making major revisions.

T F **8.** JAZZ@2 is not a valid filename.

T F **9.** When opening and closing files from a floppy disk, it is all right to remove the disk before exiting Word.

T F **10.** Scrolling the screen does not remove the insertion point.

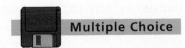 **Multiple Choice**

1. The mouse takes on the shape of a(n) _____ when in the text area.

   a. I-beam

   b. double arrow

   c. left-pointing arrow

   d. right-pointing arrow

2. The title bar of each new document reads _____.

   a. Untitled

   b. FileX

   c. DocumentX

   d. TextX

3. The file name extension Word assigns to files is _____.

   a. wrd

   b. doc

   c. wor

   d. wpd

4. _____ buttons offer mutually exclusive options.

   a. Option

   b. Command

   c. List

   d. Spin

5. Pressing _____ moves the insertion point to the end to the document.

   a. `PgDn`

   b. `Home`, `Home`, `↓`

   c. `Ctrl`+`End`

   d. `Ctrl`+`Home`

6. A _____ is a stored document layout with preset margins and fonts.

   a. File

   b. Template

   c. Macro

   d. Module

7. When you _____ a document, it clears the document from the screen and removes it from the computer's memory.

   a. Close

   b. Exit

   c. Save

   d. Resave

8. _____ buttons execute commands when you click them.

   a. Option

   b. Command

   c. List

   d. Spin

9. Which of the following is not a legal filename character:

   a. ^

   b. @

   c. !

   d. *

10. To save a file under a new name, click the _____ command.

    a. **Save**

    b. **Save As**

    c. **Save Over**

    d. **New Save**

 Fill In the Blank

1. The Word screen is called the _____.

2. The _____ bar lists the name of the application and any open document.

3. The _____ displays information about the document and the program.

4. The _____ indicates the last line in the document.

5. The _____ most recent files are listed on the bottom of the **File** menu when you pull it down.

6. The vertical scroll bar contains three basic elements: _____, _____, and _____.

7. Pressing _____ will move the insertion point to the top of the document.

8. When documents are created, the _____ template is used.

9. The _____ toolbar contains buttons that open new or existing documents, save documents, or print documents.

10. The _____ toolbar contains buttons and drop-down arrows for such items as Font, Font Size, Align Left, and Style.

PicTorial 1 Lab Activities

▶▶ **COMPUTER-BASED TUTORIALS**

Word includes built-in computer-based previews, examples, and demos that teach you more about Word. In this tutorial we suggest you complete the Quick Preview of the program. This takes about ten minutes and covers a lot of points that you haven't been introduced to yet, but it gives you a good overview of the things you will learn how to do.

1. Pull down the **Help** menu and click the **Quick Preview** command to display the Quick Preview opening screen.

2. Click the **GETTING STARTED** button to begin the preview. Two command buttons are displayed on the screen at all times; **Next >** and **Cancel**.

   ▶ When you have finished reading a screen or seeing a demonstration, click the **Next >** command button to advance to the next screen.

   ▶ To quit the Quick Preview at any point, click the **Cancel** command button.

3. When finished, click the **Return to Word** command button on the Quick Preview opening screen.

 ▶▶ **SKILL-BUILDING EXERCISES**

1-1. Loading Word on Your Own System

List the steps here that you use to load Word so that you have them for future reference.

1. _____

   _____

2. _____

   _____

3. _____

   _____

4. _____
   _____
5. _____
   _____

1-2. Describing the Anatomy of the Word for Windows Display

This illustration shows the Word for Windows display that appears when you first load the application. In the spaces provided, write down the name of each of the lettered elements.

a. _____   b. _____

c. _____   d. _____

e. _____   f. _____

g. _____   h. _____

i. _____   j. _____

k. _____   l. _____

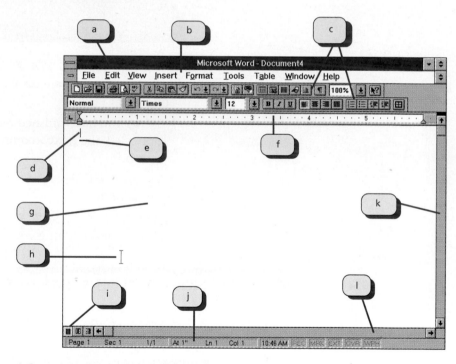

1-3. Exploring Word's Dialog Boxes

Many of Word's commands display dialog boxes where you make choices. In this exercise, you explore a number of these dialog boxes to familiarize yourself with their elements.

1. Pull down the **File** menu and click the **Page Setup** command to display the Page Setup dialog box. Click each of the tabs looking for command buttons, lists with scroll bars, spin buttons (⬍), check boxes (☐ and ☒), drop-down arrows (⬇), and option buttons (○ and ◉). When finished, click the **Cancel** button to close the dialog box.

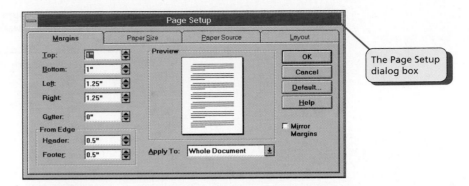

The Page Setup dialog box

2. Pull down the **Format** menu and click the **Paragraph** command to display the Paragraph dialog box. Click each of the tabs looking for command buttons, spin buttons (⬍), check boxes (☐ and ☒), and drop-down arrows (⬇). When finished, click the **Cancel** button to close the dialog box.

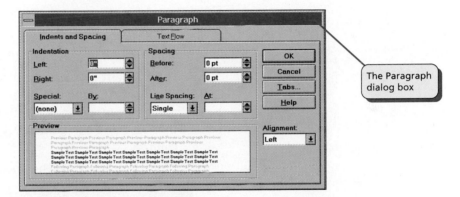

The Paragraph dialog box

3. Pull down other menus and click any command that ends with an ellipsis (...). The ellipsis indicates that selecting the command displays a dialog box. When finished, click the **Cancel** button to close the dialog box.

1-4. Getting Around a Document with a Mouse

To navigate Word for Windows you have to know how to use the scroll bars and how to move the insertion point by pointing and clicking. In this exercise you practice those procedures.

1. Open the *mousemov.doc* document stored in the *exercise* directory of the *Word Student Resource Disk (Part 2)*.

2. The document contains three numbers: ①, ②, and ③. Use the scroll bar to locate them. Click on the left side of each number and then on the right side. Write down in the table "Status Bar Information" the information displayed on the status bar about the position of the insertion point.

3. Position the insertion point in any space between words and press ← or → to move it to the other side of the space. As you do so, watch the *Col* position change on the status bar even though the insertion point is in a space.

4. Close the document without saving it.

STATUS BAR INFORMATION			
Number	At	Ln	Col
]①	_____	_____	_____
①[	_____	_____	_____
]②	_____	_____	_____
②[	_____	_____	_____
]③	_____	_____	_____
③[	_____	_____	_____

1-5. Getting Around a Document with the Keyboard

When typing, it's often faster to move the insertion point with keyboard commands than it is to reach for the mouse. In this exercise you match the keyboard commands in the "Press" column of the table "Keyboard Commands" with appropriate lines in the column "To Move To."

1. Open the *select.doc* document stored in the *exercise* directory on the *Word Student Resource Disk (Part 2)*.

2. Experiment with the keys in the *Press* column of the table "Keyboard Commands." As you discover where each command moves the insertion point, find the description of the movement in the "To Move To" column, and write in the letter from the "Press" column.

3. When finished, close the document without saving it.

KEYBOARD COMMANDS		
To Move To		Press
_____ Top of the previous page	a	Ctrl + Home
_____ Top of the next page	b	Ctrl + ↓
_____ Previous line	c	Ctrl + →
_____ Beginning of the next paragraph	d	Alt + Ctrl + PgDn
_____ End of the document	e	Ctrl + End
_____ Previous character	f	Ctrl + ↑
_____ Next screen up or down	g	Ctrl + ←
_____ Next line	h	Home
_____ Next character	i	End
_____ Beginning of the previous word	j	PgUp or PgDn
_____ End of text on the line	k	→
_____ Beginning of the text on the line	l	↓
_____ Beginning of the previous paragraph	m	←
_____ Beginning of the next word	n	↑
_____ Beginning of the document	o	Alt + Ctrl + PgUp

1-6. Using On-Line Help

The best thing about Word's on-line Help system is that it's always available, even long after you've lost the manual. In this exercise you search on-line Help to locate help.

1. Use the **Help**, **Search for Help on** command to locate the topics listed in the table "Help Topics to Look Up."

2. When you locate a topic, click the **Show Topics** button, count the number of topics shown in the **Go To** section, and write down the number in the table.

3. When finished, double-click the Help window's Control-menu box (⊟) to close the window.

HELP TOPICS TO LOOK UP	
Help Topic	**Number of Topics**
Application Control menu	_____
Application Minimize button	_____
checking spelling	_____
choosing commands	_____
creating documents	_____
Help	_____
opening documents	_____
screen	_____
document windows	_____
Print command (File menu)	_____
Save command (File menu)	_____

1-7. Exploring the Standard Toolbar

Point to each of the buttons on Word's Standard toolbar so its name is displayed on the mouse pointer and its description is displayed on the status bar. Write down the name of each button on the list below.

a b c   d e f   g h i j   k   l   m n   o p q   r s   t   u   v

a. _____ b. _____

c. _____ d. _____

e. _____ f. _____

g. _____ h. _____

i. _____ j. _____

k. _____ l. _____

m. _____ n. _____

o. _____ p. _____

q. _____ r. _____

s. _____ t. _____

u. _____ v. _____

1-8. Exploring the Formatting Toolbar

Point to each of the buttons on Word's Formatting toolbar so its name is displayed on the mouse pointer and its description is displayed on the status bar. Write down the name of each button on the list below.

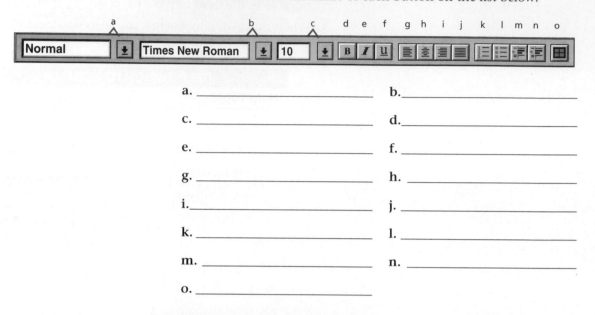

a. _____ b. _____

c. _____ d. _____

e. _____ f. _____

g. _____ h. _____

i. _____ j. _____

k. _____ l. _____

m. _____ n. _____

o. _____

1-9. Opening and Closing Documents

In this exercise, you open and close a number of documents. (For practice in saving documents, see Exercise 1-11, "Entering Text and Saving Documents.") On some systems this can be a very slow process. If your system is slow, you need not open and close all of the documents if you feel that you have mastered the procedures.

1. Insert the floppy disk labeled *Word Student Resource Disk (Part 1)* into the floppy disk drive you use to open and save documents.

2. Use the **Open** command on the **File** menu to open each of documents listed in the table "Documents to Open and Close—Part 1." The files are in the specified directories. Write down the magic word you find at the end of each document, and then close each document using the **Close** command on the **File** menu or by double-clicking its Control-menu box (⬜).

DOCUMENTS TO OPEN AND CLOSE—PART 1		
Directory	**Filename**	**Magic Word**
tutorial	*open1.doc*	_____
tutorial	*open2.doc*	_____
drill	*open3.doc*	_____
drill	*open4.doc*	_____

3. Insert the floppy disk labeled *Word Student Resource Disk (Part 2)* into the floppy disk drive you use to open and save documents.

4. Use the **Open** command on the **File** menu to open each of documents listed in the table "Documents to Open and Close—Part 2." The files are in the specified directories. Write down the magic word you find at the end of each document, and then close each document using the **Close** command on the **File** menu or by double-clicking its Control-menu box (⊟).

DOCUMENTS TO OPEN AND CLOSE—PART 2		
Directory	**Filename**	**Magic Word**
exercise	*open5.doc*	_____
exercise	*open6.doc*	_____
project	*open7.doc*	_____
project	*open8.doc*	_____

1-10. Saving and Opening Documents on Your Own System

Some systems are connected to a network, and you save and retrieve documents from the hard disk drive on the system. If you are working on such a system, enter the following information about the location of your files.

Drive: _____

Directory: _____

Other: _____

_____

_____

1-11. Entering Text and Saving Documents

In this PicTorial you have already performed almost all of the essential procedures that make word processing programs so powerful. If you are fearless (and there is no reason not to be), you can create documents right now! Entering text is as easy as typing it in and pressing [Enter ←] where necessary. In this exercise you enter three very short poems and save each in a specified directory on your disk.

1. Insert the *Word Student Resource Disk (Part 1)* into the floppy disk drive you use to open and save documents.

2. Use the **New** button on the toolbar to open a new document, enter your name at the top of the document, and press [Enter ←] twice to insert a blank line.

3. Enter Poem 1 shown below. (To enter --, press the hyphen key twice.)

4. Use the **Save** command on the **File** menu to save the finished document as *poem1* in the *drill* directory.

5. Click the **Print** button on the toolbar to print the document.

6. Double-click the document window's Control-menu box (⊟) to close the document.

7. Repeat Steps 2 through 6 for Poem 2 but save it as *poem2* in the *tutorial* directory.

8. Repeat Steps 2 through 6 for Poem 3 (feel free to edit the word *Men* on the second line of the poem to read *We*) but save it as *poem3* in the *drill* directory.

IT ISN'T THE COUGH

It isn't the cough

That carries you off;

It's the coffin

They carry you off in.

--Anonymous

Poem 1

RELATIVITY

There was a young lady named Bright

Who traveled much faster than light.

She started one day

In the relative way,

And returned on the previous night.

--Anonymous

Poem 2

DON'T GIVE UP

'Twixt failure and success the point's so fine

Men sometimes know not when to touch the line,

Just when the pearl was waiting one more plunge,

How many a struggler has thrown up the sponge!

Then take this honey from the bitterest cup:

"There is no failure save in giving up!"

--Anonymous

Poem 3

PICTORIAL 2

MASTERING THE ESSENTIALS

After completing this PicTorial, you will be able to:

▸ Enter and edit text

▸ Spell-check documents

▸ Preview and print documents

▸ Select text and copy and move it

▸ Find and replace text

▸ Look up synonyms and antonyms in the thesaurus

There are only a few procedures that you absolutely must know to begin getting value from a program such as Word, and they are covered in this PicTorial. These procedures include entering and editing text, and printing documents. It is also helpful to know how to use Word's built-in spelling checker and thesaurus and how to copy, move, or delete larger sections of text.

2-1. ENTERING TEXT

The basic rule of entering text is to move the insertion point to where you want to enter it and then type it in. If you have just started Word or opened a new document, the insertion point is at the top of the document waiting for you to enter text. As you type a character, the character appears where the insertion point is, and the insertion point then moves one space to the right.

WORD WRAP

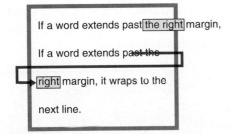

When you are typing paragraphs, you do not have to press ⌈Enter ↵⌉ at the end of each line. Word has a feature, called *word wrap*, that automatically does this for you. When the end of a line is reached, Word calculates whether the word being entered fits on the line. If it will not fit, Word automatically begins a new line of text by moving the entire word to the next line.

HARD AND SOFT RETURNS

Returns (sometimes called carriage returns) are codes in the document that indicate where lines end. When you print the document, these codes are not printed, but they tell the printer when to move down one line and back to the left margin. Word (like all word processing programs) has two kinds of returns: soft and hard.

Word automatically enters *soft returns* at the end of a line as you enter text whenever it reaches the right margin and wraps a word to the next line. Soft returns automatically adjust their position if you revise the text. For example, when you insert or delete text or when you change the margins, existing soft returns are automatically rearranged so that they are always positioned at the end of each line.

LOOKING AHEAD: DISPLAYING PARAGRAPH MARKS

To see where you have entered paragraph marks, click the **Show/Hide ¶** button on the toolbar. They are indicated with ¶ symbols. Click the **Show/Hide ¶** button again to hide them.

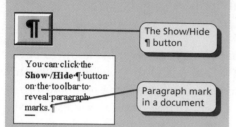

The Show/Hide ¶ button

You·can·click·the· **Show·/Hide·¶**·button· on·the·toolbar·to· reveal·paragraph· marks.¶

Paragraph mark in a document

Unlike soft returns, *hard returns*, also called paragraph marks (¶), remain fixed in the place where you enter them by pressing Enter⏎. You enter a hard return whenever you want to end a line before you reach the right margin—for example:

▶ To end a paragraph and start a new one.

▶ To enter an inside address, a salutation, or a heading.

▶ To insert a blank line, as you would following an inside address, the date, and the closing of a letter. Each time you press Enter⏎, you insert another blank line.

ENTERING LETTERS, NUMBERS, AND SYMBOLS

You can enter letters, numbers, and shifted characters such as % and &.

To enter uppercase letters, either hold down ⇧ Shift while typing a letter or press CapsLock to enter all uppercase letters. Press CapsLock again to return to lowercase. If you press ⇧ Shift to enter text when CapsLock is engaged, you enter lowercase letters. Most keyboards have lights that indicate when CapsLock is engaged.

To enter shifted characters like !, @, and # that appear on the top half of some keys, hold down ⇧ Shift while you press the keys.

To enter numbers, either use the number keys on the top row of the keyboard or use the numeric keypad. The keys on the numeric keypad not only enter numbers; they also move the insertion point. When NumLock is engaged, pressing the keys enters numbers. When NumLock is not engaged, pressing the keys moves the insertion point. Most keyboards have lights that indicate when NumLock is engaged.

If you are an experienced typist and are used to typing a lowercase letter ell (l) for the number one (1), or an uppercase letter oh (O) for zero (0), do not do this on your computer. The computer treats numbers and letters differently, and although you usually won't have problems, you could run into difficulties by disregarding this distinction.

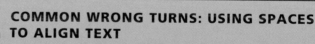

COMMON WRONG TURNS: USING SPACES TO ALIGN TEXT

With a program such as Word, you should never use spaces to align text as you might on a typewriter. Word will expand and compress spaces at times so your text may look aligned on the screen but then print out of alignment. When using Word, use tab stops or paragraph indents to align your text, as you will see in PicTorial 3.

TIP: THE CHANGING RULES ON SPACES FOLLOWING PERIODS AND COLONS

When documents were typed on typewriters, it was common practice to enter two spaces following periods and colons. However, in publishing, it has always been standard practice to use only one space. As the power of word processors has begun to rival that of desktop publishing programs, it is more common to follow publishing practices, so one space is becoming increasingly acceptable.

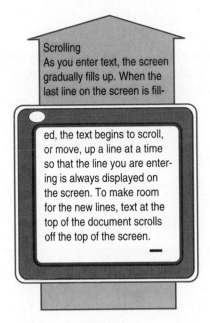

Scrolling

As you enter text, the screen gradually fills up. When the last line on the screen is fill-

ed, the text begins to scroll, or move, up a line at a time so that the line you are entering is always displayed on the screen. To make room for the new lines, text at the top of the document scrolls off the top of the screen.

SCROLLING

As you enter text, the screen gradually fills up. When the last line on the screen is filled, the text begins to scroll, or move, up a line at a time so that the line you are entering is always displayed on the screen. To make room for the new lines, text at the top of the document scrolls off the top of the screen. But it is not gone for good; you can scroll back to it whenever you want using the scroll bar or keyboard commands.

PAGE BREAKS

When you enter enough lines of text so that they will fill a page when you print the document, Word automatically inserts a page break. This is called a *soft page break*. If you insert or delete text above this soft page break, it adjusts its position automatically. The soft page break is indicated by a thin dotted line across the screen in Normal view and a separation between pages in Page Layout view. You cannot delete a soft page break. The only way to change its position is to add or delete text above it.

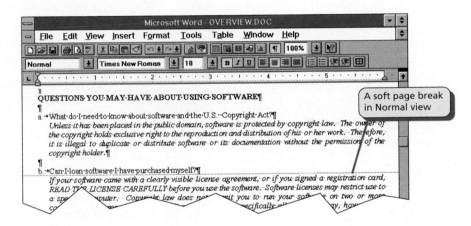

A soft page break in Normal view

CORRECTING MISTAKES

If you make a mistake when typing, press ⌫Bksp to delete characters to the insertion point's left; then type the characters correctly. You can also move the insertion point through the text and press Del to delete any character to the right of the insertion point. If you hold ⌫Bksp or Del down, it will delete one character after another until you release it.

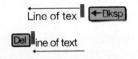

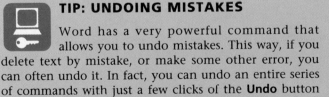

Deleting text

TIP: UNDOING MISTAKES

Word has a very powerful command that allows you to undo mistakes. This way, if you delete text by mistake, or make some other error, you can often undo it. In fact, you can undo an entire series of commands with just a few clicks of the **Undo** button on the toolbar.

Click the Undo button to undo a change you just made.

▸ To undo the last command, click the **Undo** button on the toolbar.

▸ To undo the last command and any number of commands before it, click the drop-down arrow (⬇) next to the **Undo** button to display a list of commands you can undo. Press ⬇ to highlight the commands to be undone and press Enter⏎, or click the last command on the list to be undone.

You can also pull down the **Edit** menu and click the **Undo** command. The word **Undo** on the menu is followed by the name of the command that will be undone. If no command can be undone, the command will read **Can't Undo**.

TUTORIAL

Entering text is what word processing is all about. You can't do anything else until you have mastered this basic skill. In this tutorial you open a document with a pre-existing letterhead and heading and enter your own body text.

Getting Started

1. Open the *enterdoc.doc* document stored in the *tutorial* directory on the *Word Student Resource Disk (Part 1)*.

2. Click just to the left of the *y* in *your name*, press [Del] nine times to delete the phrase, then type your own name.

3. Click anywhere in the date and press [F9] to update it.

> **LOOKING AHEAD: UPDATING DATE FIELDS IN WORD**
>
> In many of the documents used in this book, the date has been entered in a special format called a field. When you open the document, Word displays the date on which the document was created. It will automatically update that date when you print or repaginate the document, but you can update it yourself by clicking anywhere in the date and pressing [F9]. Word reads the current date from your computer's clock, so if the clock is not accurate, the date shown won't be either.

4. Press [Ctrl]+[End] to move the insertion point to the end of the document. (Remember—to press keys such as this connected by a plus sign, hold down [Ctrl] and quickly press [End].)

Entering a Document

5. The document already has a letterhead and a heading. However, you must enter the body of the document shown here. As you do so:

   ▶ Press [Enter ↵] only where indicated—at the end of paragraphs and to insert blank lines.

   ▶ Press [Tab ⇆] where indicated—at the beginning of each body paragraph.

   ▶ Your lines will probably wrap at places other than the ones shown in the figure; don't worry if they do. Where they wrap depends on your system.

   ▶ If you make any typos, press [← Bksp] to back up the insertion point to erase them, and then enter the correct letters.

Computer Curriculum Center
MEMORANDUM

123 North Monroe Street
Cleveland, Ohio 65743

Phone: 456 385-2578
Fax: 456 385-3456

TO: Janie Czarnecki, Word Instructor

FROM: your name, Educational Director

SUBJECT: Interesting documents needed

DATE: November 11, 1995

`Enter ↵`

`Tab ⇥`We need to come up with a document to use in the introductory Word class in the section on entering text. The document should be short because some students don't type well. It should also be interesting or useful. Too many documents used in textbooks are DULL! I'd like to suggest the paragraphs describing OLE, one of the newest features of application programs. `Enter ↵`

`Enter ↵`

`Tab ⇥`"Windows gives you more than one way to move information from one application into another. Some Windows applications support object linking and embedding (OLE). OLE allows you to open one application from within another, so that an object created in one application can be edited from within the second, within which it is embedded. `Enter ↵`

`Tab ⇥`Applications that support OLE can be either servers or clients or both. Servers create documents or graphics (called objects) that can be embedded in documents created with client applications. Paintbrush and Excel are servers. Word is a client. Paintbrush and Excel objects can therefore be embedded in Word documents. The resulting Word document, containing material created in another application, is called a compound document. `Enter ↵`

`Tab ⇥`Embedding data has one major advantage over copying data. When data is copied, it is no longer connected to the application that created it. When it is embedded, the creating application can be opened from within the client application's document so you can edit it. After embedding an object in a document, you can just double-click the object to automatically load it and its server application. After making any changes, you use the application's command to carry the changes to the client document." `Enter ↵`

Finishing Up

6. Click the **Save** button on the toolbar to save the document.

7. Pull down the **File** menu and click the **Close** command to close the document and clear the screen.

2-2. EDITING TEXT

To edit text, you move the insertion point through the document and insert characters by typing them in or delete them by pressing `← Bksp` or `Del`. You can also switch between insert and overtype modes, make new paragraphs from existing ones, and join existing paragraphs into one paragraph.

SWITCHING BETWEEN INSERT AND OVERTYPE MODES

Word's default setting is the insert mode, so if you enter characters into existing text, the text moves over to make room for them. However, you can switch to overtype mode so that characters you enter type over and replace any existing characters in their way. The current status is listed on the status bar. When *OVR* is dimmed, you are in insert mode. When it's not dimmed, you are in overtype mode.

QUICKSTEPS: SWITCHING BETWEEN INSERT AND OVERTYPE MODES

Do either of the following:

▶ Press [Ins].

▶ Double-click *OVR* on the status bar.

TIP: RETURNING TO A PREVIOUS REVISION

To return the insertion point to each of the last three locations where you entered or deleted text, press [⇧ Shift]+[F5].

TIP: INSERTING TEXT

When you position the insertion point to insert text between two existing words, you can position it on either side of the space that separates the words. If you position it on the left side of the space, you press [Spacebar] before typing the new word. If you position it on the right side of the space, you press [Spacebar] after typing the new word.

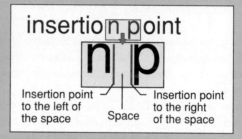

DISPLAYING NONPRINTING CHARACTERS

When you press [Enter ↵], [Tab ⇆], and [Spacebar], you enter nonprinting characters into the document that control printouts. When these characters are displayed, it's easy to see if you have inserted extra spaces, tabs, or returns. It also makes it easy to delete these hidden characters. Some of the nonprinting characters that you can display are listed and described in the box "Nonprinting Characters."

Nonprinting Characters	
Character name	**Character**
Tab characters	→
Spaces	•
Paragraph marks	¶

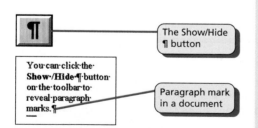

QUICKSTEPS: DISPLAYING NONPRINTING CHARACTERS

Fastest

▶ Click the **Show/Hide ¶** button on the toolbar to display or hide nonprinting characters.

Menus

1. Pull down the **Tools** menu and click the **Options** command to display the Options dialog box.

2. On the **View** tab, click any of the check boxes in the *Nonprinting Characters* section to turn them on, and then click the **OK** command button.

MAKING ONE PARAGRAPH INTO TWO

You can enter hard returns as you type a document, or you can enter them into existing text. You enter hard returns in existing text whenever you want to break an existing paragraph into two paragraphs. To do so, move the insertion point just to the left of the character that you want to be the first character in the new paragraph and press [Enter←]. This moves the insertion point, and all text to its right, down one line and back to the left margin. If you press [Enter←] a second time, a blank line is inserted above the new paragraph.

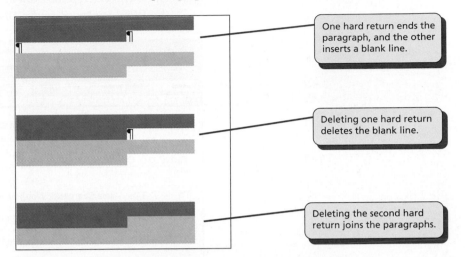

One hard return ends the paragraph, and the other inserts a blank line.

Deleting one hard return deletes the blank line.

Deleting the second hard return joins the paragraphs.

JOINING TWO PARAGRAPHS INTO ONE

To join two paragraphs into one, you can use [←Bksp] or [Del] to delete the paragraph marks (hard returns) that separate them. (Click the **Show/Hide ¶** command on the toolbar to turn it on so you can see them). When you join paragraphs like this, strange things can happen because Word stores all paragraph formats, like alignment, indents, and spacing, in the paragraph mark symbol. When you delete the paragraph mark (or marks) at the end of a paragraph, it becomes part of the paragraph that follows. The paragraph mark at the end of that paragraph determines the format of the combined paragraphs.

Before Paragraphs Are Joined:

This paragraph is aligned with the left margin and separated from the paragraph below by a paragraph mark.¶
> The paragraph below is aligned with the right margin.¶

After Paragraphs Are Joined:

> This paragraph is aligned with the left margin and separated from the paragraph below by a paragraph mark. The paragraph below is aligned with the right margin.¶

TUTORIAL

In this tutorial you open the document you created in a previous tutorial and revise it by inserting and deleting text.

Getting Ready

1. Open the *enterdoc.doc* document stored in the *tutorial* directory on the *Word Student Resource Disk (Part 1)*.

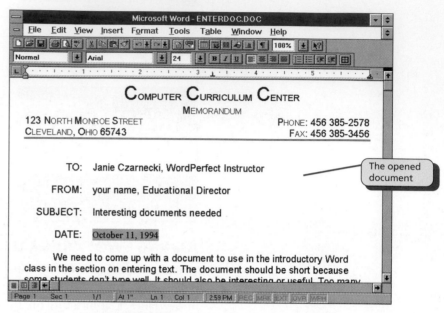

2. Click the **Show/Hide ¶** command on the toolbar to display hard returns, spaces, and tabs.

Editing a Document

3. Edit the first paragraph of the document by inserting and deleting text:

   ▶ To insert the text shown underlined in this illustration, move the insertion point to the appropriate place in the document and type it in. As you do so, notice how existing text moves aside to make room for the inserted text.

   ▶ To delete each of the words shown struck out in this illustration, move the insertion point to the beginning or end of the section to be deleted and press [Del] or [←Bksp]. (If you delete any text by mistake, immediately click the **Undo** button on the toolbar.)

We need to come up with a <u>useful</u> document to use in the introductory Word class in the section on entering text. The document should be <u>as</u> short <u>as possible</u> because some students don't type well. ~~It should also be interesting or useful.~~ Too many <u>textbooks use</u> documents <u>that</u> ~~used in textbooks~~ are DULL! I'd like to suggest the <u>following</u> paragraphs describing OLE, one of the newest features of applications programs.

Separating and Joining Paragraphs

4. Move the insertion point to the space following the exclamation point at the end of the sentence that reads *Too many textbooks use*

documents that are DULL! in the first body paragraph. It should be at the right side of the space (indicated by a ▪ character).

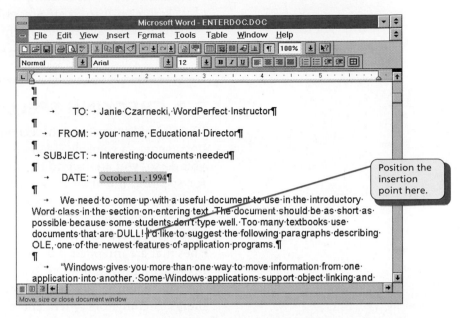

5. Press `Enter ←┘` twice to break the paragraph into two paragraphs with a blank line between them. Then press `Tab⇥` to indent the second paragraph.

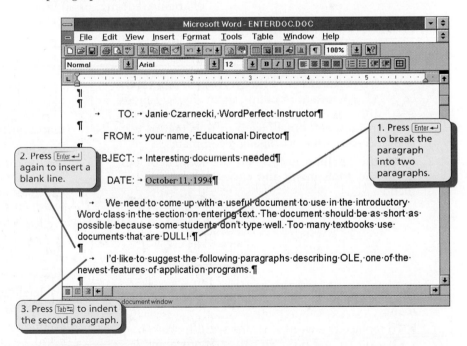

6. Press `←Bksp` three times to delete the symbols for the tab code and two hard returns so the two paragraphs are again joined into one. The document should now look as it did before you separated the paragraphs.

Finishing Up

7. Click the **Show/Hide ¶** button on the toolbar to hide nonprinting characters.

8. Click the **Save** button on the toolbar to save the document.

9. Click the **Print** button on the toolbar to print the document. Proofread it to locate any errors and correct them using the procedures you have studied in this section.

10. Save and close the document.

2-3. CHECKING SPELLING

Word's built-in spelling checker will correct the spelling of words in your documents—a valuable aid upon which you should not rely too much. If you do so, you are sure to be embarrassed at some point. It checks only for spelling, not usage. For example, spelling checkers would find no problems in the sentences *Eye wood like two except you're invitation, butt can not. unfortunately, their are another things I half too due* or *Too bee oar knot two bee.* These sentences, concocted from words that sound like the ones that are intended, will not be flagged by Word's **Spelling** command because each word in them is an actual word, correctly spelled, that is in Word's dictionary. Because of this limitation, you must proofread documents carefully for content and context.

When you use the **Spelling** command, Word checks each word in the document against its dictionary. If Word can't find the word in its dictionary, it highlights the word, and you are given the option of ignoring, changing, editing, or adding it to the dictionary if it is spelled correctly. Adding a word to the dictionary keeps it from being flagged in other documents.

QUICKSTEPS: CHECKING SPELLING

1. The insertion point can be anyplace in the document but if you want to check the spelling of a single word or a section of text, select it before using the **Spelling** command.

2. Click the **Spelling** button on the toolbar or pull down the **Tools** menu and click the **Spelling** command.

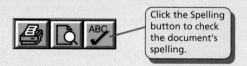

Click the Spelling button to check the document's spelling.

3. If a "misspelled" word is highlighted in the document:

   ▶ To replace the word with the word in the **Change To** text box, click the **Change** command button. To replace it and all subsequent occurrences of the same word, click the **Change All** button.

   ▶ To replace the word with a word on the **Suggestions** list, click the replacement word to select it and then click the **Change** command button.

   ▶ To edit a word displayed in the **Change To** text box, press → to remove the highlight from the word or click in the text box to move the insertion point there. After editing the word, click the **Change** command button.

   ▶ To leave the word unchanged, click either the **Ignore** or **Ignore All** command button.

   ▶ To add the word to the dictionary, click the **Add** command button.

   ▶ To delete one of a pair of repeated words, click the **Delete** command button when it appears.

   ▶ To undo the last correction if you change your mind, click the **Undo Last** command button.

4. When spell-checking is complete, a dialog box tells you so. Click the **OK** command button to close the dialog box.

TUTORIAL

No one is perfect—that's one reason why spelling checkers are so popular. In this tutorial you use Word's spelling checker to check a document that contains built-in mistakes.

1. Open the *educom.doc* document stored in the *tutorial* directory on the *Word Student Resource Disk (Part 1)* and enter your name at the end of the line that reads *Copy belonging to:*.

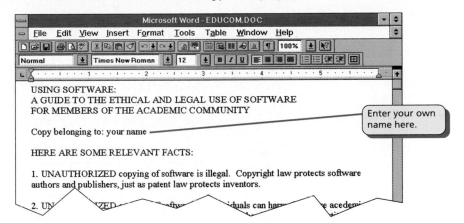

2. Click the **Spelling** button on the toolbar to begin spell-checking.

3. When a word is found that isn't listed in the dictionary, Word highlights it and displays the Spelling dialog box. You have to decide whether it is spelled correctly (or look it up in the box "Tip: Misspelled Words"). When you decide, refer to Step 3 in the QuickSteps box "Checking Spelling."

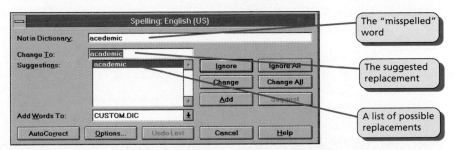

TIP: "MISSPELLED" WORDS

Not all words highlighted during a spell check are spelled wrong. Some are spelled correctly but just aren't in the program's dictionary. Here is a list of the words that should be highlighted during your spell check of the *educom.doc* document, with comments about each.

Word highlighted	Comment	Word highlighted	Comment
acedemic	academic	distribute distribute	distribute
unauthorised	unauthorized	licenseagreement	license agreement
widily	widely	legel	legal
EDUCOM	*Spelled correctly*	Shareware	*Spelled correctly*
worksof	works of	ADAPSO	*Spelled correctly*
U.S.	*Spelled correctly*	P.O.	*Spelled correctly*

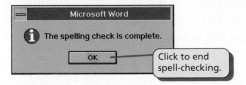

4. When the last word is corrected, a dialog box tells you spell-checking is complete. Click the **OK** command button to close the dialog box.

5. Click the **Save** button on the toolbar to save your changes and then print the document.

6. Close the document.

2-4. PREVIEWING AND PRINTING DOCUMENTS

Most document are eventually printed so a record can be filed or distributed to others. Word lets you print a document with the click of a button or preview it before you print it to be sure it will print correctly.

PREVIEWING A DOCUMENT

Print Preview lets you catch layout mistakes before wasting time and paper printing the document. In this view, you can also adjust margins, edit text, and even drag text or graphics between pages, as you will see later.

QUICKSTEPS: PREVIEWING PRINTOUTS
1. Click the **Print Preview** button on the toolbar, or pull down the **File** menu and click the **Print Preview** command.

2. Click any of the buttons described in the box "Understanding the Print Preview Toolbar." Use the scroll bar to scroll through a document that has more pages than are currently displayed.

3. Click the **Close** command to return to your previous view of the document.

UNDERSTANDING THE PRINT PREVIEW TOOLBAR

When you pull down the **File** menu and click the **Print Preview** command, the Print Preview toolbar is displayed.

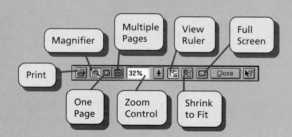

Print prints the document.

Magnifier switches the mouse pointer between a magnifier and an I-beam (I). When displayed as a magnifier, click anywhere in the document to enlarge it and again to shrink it. When displayed as an I-beam, you can select text as described in Section 2-5 and drag and drop it as described in Section 2-7.

One Page displays one page at a time.

Multiple Pages displays a grid you use to select the number of pages to be displayed. Click the lower-right corner of the rectangular grid of pages you would like displayed or point to the upper-left corner of the grid, hold down the mouse and drag the highlight over the grid. It will expand as you drag against a border. When you have highlighted the number of pages you want to display, release the mouse button.

Zoom Control drop-down arrow (⬇) displays a list of zooms from which you can choose.

View Ruler turns the horizontal and vertical rulers on and off.

Shrink to Fit reduces the number of pages when there is only a limited amount of text on the document's last page. It does this by making the document's type smaller each time you click it. These changes in type size are permanent, so use this with care (or return to Normal view and click the **Undo** button to reverse them).

Full Screen hides all screen elements except the Print Preview toolbar when you click it the first time, and reveals them when you click it again.

Close returns you to your previous view of the document.

PRINTING DOCUMENTS

When you print the document displayed on the screen, you can print the entire document, specific pages, or a selected block.

UNDERSTANDING THE PRINT DIALOG BOX

When you pull down the **File** menu and click the **Print** command, the Print dialog box appears. This box allows you to control all aspects of the printout.

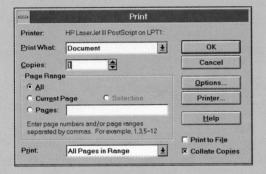

Printer Section

Printer lists the currently selected printer.

Print What normally specifies the document, but you can change it to print such things as summary information about the document, annotations, or key assignments.

Copies specifies the number of copies to be printed.

Page Range section allows you to specify pages to be printed:

▶ **All** (the default setting) prints all pages in the document.

▶ **Current Page** prints the page on which the insertion point is positioned.

▶ **Pages** prints ranges of pages using these procedures (do not enter spaces in the page specifications, for they may create problems.):

- To print a single page, enter the page number. For example, to print page 7, type **7**.

- To print several consecutive pages, enter the starting and ending pages separated by a hyphen. For example, to print pages 2 through 5, type **2-5**.

- To print several nonconsecutive pages or ranges of pages, separate them with commas. For example, to print pages 1, 5, and 10, type **1,5,10** and to print page 1 and then pages 6 through 8, type **1,6-8**.

- To print from the beginning of the document to a specific page, type a hyphen and then the ending page number. For example, to print from the beginning of the document to page 10, type **-10**.

- To print from a specific page to the end of the document, type the beginning page number followed by a hyphen. For example, to print from page 10 to the end of the document, type **10-**.

Print specifies whether you print all pages in the specified range or just odd or even pages.

Options command button displays a dialog box where you can change print options. Click the **OK** command button to return to the Print dialog box.

Printer command button displays a list of available printers. Double-click the one you want to use to select it. Click the **Close** command button to return to the Print dialog box.

TUTORIAL

In this tutorial you use the Print Preview command to check a document's layout before printing. You then print only selected pages instead of the entire document.

1. Open the *overview.doc* document stored in the *tutorial* directory on the *Word Student Resource Disk (Part 1)*.

Exploring Print Preview

2. Click the **Print Preview** button on the toolbar. The screen changes and the mouse pointer appears as a magnifying glass when in the page area of the screen.

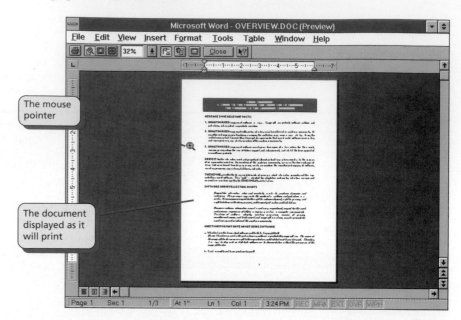

The mouse pointer

The document displayed as it will print

3. Click on the heading on the document to enlarge that section of the document. Then click anywhere in the document to return to your previous view.

4. Click the **Multiple Pages** button on the toolbar to display a grid. Point to the upper-left corner of the grid, hold down the mouse and drag the highlight down and right until the grid reads *2 x 2 Pages*. Then release the mouse button to display all three pages of the document.

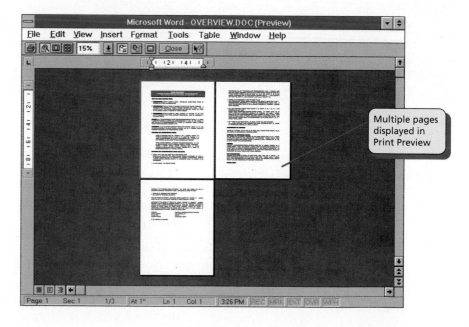

Multiple pages displayed in Print Preview

5. Click the **One Page** button on the toolbar to return to your previous view.

6. Click the **Close** command button to leave Print Preview and return to your original view.

Printing a Single Page

7. Pull down the **File** menu and click the **Print** command to display the Print dialog box.

8. Click the **Pages** option button in the *Page Range* section to turn it on, and then type **2** in the **Pages** text box.

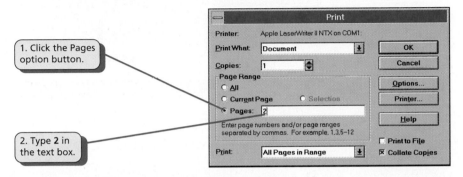

9. Click the **OK** command button to begin printing. When you do so, an hourglass briefly appears and information about the print job is displayed on the status bar while the document is being printed to the disk. When the hourglass disappears, you can resume editing while the document is sent from the disk to the printer.

Finishing Up

10. Close the document without saving it.

2-5. SELECTING TEXT

Word, like most other Windows applications, makes it easy for you to copy, move, delete, or format data in a document. To do so, you first select the text you want to work with and then choose the action to be performed on it. Selected text is displayed in reverse video—white text against a dark background.

There are four ways to select text: clicking, dragging with the mouse, using the keyboard, and using the **Edit** menu.

CLICKING THE MOUSE

The fastest way to select text is often by clicking it. Where you point and how many times you click determine what is selected. These options are described in the table "Selecting Text by Clicking the Mouse" on the next page. When clicking you should be aware of the invisible area, called the *selection bar*, between the text and the left edge of the screen. When the mouse pointer is positioned in this narrow area, the mouse pointer turns into a right-pointing arrow. Clicking the mouse then selects text to the right of the pointer (see the illustration on the next page).

Selected text is highlighted
Unselected text isn't.

TIP: REPLACING TEXT

The fastest way to replace text in a document is to select it and then type in the new text. The first character that you type deletes all of the selected text.

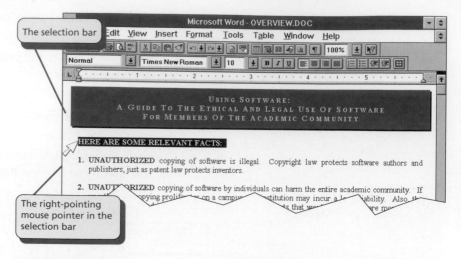

The selection bar

The right-pointing mouse pointer in the selection bar

SELECTING TEXT BY CLICKING THE MOUSE

To	Do This
Select a word	▶ Double-click the word.
Select a sentence	▶ Hold down [Ctrl] and click anywhere in the sentence.
Select a line of text	▶ Click in the selection bar next to it.
Select a paragraph	▶ Double-click in the selection bar next to it.
	▶ Triple-click anywhere in the paragraph.
Select any amount of text	▶ Click at the beginning of the text you want to select and [⇧ Shift]-click at the end.
Select an entire document	▶ Triple-click anywhere in the selection bar or hold down [Ctrl] and click once in the selection bar.
Unselect selected text	▶ Click anywhere to remove the highlight from selected text.

DRAGGING THE MOUSE

You can drag the mouse pointer while holding down the left button to expand the highlight over selected text. When doing so, if you drag it against the upper or lower frame of the window, the document will scroll. When the text that you want to select is highlighted, release the left button and it remains highlighted.

▶ Once you have selected a word by clicking or dragging the mouse, if you continue to drag the highlight it will select only whole words. You can't select partial words with this procedure.

▶ If you select a sentence or paragraph by clicking and then drag the highlight without releasing the mouse button, you will select adjacent sentences or paragraphs. You can't select partial sentences or paragraphs with this procedure.

To fine-tune your selection, you can press [F8] and move the highlight a character at a time by pressing [←] or [→]. You can do the same thing if you hold down [⇧ Shift] while pressing [←] or [→].

USING THE KEYBOARD

You can also use the arrow keys to expand the highlight. One way is to hold down ⟨⇧ Shift⟩ while you then press the arrow keys (or other keys that move the insertion point). Another way is to press ⟨F8⟩ or double-click *EXT* on the status bar (*EXT* will no longer be dimmed). When you then press the arrow keys (or other keys that move the insertion point), or click elsewhere in the document, all text is selected between the original position and where you move the highlight or click. Press ⟨F8⟩ again or double-click *EXT* on the status bar again to turn Extend Selection off if you want to press the arrow keys or click without expanding the highlight further.

USING THE EDIT MENU

To select all of the text in a document, pull down the **Edit** menu and click the **Select All** command.

TUTORIAL

In this tutorial you practice selecting text by clicking and dragging. To make it more interesting, you click buttons on the toolbar to format your selections.

Getting Started

1. Open the *enterdoc.doc* document stored in the *tutorial* directory on the *Word Student Resource Disk (Part 1)*.

Clicking to Select Fixed Amounts of Text

2. Double-click the word *DULL* in the first paragraph to select it, and then click the **Bold** button on the toolbar.

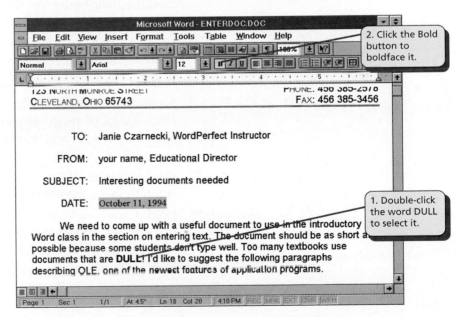

3. Double-click in the selection bar next to the opening paragraph that begins "*We need to come up with...*" to select it, and then click the **Italic** button on the toolbar to italicize it.

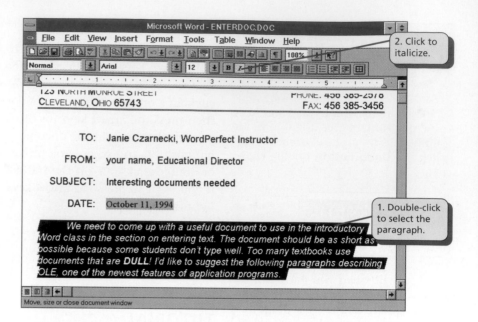

2. Click to italicize.

1. Double-click to select the paragraph.

4. Double-click the word *TO* on the first line of the heading to select it, and then click the **Bold** button on the toolbar.

5. Repeat Step 4 for *FROM*, *SUBJECT*, and *DATE*, in the heading.

Dragging the Highlight

6. Click to the left of the *W* in *We* at the beginning of the first paragraph to move the insertion point there.

7. Hold down the left button, and drag the mouse downward to expand the highlight over the entire italicized paragraph. Release the left button, and the paragraph remains highlighted. Notice how the **Italic** button on the toolbar is highlighted to indicate that format was applied to the selection.

8. Click the **Italic** button on the toolbar to remove the italic format from the paragraph.

Selecting Text by Clicking the Mouse in the Text

9. Scroll the document so you can see the last three paragraphs. If you can't see all of them, display the one that begins *"Windows gives you more than one way to move information from one application into another."*

10. Click to the left of the quotation mark at the beginning of the paragraph to move the insertion point there.

11. Hold down [⇧ Shift] and click to the right of the closing quotation mark at the end of the document. (You may have to scroll the screen to see it.) This selects all text between the two points.

12. Click the **Italic** button on the toolbar to italicize it.

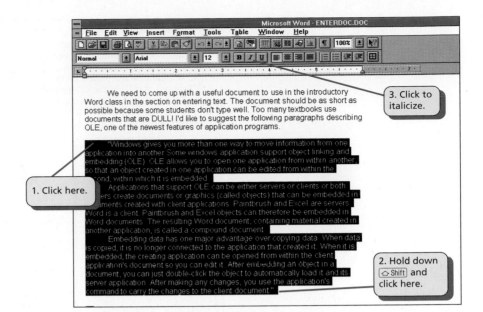

Finishing Up

13. Save and print the document.

> ✋ **PAUSING FOR PRACTICE**
>
> Selecting text is a basic procedure that you must master to become a proficient Word user. Pause here to continue practicing selecting text using all of the techniques described in this section.

14. When you have finished, close the document without saving it again.

2-6. COPYING AND MOVING TEXT WITH THE CLIPBOARD

Word, like most other Windows applications, makes it easy for you to copy or move text in a document. To begin, you first select the text you want to copy or move. You then copy or cut the selected text to Windows' Clipboard, where it remains until you copy or cut other text or exit Windows. While the text is stored on the Clipboard, you can paste it anywhere in the document you copied or cut it from. You can also paste it into another document, or even into another application's document.

Cutting and Pasting

Copying leaves the original text intact and makes a copy of it on the Clipboard. Cutting removes the original text from the application's file and transfers it to the Clipboard. A copy of the text remains on the Clipboard until you cut or copy other text so you can paste it in a number of places if you wish.

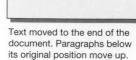

Original document with text selected

Text moved to the end of the document. Paragraphs below its original position move up.

Text copied to the end of the document. The original text remains unchanged.

QUICKSTEPS: COPYING OR MOVING TEXT

1. Select the text you want to copy or move.
2. Do one of the following to copy or cut the selected text:
   ▶ Click the **Cut** or **Copy** button on the toolbar.
   ▶ Pull down the **Edit** menu and click the **Cut** or **Copy** command.
   ▶ Click in the selected area with the right mouse button to display a shortcut menu and click the **Cut** or **Copy** command.
3. Move the insertion point to where you want it inserted.
4. Do one of the following to paste the cut or copied text:
   ▶ Click the **Paste** button on the toolbar.
   ▶ Pull down the **Edit** menu and click the **Paste** command.
   ▶ Click the right mouse button to display a shortcut menu and click the **Paste** command.

TIP: SMART CUT AND PASTE

When you select text and cut, paste, or delete it, Word will automatically adjust spaces to make the text fit the surroundings. For example, if you delete a word at the end of the sentence, Word automatically deletes the space that was in front of the word so there is no space between the new last word and the period. It will also automatically make similar adjustments when you delete text near parentheses or hyphens.

TUTORIAL

In this tutorial you are introduced to copying and moving paragraphs and phrases using the Clipboard.

Getting Started

1. Open the *cutpaste.doc* document stored in the *tutorial* directory on the *Word Student Resource Disk (Part 1)* and enter your name, then click anywhere in the date and press F9 to update it .

2. Click the **Show/Hide ¶** button on the toolbar to display hard returns, spaces, and tabs.

Moving a Phrase

3. Position the insertion point just to the left of the letter *a* in the phrase *after you select it* on the first line of the body text. Hold down the left button and drag the mouse to the right to highlight up to and including the letter just before the period at the end of the line. Release the mouse button.

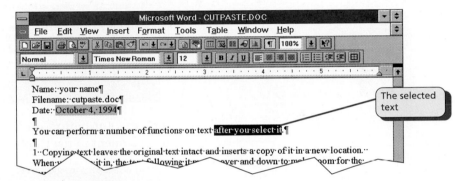

4. Pull down the **Edit** menu and click the **Cut** command to move the phrase from the document to the Clipboard.

COMMON WRONG TURNS: THE CLIPBOARD

The Clipboard retains text only until you cut or copy something else. Therefore, if you plan to paste it elsewhere in the document, do so before you use the **Cut** or **Copy** commands again.

5. Click at the beginning of the sentence to move the insertion point there, pull down the **Edit** menu, and click the **Paste** command to copy the phrase back into the document from the Clipboard.

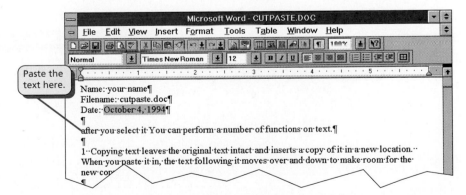

6. Edit the sentence so that it reads *After you select it, you can perform a number of functions on text.*

Moving a Paragraph

7. Double-click in the selection bar next to the paragraph numbered *1* to select the entire paragraph.

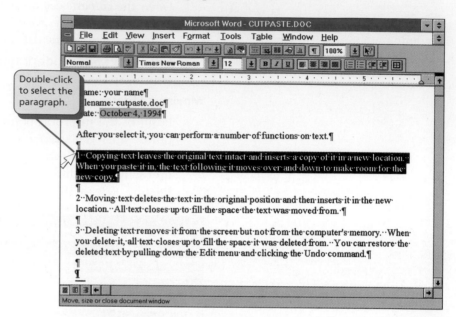

8. Click the **Cut** button on the toolbar to move the paragraph from the document to the Clipboard.

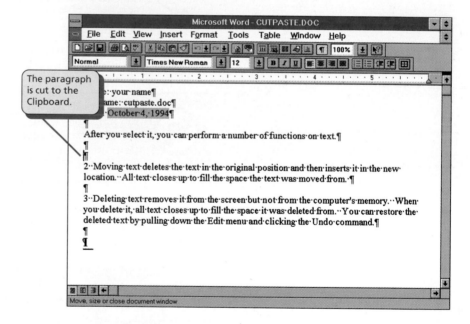

9. Press Ctrl+End to move the insertion point to the end of the document.

10. Click the **Paste** button on the toolbar to copy the paragraph back into the document from the Clipboard.

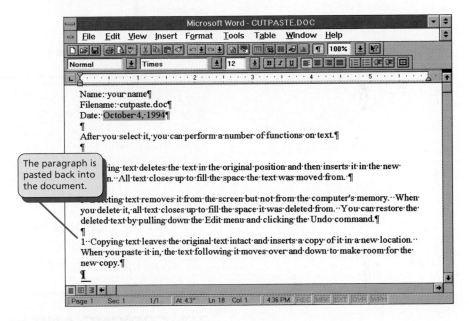

The paragraph is pasted back into the document.

Copying a Paragraph

11. Double-click in the selection bar next to the paragraph numbered *2* to select the entire paragraph.

12. Click the **Copy** button on the toolbar to place a copy of the paragraph on the Clipboard.

13. Press Ctrl+End to move the insertion point to the end of the document.

14. Click the **Paste** button on the toolbar to place a copy of the paragraph into the document from the Clipboard.

Fixing Hard Returns

15. Scroll through the document checking that there is exactly one blank line below each paragraph. Insert or delete hard return symbols (¶) as needed.

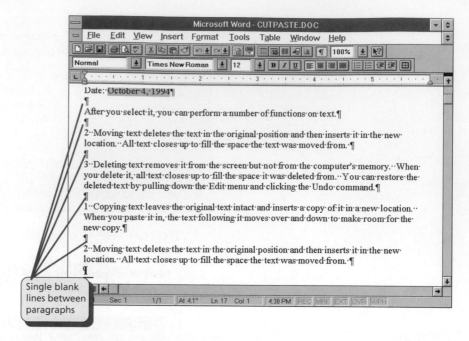

Single blank lines between paragraphs

16. Print the document.

Finishing Up

17. Click the **Show/Hide ¶** button on the toolbar to hide hard returns, spaces, and tabs.

18. Close the document without saving your changes.

2-7. COPYING AND MOVING TEXT BY DRAGGING AND DROPPING IT

Instead of using the Clipboard to move text, you can drag it from one place to another with the mouse and then release it. This is called *dragging and dropping* and is a quick way to copy and move text.

🚫 **COMMON WRONG TURN: CAN'T DRAG AND DROP**

If you can't drag and drop text, someone has turned off a setting. Pull down the **Tools** menu and click the **Options** command to display the Options dialog box. On the **Edit** tab, click the **Drag-and-Drop Text Editing** check box to turn it on, then click the **OK** command button.

QUICKSTEPS: COPYING AND MOVING TEXT BY DRAGGING AND DROPPING IT

1. Select the text to be copied or moved.
2. Point to the selected text and hold down the left button. The mouse pointer changes from an I-beam to a diagonal arrow with a small box attached to it. This indicates you can now drag and drop the selected text. The dotted vertical bar indicates exactly where the text will be pasted when you release the mouse button.
3. Move or copy the selection:
   ▶ To move the selection, drag the pointer to where you want the text moved and release the left button.

▶ To copy the selection, hold down Ctrl while you drag it. (A small plus sign is added to the mouse pointer to indicate you are copying text rather than moving it.) To drop the copied text, release first the mouse button and then Ctrl. (If you reverse the order of release, the selected text will be moved.)

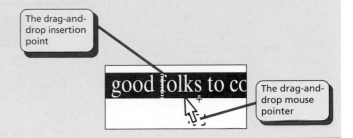

The drag-and-drop insertion point

The drag-and-drop mouse pointer

TUTORIAL

In this tutorial you are introduced to copying and moving paragraphs using the dragging and dropping.

Getting Ready

1. Open the *cutpaste.doc* document stored in the *tutorial* directory on the *Word Student Resource Disk (Part 1)* and enter your name, then click anywhere in the date and press F9 to update it..
2. Click the **Show/Hide ¶** button on the toolbar to display hard returns, spaces, and tabs if they are not displayed.

Moving a Paragraph

3. Double-click in the selection bar next to the paragraph numbered *1* to select the entire paragraph.

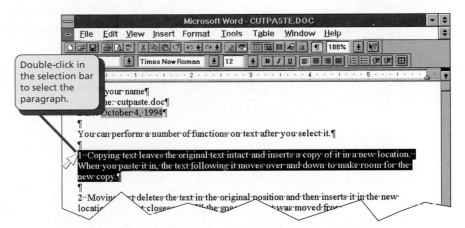

Double-click in the selection bar to select the paragraph.

4. Point anywhere in the selected paragraph and hold down the left button. A small square and a dotted insertion point appear on the mouse pointer to indicate that you are in drag-and-drop mode.

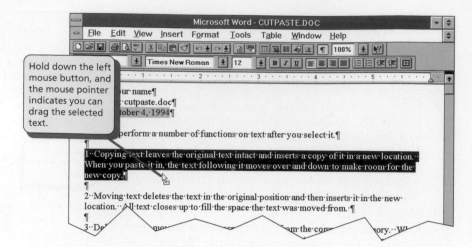

Hold down the left mouse button, and the mouse pointer indicates you can drag the selected text.

5. Drag the mouse pointer to the bottom of the document (the window will scroll if you have to drag against its bottom), and release the mouse button to move the paragraph to its new position. (If you make a mistake, quickly click the **Undo** button on the toolbar and try again.)

Copying a Paragraph

6. Double-click in the selection bar next to the paragraph numbered *2* to select the entire paragraph.

7. Point anywhere in the selected paragraph and hold down the left button. The mouse pointer changes shape to indicate that you are in drag-and-drop mode.

8. Hold down [Ctrl] while you drag the mouse pointer to the bottom of the document, and release first the mouse button and then [Ctrl] to copy the paragraph to the new position. (If you make a mistake, quickly click the **Undo** button on the toolbar and try again.)

9. Scroll through the document checking that there is exactly one blank line below each paragraph. Insert or delete hard return symbols (¶) as needed.

10. Click the **Show/Hide ¶** button on the toolbar to hide hard returns, spaces, and tabs.

11. Print the document.

PAUSING FOR PRACTICE

Dragging and dropping text are basic skills in many Windows applications. Pause here to practice these procedures until you have mastered them. You will not be saving the file when you are finished, so feel free to copy, move, and delete any text.

Finishing Up

12. Close the document without saving it.

2-8. FINDING TEXT

Word can help you find text in a document. This is especially useful in long documents. For example, you may want to find an article's title so you can put quotation marks around it or find a word you want to change. (In other cases, you may want to find a format you want to change, as described in Section 4-3.)

QUICKSTEPS: FINDING TEXT

1. Pull down the **Edit** menu and click the **Find** command to display the Find dialog box. Use any of the options described in the Box "Understanding the Find Dialog Box."

2. Enter the text you want to find in the **Find What** box, and then click the **Find Next** command button to begin the find operation. If a match is found in the document, it is highlighted. You may have to drag the Find dialog box out of the way so you can see it. You can click in the text area to edit the document without closing the dialog box.

3. You can then continue to click the **Find Next** command button to find more occurrences, or you can click the **Cancel** command button to remove the dialog box.

**UNDERSTANDING
THE FIND DIALOG BOX**

When you use the **Find** command, the Find dialog box appears. (At any point you can click in the document to move the insertion point there to edit text and then click the dialog box to make it active again.) Here is a brief description of the box's commands.

Find What text box is where you enter the text you want to find. Click the drop-down arrow (⬇) next to the text box to display previous terms you've searched for and click one to use it again.

Search drop-down arrow (⬇) lets you select the direction of search. Your choices are *All* (starting at the insertion point), *Down*, or *Up*.

Match Case check box, when on (⊠), will find only text that matches yours in capitalization. For example, when on a search for *mouse* will not find *Mouse*.

Find Whole Words Only check box, when on (⊠), will find only matching text that forms whole words. For example, when on a search for *Wind* or *Window* will not find *Windows*.

Use Pattern Matching check box, when on (⊠), allows you to use wildcards where **?** stands for any single character and ***** stands for any group of characters.

Sounds Like check box, when on (⊠), finds words that sound like the one you enter. For example, searching for *color* will find *colour*.

Find Next command button finds the next match.

Cancel command button closes the Find dialog box at any point in the procedure.

No Formatting command button is dimmed unless you have previously searched for formats (see Section 4-3).

Format command button allows you to search for formatted text. (We'll discuss formatting in the next PicTorial.)

Special command button displays a list of nonprinting characters (paragraph marks, tab characters, and so on) you can search for. Also allows you to enter wildcards in the word or phrase you are searching for

Replace changes the Find dialog box into the Replace dialog box so you can replace one word or phrase with another. Replace is discussed in Section 2-9.

TIP: SEARCHING PART OF A DOCUMENT

If you select part of a document before using the **Find** command, only the selected part will be searched.

TIP: REPEATING THE PREVIOUS FIND COMMAND

After you have used the Find command and then closed the dialog box, you can repeat the same Find command by just pressing ⟨⇧ Shift⟩+⟨F4⟩.

TUTORIAL

In this tutorial you are introduced to finding words in a document.

Getting Started

1. Open the *educom.doc* document stored in the *tutorial* directory on the *Word Student Resource Disk (Part 1)*.

Finding Words

2. Pull down the **Edit** menu and click the **Find** command to display the Find dialog box.

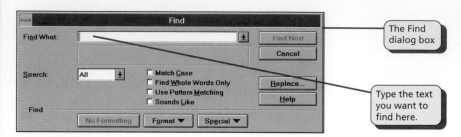

The Find dialog box

Type the text you want to find here.

3. Type **copy** into the **Find What** text box, and then click the **Find Next** command button. The first word containing *copy* is highlighted. (Drag the dialog box out of the way if you can't see the highlighted word.)

4. Continue clicking the **Find What** command button to find additional words containing *copy*. Notice how words such as *copying* and *copyright* are highlighted because they also contain the characters *copy*. (If a dialog box appears telling you that Word has finished searching the document, click the **OK** command button.)

5. Click the **Cancel** command button to cancel the find operation.

Finding Only Words That Match Exactly

6. Press ⟨Ctrl⟩+⟨Home⟩ to move the insertion point to the top of the document.

7. Pull down the **Edit** menu and click the **Find** command to display the Find dialog box.

8. Type **Copy** into the **Find What** text box.

9. Click the **Match Case** and **Find Whole Words Only** check boxes to turn them on.

10. Click the **Find Next** command button, and the first word that exactly matches *Copy* is highlighted.

11. Continue clicking the **Find Next** command button to find additional occurrences of the word *Copy*. Since there aren't any, a dialog box appears telling you that Word has finished searching the document. Words such as *copy* or *Copying* have been skipped over because they don't match either the case or the whole word criterion.

12. Click the **OK** command button to return to the Find dialog box and then click the **Cancel** command button to close that dialog box.

Finishing Up

13. Close the document without saving it.

2-9. REPLACING TEXT

Replacing text is much like finding it but goes a step further—one word or phrase is replaced with another. All of the commands and options you can use are the same as when finding text. One difference is the **Match Case** check box. When this setting is off, the case of words is preserved. For example, if you replace *Old* with *new*, *Old* in the document becomes *New*. When **Match Case** is on, *Old* becomes *new*.

QUICKSTEPS: REPLACING TEXT

1. Pull down the **Edit** menu and click the **Replace** command to display the Replace dialog box. Use any of the options described in the Box "Understanding The Find Dialog Box" in Section 2-8.

2. Enter the text you want to find in the **Find What** text box, and the text you want to use instead in the **Replace With** text box.

3. Click the **Find Next** command button to begin the operation. If a match is found in the document, it is highlighted. (You may have to drag the Replace dialog box out of the way so you can see it.)

   ▶ Click the **Find Next** command button to leave the word unchanged and look for the next occurrence.

   ▶ Click the **Replace** command button to replace the word and look for the next occurrence.

   ▶ Click the **Replace All** command button to replace the word and all further occurrences of it.

   ▶ Click the **Cancel** command button to end the procedure and close the dialog box.

   ▶ Click in the text area to edit the document without closing the dialog box, then click the **Find Next** command button to continue.

TIP: REPLACING WITH CLIPBOARD CONTENTS

You can replace text with anything you have copied to the Clipboard. For example, if you want to find a special symbol, or other item, copy it to the Clipboard. Then pull down the **Edit** menu and click the **Replace** command to display the Replace dialog box. With the insertion point in the **Replace With** text box click the **Special** command button, then select **Clipboard contents**.

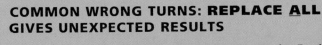

COMMON WRONG TURNS: REPLACE ALL GIVES UNEXPECTED RESULTS

Clicking the **Replace All** command button in the Replace dialog box automatically replaces all text in the selected section of the document without prompting you. This can lead to problems. Immediately click the **Undo** button on the toolbar if you click this command in error.

TUTORIAL

In this tutorial you are introduced to replacing words in a document.

Getting Started

1. Open the *educom.doc* document stored in the *tutorial* directory on the *Word Student Resource Disk (Part 1)*.

Replacing Text

2. Pull down the **Edit** menu and click the **Replace** command to display the Replace dialog box.

3. If **Match Case** or **Find Whole Words Only** check boxes are on, click them to turn them off.

4. Type **school's campus** into the **Find What** text box and **campus** into the **Replace With** text box.

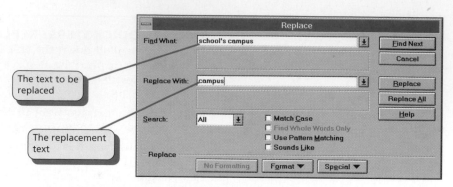

The text to be replaced

The replacement text

5. Click the **Find Next** command button, and the first occurrence of the phrase is highlighted.

6. Click the **Replace** command button to replace each occurrence of *school's campus* with the word *campus*, and eventually a dialog box appears with a message telling you that Word has finished searching the document.

7. Click the **OK** command button to return to the Replace dialog box (see the margin illustration), and then click its **Close** command button.

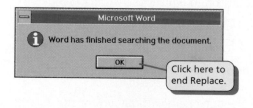

Click here to end Replace.

Finishing Up

8. Close the document without saving it.

2-10. LOOKING UP SYNONYMS AND ANTONYMS IN THE THESAURUS

Word includes a thesaurus for looking up synonyms (words with the same meaning) and antonyms (words with opposite meanings). For example, when you look up the word *wicked*, the Thesaurus may display the synonyms *evil, corrupt, depraved, atrocious, heinous, immoral, amoral,* and *abandoned*. You can choose one of the suggested words to replace the word in the document, look up another word, or quit the thesaurus and return to the document.

QUICKSTEPS: LOOKING UP SYNONYMS AND ANTONYMS IN THE THESAURUS

1. Position the insertion point anywhere in a word you want to look up.

2. Pull down the **Tools** menu and click the **Thesaurus** command to display the Thesaurus dialog box.

3. Click a word in the **Replace with Synonym** list to select it, and then click the **Replace** command button, or use any of the commands described in the box "Understanding the Thesaurus Dialog Box."

UNDERSTANDING THE THESAURUS DIALOG BOX

When you look up a word in the thesaurus, Word displays the Thesaurus dialog box with the following options and commands.

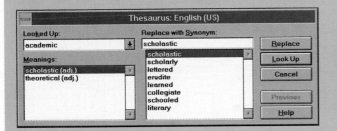

Looked Up text box displays the word being looked up. Click the drop-down arrow (⬇) to display words previously looked up in the session/document. To change the word in this box, click the drop-down arrow (⬇) to select another, or double-click any word on the list below the **Replace with Synonym** text box.

If the selected word is not found in the thesaurus, the text box's name changes to **Not Found** and the list below changes its name to **Alphabetical List** and lists similarly spelled words from which to choose.

Meanings list allows you to select the meaning that best matches the context of the word you are looking up—for example, antonyms. If the selected word is not found in the thesaurus, the list's name changes to **Alphabetical List** and lists similarly spelled words or phrases from which to choose.

Replace with Synonym or **Replace with Antonym** text boxes list all synonyms, antonyms, or related words for the word listed in the **Meanings** list. To change the word in the text box, click any other word on the list below it. If the insertion point is not in a word, or a space next to a word, when you use the **Thesaurus** command, this box is named **Insert**. You can then type a word in the box and click the **Look Up** command button to look it up.

Replace command button replaces the word in the document with the word in the **Replace with Synonym** text box. If the document is empty when you use the **Thesaurus** command, this button is named **Insert**.

Look Up command button displays synonyms for the word listed in the **Replace with Synonym** text box.

Cancel command button close the dialog box.

Previous command button displays the last word you looked up, its meaning, and its synonyms.

TUTORIAL

In this tutorial you are introduced to looking up synonyms in a document so you can find the best possible word.

Getting Started

1. Open the *educom.doc* document stored in the *tutorial* directory on the *Word Student Resource Disk (Part 1)*.

Looking Up Synonyms

2. Position the insertion point in the word *illegal* in the opening paragraph, and then pull down the **Tools** menu and click the **Thesaurus** command to display the Thesaurus dialog box.

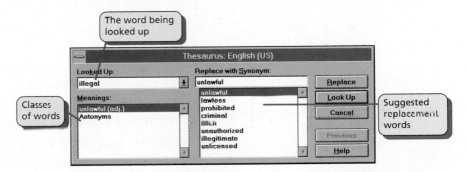

3. Click a word in the **Replace with Synonym** list to select it, and then click the **Replace** command button to replace it in the document.

Looking Up Antonyms

4. Position the insertion point in the word *decrease* in the paragraph that begins *3. UNAUTHORIZED*, and then pull down the **Tools** menu and click the **Thesaurus** command to display the Thesaurus dialog box.

5. Click *Antonyms* in the **Meanings** list to display antonyms in the **Replace with Antonym**. (Yes, the list's heading changed.)

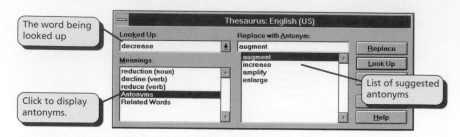

The word being looked up

Click to display antonyms.

List of suggested antonyms

6. Click *increase* to select it, and then click the **Replace** command button to replace *decrease* with *increase* in the document.

 PAUSING FOR PRACTICE

Continue to look up words in the thesaurus until you have mastered using the dialog box.

Finishing Up

7. Print the first page of the document and then close it without saving it.

PicTorial 2 Review Questions

 **True-False**

T   F   **1.** Word automatically inserts hard returns at the end of a line as you enter text whenever it reaches the right margin and wraps a word to the next line.

T   F   **2.** To align text in a Word document, it doesn't matter whether you use spaces or tab stops.

T   F   **3.** You can delete soft page breaks.

T   F   **4.** The fastest way to replace text in a document is to select the text and then type in the new text.

T   F   **5.** When removing text, Word will automatically adjust spaces to make the text fit the surroundings.

T   F   **6.** The Clipboard retains text only until you cut or copy something else.

T   F   **7.** Word's Find feature will allow you to perform only downward searches.

T F   8. You can print specific pages by clicking the **Print** button on the toolbar.

T F   9. If you make a mistake, quickly click the **Undo** button on the toolbar.

T F   10. When using the **Find** command, Word cannot help you find words that sound like the one you entered.

 Multiple Choice

1. Which of the following commands would print from the beginning of a document to page 8?

   a. -8

   b. 8

   c. +8

   d. None of the above

2. Which of the following is not an example of a nonprinting character:

   a. Tab character

   b. Caps Lock

   c. Space

   d. Paragraph mark

3. When using the Word Spelling feature, to leave a word and all subsequent displays of the word unchanged, click the _____ command button.

   a. Change

   b. Ignore

   c. Ignore All

   d. Skip All

4. Which of the following would print pages 2 through 5 of a file?

   a. 2-5

   b. 2,5

   c. (2.5)

   d. –5

5. When using the mouse to select a paragraph, _____.

   a. Double-click in the selection bar next to it

   b. Triple-click anywhere in the paragraph

   c. Double-click the paragraph

   d. Either a or b

6. To print several nonconsecutive pages, separate the page numbers with _____.

   a. Colons

   b. Asterisks

   c. Number signs

   d. Commas

7. To return the insertion point to each of the last three locations where you entered or deleted text, press _____.

   a. Undelete

   b. ⌹Shift⌹+⌹F5⌹

   c. ⌹F5⌹

   d. ⌹Ctrl⌹+⌹F5⌹

8. When using the mouse to select a word, _____ the word.

   a. Click

   b. Double-click

   c. Triple-click

   d. Hold down ⌹Ctrl⌹ and click

9. To turn on the Extend Selection feature, press _____.

   a. ⌹F5⌹

   b. ⌹F6⌹

   c. ⌹F7⌹

   d. ⌹F8⌹

10. After using the **Find** command and then closing the dialog box, you can repeat the same **Find** command by pressing _____.

   a. ⌹Alt⌹+⌹F4⌹

   b. ⌹F4⌹

   c. ⌹Ctrl⌹+⌹F4⌹

   d. ⌹Shift⌹+⌹F4⌹

Fill In the Blank

1. Because of the _____ feature, you do not need to press ⌹Enter◄┘⌹ at the end of each line of a paragraph.

2. Hard returns (carriage returns) are also called _____.

3. To see where you have entered paragraph marks, click the _____ button on the toolbar.

4. When in Normal view, the _____ is indicated by a thin dotted line across the screen.

5. Nonprinting characters control _____.

6. To identify layout mistakes before printing a document, use the _____ command.

7. There are four ways to select text: clicking, dragging with the mouse, using the Edit menu, and _____.

8. When using the mouse to select an entire document, hold down _____ and click once in the selection bar.

9. Word has a feature called _____ that allows you to drag text to a new position in the document.

10. One way to expand a highlight is to hold down _____ while you then press the arrow keys.

▶▶ COMPUTER-BASED TUTORIALS

Word has built-in computer-based Examples and Demos that you can use to learn more about the application. In this PicTorial and those that follow, we suggest Examples and Demos you might complete in this "Computer-Based Tutorials" section. To complete the suggested activities:

1. Pull down the **Help** menu and click the **Examples and Demos** command to display a list of topics from which you can choose.

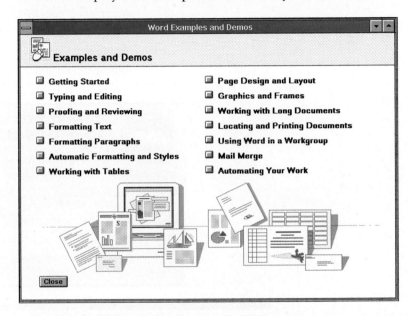

2. Each topic has a button in front of it that you click to select the topic. Click the button in front of any *Topic* listed in the table "Suggested Examples and Demos to Complete." This opens a window listing subtopics.

3. Click the button in front of any *Subtopic* listed in the table "Suggested Examples and Demos to Complete" and read the information displayed on the screen—including any instructions. To explore or quit the lesson:

   ▶ Click any gray button (☐) that appears on the screen to display other windows. To close these windows, click again anywhere in the window.

   ▶ Use any of the command buttons described in the box "Understanding Examples and Demos Command Buttons."

   ▶ Some of these Examples and Demos run even powerful systems out of memory. If that happens, Word displays a message to that effect. Should this happen to you, just close the Examples and Demos window and try another one on the list.

4. When finished with each of the Examples and Demos, check it off the list.

5. To return to Word when finished Examples and Demos, click the **Close** command button to close Examples and Demos and double-click the Control-menu box (⊟) to close the Help window.

Suggested Examples and Demos to Complete		
Done	**Topic**	**Subtopic**
☐	Getting Started	Checking spelling
☐	Getting Started	Overview of Printing
☐	Getting Started	Overview of Editing and Proofing Tools
☐	Getting Started	Looking up words in the thesaurus
☐	Getting Started	Moving or copying text and graphics using drag-and-drop editing
☐	Automating Your Work	Different ways to view a document
☐	Typing and Editing	Overview of Finding and Replacing
☐	Typing and Editing	Finding text and formatting
☐	Typing and Editing	Replacing text and formatting

UNDERSTANDING EXAMPLES AND DEMOS COMMAND BUTTONS

Close returns you to the Help Contents window from the Examples and Demos window or to the Examples and Demos window page from a demo. Click **Close** on the Examples and Demos opening screen to return to Word.

Demo loads a demonstration of a procedure.

Start starts a demo once it has been loaded.

Next > runs a demonstration and/or advances you to the next step in a demo.

▶▶ QUICKSTEP DRILLS

2-1. Entering Text

To enter text, you just type it in, pressing [Enter ←] whenever you want to end a paragraph or insert a blank line. In this drill, you practice these procedures by typing a short document describing geysers.

1. Enter the document shown here, press [Enter ←] only where indicated.

2. Save the document as *geysers.doc* in the *drill* directory of *the Word Student Resource Disk (Part 1)*.

3. Print and close the document.

What Is a Geyser? [Enter ↵]
[Enter ↵]
A geyser is a special kind of hot spring that from time to time spurts water above ground. It differs from most hot springs in having periodic eruptions separated by intervals without flow of water. The temperature of the erupting water is generally near the boiling point for pure water. Some geysers erupt less than a foot, and a few erupt more than 150 feet. Some small geysers erupt every minute or so, but others are inactive for months or even years between eruptions. Contrary to popular opinion, most geysers are very irregular in their behavior, and each is different in some respect from all others. Among the major geysers, only a few, such as Old Faithful in Yellowstone National Park, are predictable enough for the impatient tourist. But even for Old Faithful the interval between eruptions varies from about 30 to 90 minutes, with an average of about 65 minutes. [Enter ↵]
[Enter ↵]
Donald E. White [Enter ↵]
U.S. Department of the Interior [Enter ↵]

2-2. Editing Text

Any successful newspaper, magazine, or book writer can tell you that writing is revising. No one sits down and jots down deathless prose. Writers write and then they revise, revise, revise. It's word processing's ability to make the mechanics of revisions painless that makes writers love it. Only a few years ago each major draft had to be typed all over again. Now writers just insert and delete on the fly. In this drill you practice some of the basic editing procedures.

1. Open the *insdel.doc* document stored in the *drill* directory of the *Word Student Resource Disk (Part 1)* and enter your name, then click anywhere in the date and press [F9] to update it.

2. Move the insertion point to the left of the symbol | in the first paragraph that begins with the symbol ☞. Press [Spacebar] to insert a space, and type **(the word "OVR" is dimmed on the status bar)** and watch text move aside to make room for it.

3. Next to the second paragraph that begins with the ☞ symbol is a section of underlined text. Point to the left of the first underlined character, hold down the left mouse button, and drag the mouse pointer to expand the highlight over all of the underlined text including the comma and space at the end. Release the mouse button, and the text remains highlighted.

4. Type **The best way to replace text** and see how all of the selected text is replaced with the text you typed.

5. Move the insertion point to the right of the symbol | in the third paragraph that begins with the symbol ☞.

6. Hold down [←Bksp] until you have deleted all text up to and including the hand symbol at the beginning of the sentence. (This key works with different speeds on different systems and may also continue deleting some text after you release it. If you delete too much text, click the **Undo** button on the toolbar and try again.)

7. Hold down [Del] until you have deleted all text up to the end of the paragraph.

8. Use the **Print** button on the toolbar to print the document, then double-click the document window's Control-menu box (⊟) to close the document without saving your changes.

2-3. Checking Spelling

Checking the spelling in your documents should be a routine procedure. In this drill you spell-check a document that has a number of built-in spelling errors.

1. Open the *spelling.doc* document stored in the *drill* directory of the *Word Student Resource Disk (Part 1)* and enter your name, then click anywhere in the date and press F9 to update it.

2. Click the **Spelling** button on the toolbar to spell-check the document, making whatever changes you think are appropriate. When spell-checking is complete, proofread the document. What is your opinion of the second paragraph?

3. Use the **Save** and **Print** buttons on the toolbar to save and print the document, then double-click the document window's Control-menu box (⊟) to close the document.

2-4. Previewing and Printing Documents

When working on documents, it's smart to use the **Print Preview** command to check them before making printouts. This not only saves time, but also saves paper. In this drill you practice previewing and printing.

1. Open the *devildic.doc* document stored in the *drill* directory on the *Word Student Resource Disk (Part 1)* and enter your name, then click anywhere in the date and press F9 to update it.

2. Click the **Print Preview** button on the Standard toolbar to preview the document.

3. Click the **Multiple Pages** button on the Print Preview toolbar, highlight the first two page icons so the message reads *1 x 2 Pages*, and release the mouse button.

4. Click the **Single Page** button on the Print Preview toolbar to return to displaying a single page.

5. Click the **Print** button on the Print Preview toolbar to print it.

6. Click the **Close** button on the Print Preview toolbar to close the Print Preview window.

7. Click the document window's Control-menu box (⊟) to close the document without saving your changes.

2-5. Selecting Text

Normally with Word, you select text and then use commands to act on it. Since selecting text is such a fundamental skill, you should master it as soon as possible. In this drill you practice the procedures you use to select various text elements such as words, line, paragraphs, and documents. When completing this drill, refer to the table "Selecting Text by Clicking The Mouse" in Section 2-5 for help.

1. Open the *devildic.doc* document stored in the *drill* directory of the *Word Student Resource Disk (Part 1)*. Click the **Show/Hide ¶** button on the Standard toolbar to display spaces and paragraph marks.

2. Practice clicking in the document to select a word, sentence, or paragraph. Then write down how you did it.

   Select a word _____

   Select a sentence _____

   Select a paragraph _____

3. Practice clicking in the selection bar to select a sentence, a paragraph, or the entire document. Then write down how you did it.

   Select a line_____

   Select a sentence _____

   Select a paragraph _____

   Select entire document _____

4. Practice using ⇧ Shift to select text and then write down how you did it.

   _____

   _____

5. Practice using F8 to select text and then write down how you did it.

   _____

   _____

6. Close the document without saving it.

2-6. Copying and Moving Text with the Clipboard

Windows' Clipboard is designed to store text and other data that you copy or cut while working on a document. As long as the data remains on the Clipboard, you can paste it elsewhere in the document. In this drill you practice using the Clipboard to copy and move text in a document.

1. Open the *abuse.doc* document stored in the *drill* directory of the *Word Student Resource Disk (Part 1)* and enter your name, then click anywhere in the date and press F9 to update it.

2. Use the **Cut** and **Paste** buttons on the Standard toolbar to arrange the paragraphs in both sections in the correct numeric order. (If you make any mistakes that are so bad you wish you could start over, you can! Just close the document without saving it and then open it again.)

3. Use the **Copy** and **Paste** buttons on the Standard toolbar to copy the decorative dividing line from below the heading to above it and also to the end of the document.

4. Click the **Show/Hide ¶** button on the Standard toolbar to show paragraph marks. Then scroll through the document and insert or delete blank lines so all paragraphs are separated from headings and the decorative dividing line by only one blank line.

5. Save, print, and close the document.

2-7. Copying and Moving Text by Dragging and Dropping It

In this drill you practice moving text by dragging and dropping numbered paragraphs so they appear in numerical order.

1. Open the *spanish.doc* document stored in the *drill* directory of the *Word Student Resource Disk (Part 1)* and enter your name, then click anywhere in the date and press F9 to update it.

2. Arrange the numbered paragraphs in order by dragging and dropping them. (If you make any mistakes that are so bad you wish you could start over, you can! Just close the document without saving it and then open it again.)

3. Click the **Show/Hide ¶** button on the Standard toolbar to show paragraph marks. Then scroll through the document and insert or delete blank lines so all numbered paragraphs are separated by only one blank line.

4. Save, print, and close the document.

2-8. Finding Text

Times have changed, and we should be glad they have. The document you use in this drill has been copied from an actual list of rules passed out to freshmen "girls" at a liberal arts college in the 1920's.

1. Open the *freshman.doc* document stored in the *drill* directory of the *Word Student Resource Disk (Part 1)* .

2. With the insertion point at the top of the document, use the **Edit**, **Find** command to find the letters *on* and note how many times they appear in the document.

   Number of times: _____

3. Repeat Step 2 but when the Find dialog box is displayed click the **Find Whole Words Only** check box to turn it on. Note how many times *on* appears as a word.

   Number of times as a whole word: _____

4. Close the document without saving it.

2-9A. Replacing Text

Given the age of most freshman today, it would not be appropriate to refer to them as boys and girls. In this drill you replace all occurrences of the word *girl* with *woman* and *boys* with *men*.

1. Open the *freshman.doc* document stored in the *drill* directory of the *Word Student Resource Disk (Part 1)* and enter your name, then click anywhere in the date and press F9 to update it.

2. Use the **Edit**, **Replace** command to find the word *girls* and replace it with *women*.

3. Use the **Edit**, **Replace** command to find the word *girl* and replace it with *woman*.

4. Use the **Edit**, **Replace** command to find the word *boys* and replace it with *men*.

5. Save, print, and close the document.

2-9B. Replacing Text

The Replace command is very useful when you want to make a lot of changes of the same kind in a document. In this drill you change all director names from being listed as *first name last name* to *last name, first name*.

1. Open the *bugs.doc* document stored in the *drill* directory of the *Word Student Resource Disk (Part 1)* and enter your name, then click anywhere in the date and press F9 to update it.

2. Use the **Edit**, **Replace** command to find the words listed in the "Bugs Replacements" table and replace them with the indicated words. (Tips: You needn't close the Replace dialog box after each pass; just enter a new pair of names. Also, using **Replace All** will not cause any problems in this document when replacing people's names.)

BUGS REPLACEMENTS	
Search For	**Replace With**
Tex Avery	Avery, Tex
Chuck Jones	Jones, Chuck
Friz Freleng	Freleng, Friz
Bob Clampett	Clampett, Bob
Frank Tashlin	Tashlin, Frank
Robert McKimson	McKimson, Robert
Phil Monroe	Monroe, Phil
Gerry Chiniquy	Chiniquy, Gerry

3. Save the document, print the first page, and then close the document.

2-10. Looking Up Synonyms and Antonyms in the Thesaurus

A synonym of a word is another word with the same meaning. An antonym of a word is another word that has an opposite meaning. The document used here is a list of words which you look up in Word's thesaurus to find one or more synonyms and antonyms.

1. Open the *thesaur.doc* document stored in the *drill* directory of the *Word Student Resource Disk (Part 1)* and enter your name, then click anywhere in the date and press F9 to update it.

2. Use the **Tools, Thesaurus** command to look up a synonym or antonym for some or all of the words in the *Changed To* column on the list. Leave the words in the *Original* column unchanged so you have a record of what you changed the word from.

3. Save, print, and close the document.

2-1. Entering and Editing a Memo on Training

As the educational director of the Computer Curriculum Center, one of your responsibilities is to coordinate class schedules. Since many of your courses are taken by people in business, they may have to be rescheduled if there is a conflict within the company you are offering them to. Here you have had to reschedule a class and write a memo notifying the instructor that you have done so.

1. Open the memo *memoform.doc* stored in the *exercise* directory on the *Word Student Resource Disk (Part 2)*. Enter your name in the heading where it reads *your name*, then click anywhere in the date and press F9 to update it.

2. Enter the rest of the memo shown below, beginning on the second line below the date.

Janie, the program scheduled for March 27 has been scheduled for May 1. Francis Boyle, coordinator, has affirmed that Room 324 will be available for you.

Please examine the empty classroom, making sure that all equipment is available. Let me know about any equipment needed.

your initials

The Memo

3. Edit the body paragraphs by deleting the words shown here struck-through and inserting the ones shown underscored. (Click the **Show/Hide ¶** button on the Standard toolbar to show spaces.)

Janie, the <u>training</u> program scheduled for March 27 has been <u>re</u>scheduled for May 1. Francis Boyle, <u>classroom</u> coordinator, has <u>already</u> affirmed that Room 324 will be available for you<u>r class</u>.

Please examine the ~~empty~~ classroom, making sure that all equipment <u>you need </u>is available. Please let me know <u>as soon as possible</u> about any <u>additional</u> equipment needed.

The Edited Memo

4. Use the **Edit**, **Replace** command to replace *Janie* with *Jane*.

5. Use the **Spelling** button on the Standard toolbar to spell-check the document.

6. Save, print, and close the document.

2-2. Entering and Editing a Memo on Punctuation Marks

As the educational director of Computer Tutors you are occasionally called upon to settle disagreements among the faculty. Recently, teachers in the Business English course have been offering conflicting advice on the use of space around punctuation marks in business memos, letters, and reports. At a faculty meeting, it was decided that each teacher should have the right to choose the approach used in his or her own classes. Once a decision such as this is made, you always send a confirming memo informing the entire staff of the final decision.

NOTE: ONE SPACE OR TWO

The issue discussed here is real. Ask your instructor which style he or she prefers and then use:

☐ One space   ☐ Two spaces after a colon
☐ One space   ☐ Two spaces at the end of every sentence

---

1. Open the memo *spaces.doc* stored in the *exercise* directory on the *Word Student Resource Disk (Part 2)*. Enter your name in the heading where it reads *your name*, then click anywhere in the date and press F9 to update it.

2. Enter the rest of the memo beginning on the second line below the date. The memo is shown in the figure "The Punctuation Marks Memo."

At today's meeting it was tentatively decided that more variety is desired. For that reason, all faculty members have the right to choose which punctuation styles are to be used in their classes. It is important that you inform students of the styles. That way, when they later take a course from another teacher, they will understand.

Leave one or two spaces:
- after a colon
- after a period ending a sentence. Typewritten business letters, memos, and reports always used two spaces. However, publishers of newspapers, books, and magazines always used one. As publishing has moved to the desktop, so have many publishing styles.

Leave one space:
- after a comma
- after a semicolon
- after a period following an abbreviation or initial
- after an exclamation point within a sentence
- after a question mark within a sentence

Leave no spaces:
- after a period within an abbreviation
- before or after a hyphen
- before or after a dash (two hyphens)
- between any word and the punctuation following it
- between parentheses and the enclosed matter
- between quotation marks and the enclosed matter

Also, do not separate punctuation from the word it follows—for instance, allowing a dash to begin a new line.

The Punctuation Marks Memo

3. Use the **Cut** and **Paste** buttons on the Standard toolbar to reverse the order of the two paragraphs after the heading *Leave one or two spaces*.

4. In the first body paragraph shown in the figure "The Edited Punctuation Marks Memo," delete the words struck-through and insert the ones shown underscored.

At today's <u>faculty</u> meeting it was ~~tentatively~~ decided that ~~more~~ variety is ~~desired~~ <u>the spice of life</u>. For that reason, all <u>members of the</u> faculty ~~members~~ have the right to choose which punctuation styles are to be used in their classes. ~~It is~~ <u>It's</u> important that you inform students of the <u>different</u> styles <u>and explain why you have picked the one you have</u>. That way, when they later take a course from another teacher <u>using a different set of rules</u>, they will understand <u>the issues involved</u>.

The Edited Punctuation Marks Memo

5. Use the **Spelling** button on the Standard toolbar to spell-check the finished letter.

6. Save, print, and close the document.

2-3. Entering and Editing a Business Letter on Training

As the educational director of a computer training firm, one of your responsibilities is to recruit new students. Frequently, people write in and ask for specific information about your program. Today, a Ms. Carraway from the Department of Transportation did just that. She inquired about courses on Word for Windows, including when they were offered and how much they cost. In your response you provided her with that information but also told her how to enroll and mentioned that your firm was certified to train state employees.

1. Open the document *ltrform.doc* stored in the *exercise* directory on the *Word Student Resource Disk (Part 2)*.

2. Enter the letter shown in the figure "The Training Letter" beginning with the current date in the format *January 12, 1996*. Enter your own name at the end of the document above the line *Educational Director*.

3. In the body paragraphs shown in the figure "The Edited Training Letter," delete the words shown here struck-through and insert the ones shown underscored.

4. Use drag and drop to move the paragraph that begins *As you may know* below the paragraph that begins *To enroll in this training program*. Make sure there is one blank line between each of the body paragraphs.

5. Use the **Spelling** button on the Standard toolbar to spell-check the finished letter.

6. Save, print, and then close the document.

Current date

Ms. Karen Kay Carraway
32773 Newport Drive
Browning, OH 34526

Dear Ms. Carraway:

The Computer Curriculum Center offers training programs on a variety of software programs. The date for the next scheduled program on Word for Windows is April 3.

To enroll in this program, please call (456) 385-2578, extension 327. The full tuition for the course is $75, which includes a textbook and the instruction.

As you may know, the Computer Center has been officially certified by the State of Ohio to provide training for all employees. We are confident you will be pleased with our program.

Please call to reserve your position in the next training session.

Sincerely yours,

your name
Educational Director

your initials

The Training Letter

The Computer Curriculum Center offers <u>numerous</u> training programs on a variety of ~~software~~ <u>application</u> programs. The date for the <u>beginning of the</u> next scheduled program on Word for Windows is April 3.

To enroll in this <u>training</u> program, please call (456) 385-2578, extension 327. The ~~full~~ tuition for the course is $75, which includes a textbook ~~and the instruction~~.

As you may know, the Computer <u>Curriculum</u> Center has been ~~officially~~ certified by the State of Ohio to provide training for all <u>state</u> employees. We are confident you will be pleased with our program.

Please call <u>soon</u> to reserve your position in the next training session.

The Edited Training Letter

2-4. Entering and Editing an Announcement

Each semester, the educational director publishes a list of the course offerings. This announcement is sent to all staff members and to all people who write in requesting information. It is also used as the basis for advertisements, catalogs, and press releases designed to attract students to the classes.

1. Open the document *announce.doc* stored in the *exercise* directory on the *Word Student Resource Disk (Part 2)*.

2. Enter the rest of the announcement beginning on the second line below the letterhead. When you are entering a course name, press [Tab⇆] after typing the course name and before typing the day it is offered. (The dots that appear when you do this are called dot leaders, and they only appear because we made a tab setting that you will learn about later in the course.)

The Computer Center is pleased to announce its fall schedule of courses on Windows and Windows applications. All classes are lab-oriented, with lots of hands-on experience. Each class begins at 6 p.m. and lasts two hours.

Basic Courses
Introduction to Computers ....Mon
Windows: A Graphical User Interface ....Tue
DOS: Looking Under Windows' Hood ....Wed

Word Courses
WordPerfect for Windows ....Mon
Word for Windows..Tue
Ami Pro ....Wed

Spreadsheet Courses
Excel ....Thur
Lotus 1-2-3 for Windows..Fri
Quatro Pro for Windows ....Sat

Database Courses
Paradox for Windows..Tue
Access ....Thur
FoxPro...Fri

Graphics Courses
CorelDRAW ....Sat
Adobe Illustrator..Fri

Desktop Publishing Courses
QuarkXpress for Windows..Sat
PageMaker for Windows ....Fri

your initials

The Announcement Document

3. In the first body paragraph, where it reads *Computer Center*, insert the word *Curriculum* between *Computer* and *Center*.

4. Change the heading for word processing courses that now reads *Word Courses* to read *Word Processing Courses*.

5. Use the **Cut** and **Paste** buttons on the Standard toolbar to arrange the courses in each section in alphabetical order.

6. Use the **Edit**, **Find** command to see if there is a word spelled *Quatro* in the document. If you find one, change it to *Quattro*.

7. Use the **Edit**, **Replace** command to change all of the day-of-the-week abbreviations (Mon, Tue, and so on) to full spellings (Monday, Tuesday, and so on).

8. Use the **Tools**, **Thesaurus** command to find a synonym for the word *pleased* in the opening paragraph.

9. Enter the date on the line below your initials at the bottom of the document.

10. Use the **Spelling** button on the Standard toolbar to spell-check the document.

11. Save, print, and then close the document.

2-5. Writing and Editing a Personal Letter Home for Money

Every college student needs money. Many students must earn it, but some have comparatively rich aunts, uncles, or parents to whom they can appeal for funds. Here you take the role of an eighteen-year-old freshman who has overspent and needs a new infusion of cash.

1. Open a new document and enter the letter shown here, using the customized information in places where it is indicated. Use Tab to indent each new body paragraph in the letter. Use one of the suggestions for customizing the letter from the list at the top of page 88 or make up your own.

Today's Date

Dear Mom and Dad,

    This year is progressing extremely well, and I'm working harder than ever (really!) All I do is work, but it's paying off. For example, I've written this letter on a state-of-the-art (*enter the name of your computer*) computer using Word for Windows. I am mastering word processing in half the time it is taking the others in the class. The only glitch is that I'm out of money. To raise the lousy (*fill in the amount needed—make it big!*) I need, I am considering taking a job as a (*choose a job from the jobs list*).

    I realize that this will detract from my studies and jeopardize the thousands of dollars you have already invested in my education, but I really have no other choice. I have overspent on textbooks, reference books, seminars on (*choose a seminar from the seminars list*), computer supplies, and other things needed to ensure the quality of my education. I guess working as a (*enter the job you used above*) for a few months is a small price to pay. Although it will result in my being less well educated, it at least makes it possible to muddle through. Your dreams of my becoming a (*choose a profession from the professions list*) will probably not now be realized, but there are plenty of lower paying and less fulfilling jobs that I will be qualified for.

    Sorry to share my minor problem with you, but other than this, everything is going VERY well! Don't worry—be happy.

Love,

Your Name

The Letter Home Document

Customize Choices		
Jobs List	**Seminars List**	**Professions List**
sewer cleaner	space science	lawyer
dog-catcher's assistant	nuclear physics	business executive
blast-furnace operator	computer programming	doctor
dynamite detonator	environmental studies	teacher

2. Using what you have learned, locate and correct any mistakes you might have made.

3. Use the **Tools**, **Thesaurus** command to look up the following words and substitute synonyms.

   ‣ extremely

   ‣ realized

   ‣ minor

4. Use the **Spelling** button on the Standard toolbar to spell-check the document.

5. Save the document as *ltrhome.doc* in the *exercise* directory of the *Word Student Resource Disk (Part 2)*.

6. Print the document and then close it.

2-6. Editing and Printing the Job-Guide Document

In the Real-World Projects that follow, you are introduced to a job-search kit that you will be working on throughout this text. This kit has three parts: a cover letter, a résumé, and a followup letter. Each of these documents is explained in the document *jobs.doc*. Here you edit and print out a copy.

1. Open the *jobs.doc* document stored in the *exercise* directory on the *Word Student Resource Disk (Part 2)* and enter your name in the letterhead line COPY BELONGING TO YOUR NAME in place of YOUR NAME.

2. In the first paragraph under the heading *The Cover Letter* shown in the figure "The Edited Cover Letter," delete the words shown struck-through and insert the ones shown underscored.

You will need a <u>cover</u> letter whenever you send a resume <u>or application form</u> to a <u>potential</u> employer. Your cover letter should capture the ~~recipients~~ <u>employer's</u> attention, show why you are ~~contacting them~~ <u>writing</u>, indicate why your employment will ~~add to~~ <u>benefit</u> the company, and ~~beg for~~ <u>suggest</u> an interview. The kind of specific information that must be included in a letter means that each must be written individually. Each letter must also be typed <u>perfectly</u>, so word processing helps. Frequently, only the address, first paragraph, and specifics concerning an interview will vary. These items are easily changed on a ~~typewriter~~ <u>word processor</u>.

The Edited Cover Letter

---

3. Drag and drop items in the first list so they match the order shown in the figure "The Reorganized Cover Letter."

- Address your letter to a specific person, if possible (use city directories or other sources).
- State exactly the kind of position you are seeking and why you are applying to a particular firm.
- Use care in sentence structure, spelling, and punctuation.
- Be clear, brief, and businesslike.
- Use a good grade of letter-sized white bond paper for the final printout.
- Enclose a résumé.

The Reorganized Cover Letter

4. Insert the date at the very bottom of the document with one line between it and the last line of text above it.

5. Save the document, print the first page, and then close the document.

2-7. Editing the Careers Document

In this exercise you edit a document that describes various career opportunities in computing and information processing.

1. Open the *careers.doc* document stored in the *exercise* directory on the *Word Student Resource Disk (Part 2)* and enter your name following the word *By*.

2. In the opening paragraph shown in the figure "The Edited Careers Document," delete the words shown here struck-through and insert the ones shown underscored.

The increased computerization of the ~~business~~ workplace has led to the development of new positions and a change in responsibilities for existing positions. One major company divides its ~~workers~~ employees into two categories—originators and processors. Originators are those people who draft original documents, reports, numeric analysis, and ~~other stuff~~ so on. Processors are those who prepare this material for presentation. For example, an average originator/processor relationship is that of a ~~manager~~ supervisor and secretary. The supervisor writes a letter to a client and the secretary then uses a word ~~processor~~ processing program to print it and the ~~thing~~ envelope in which it is mailed.

The Edited Careers Document

3. Scroll through the document to find the section with the heading *SPECIALIST POSITIONS*. This section begins with an introductory paragraph followed by a series of paragraphs containing job descriptions. Move these paragraphs (other than the introduction) as needed to arrange them in alphabetical order. Make sure the paragraphs remain separated by single blank lines

4. Use the **Edit**, **Find** command to locate the following words and then use the **Tools**, **Thesaurus** command to look up a suitable synonym to substitute.

▶ *personnel*

▶ *client*

5. Use the **Edit**, **Replace** command to replace *secretary* with *assistant*. Check the words around the replacements and make changes if any are needed.

6. Enter the date at the very bottom of the document with one line between it and the last line of text above it.

7. Save the document, print the second page, and close the document.

2-8. Editing the Rights Document

In this exercise you edit the ten amendments in the Bill of Rights to the United States Constitution.

1. Open the *rights.doc* document stored in the *exercise* directory on the *Word Student Resource Disk (Part 2)* and enter your name, then click anywhere in the date and press ⌐F9⌐ to update it.

2. In Clause 2, shown in the figure "The Edited Bill of Rights" delete the words struck-through and insert the ones shown underscored.

Clause 2
Militia and the Right to Bear Arms
A ~~poorly~~ well regulated ~~neighborhood gang~~ Militia, being necessary to the ~~destruction~~ security of a free State, the right of the people to keep and bear ~~automatic weapons~~ Arms, shall not be abridged.

The Edited Bill of Rights

3. Use the **Cut** and **Paste** buttons on the Standard toolbar to reorganize the ten clauses into the correct numeric order. Make sure the clauses remain separated by single blank lines.

4. Use the **Edit**, **Replace** command to replace the word *Clause* in all the headings with *Amendment*.

5. Enter the date at the very bottom of the document with one line between it and the last line of text above it.

6. Save the document, print page 1, and then close the document.

2-9. Editing the Desktop Publishing Document

In this exercise you edit a document describing desktop publishing.

1. Open the *dtp.doc* document stored in the *exercise* directory on the *Word Student Resource Disk (Part 2)* and enter your name on the second line following *By*.

2. In the second body paragraph shown in the figure "The Edited DTP Document," delete the words shown here struck-through and insert the ones shown underscored.

The ~~preparation~~ publication of documents using ~~old-fashioned~~ traditional procedures takes <u>a great deal of time, money, and</u> experience. The popularity of desktop publishing ~~derives~~ <u>stems</u> from the fact that it reduces the time and money required to do a ~~good~~ <u>professional-looking</u> job. However, desktop publishing still requires skill<u>, and a lot of it</u>. In traditional publishing, the ~~chores~~ <u>tasks</u> involved in publishing a document are handled by many separate ~~people~~ <u>specialists</u>. For example, one person will design a ~~document~~ <u>publication</u>, another will indicate on the manuscript how each element is to be treated, a third will set the type, and a fourth will print it. When a document is desktop published, the same person is <u>frequently</u> responsible for all these tasks <u>and any others</u> in the process.

The Edited DTP Document

3. Use the **Tools**, **Thesaurus** command to find synonyms for the following words in the opening paragraph. (Use the **Edit**, **Find** command to locate them.)

   ▶ *device*

   ▶ *created*

   ▶ *situation*

4. Use the **Edit**, **Replace** command to replace all but the first occurrence of the phrase *desktop publishing* (not counting the title) with the abbreviation *DTP*.

5. Save, print, and close the document.

 ▶▶ **REAL-WORLD PROJECTS**

2-1. The Job-Search Kit—The Cover Letter

When looking for a job, it's common to send out résumés to companies you are interested in. If you do so, you must always accompany the résumé with a cover letter. Since this cover letter is usually read first, it must capture the reader's attention or your résumé goes into the circular file. In this project you enter a sample cover letter.

1. Open the *coverltr.doc* document stored in the *project* directory on the *Word Student Resource Disk (Part 2)*. Replace YOUR NAME at the top of the document and *your name* at the bottom with your actual name.

2. Enter the letter shown in the figure "The Cover Letter" so it exactly matches the contents shown in the figure. (Your lines may wrap at different points.) Use whatever tools you have to ensure the letter's accuracy.

3. Save, print, and then close the document.

4. Now that you have finished a sample cover letter, write your own, using what you have learned. Save it under its own filename, make a printout, and then close the document.

YOUR NAME
304 AMEN STREET
SAN FRANCISCO, CALIFORNIA 94102

March 14, 1997

Mr. Wilbert R. Wilson
President, XYZ Company
3893 Factory Boulevard
Cleveland, OH 44114

Dear Mr. Wilson:

Recently I learned through Dr. Robert R. Roberts of Atlantic and Pacific University of the expansion of your company's sales operations and your plans to create a new position of sales director. If this position is open, I would appreciate your considering me.

Starting with over-the-counter sales and order service, I have had progressively more responsible and diverse experience in merchandising products similar to yours. In recent years I have carried out a variety of sales promotion and top management assignments.

For your review, I am enclosing a resume of my qualifications. I would appreciate a personal interview with you to discuss my application further.

Very truly yours,

your name

Enclosure

The Cover Letter

2-2. The Job-Search Kit—The Followup Letter

After you have had a job interview, you should immediately send a followup letter to the person who interviewed you. In this project you enter and format such a letter.

1. Open the *followup.doc* document stored in the *project* directory on the *Word Student Resource Disk (Part 2)*

2. Enter the document shown in the figure "The Followup Letter," entering your name at the bottom of the document in place of *Your Name*.

3. Use all of the tools at your disposal to ensure the document is accurate.

4. Save, print, and close the document.

5. Imagine that you have had a job interview that went fairly well but you want to reinforce a few points you made and cover a few you

didn't. Write a letter covering those points. Save the document under its own filename, make a printout, and then close the document.

Computer Curriculum Center
Student Employment Center

123 North Monroe Street
Cleveland, Ohio 65743

Phone: 456 385-2578
Fax: 456 385-3456

March 14, 1997

Mr. Lionel Train
Consolidated Corporation
45 Switch Street
Roundhouse, IN 12002

Dear Mr. Train:

Thank you for the interview last Friday. I am impressed with the quality of your organization and would like to express my continued interest in pursuing the position. As I mentioned to you, I feel that I could contribute to your company's objectives in a number of ways:

- I am able to work well with coworkers and am very much a team player.
- My previous working experience has given me an understanding of the responsibilities of the position. I hope you will give me the opportunity to share my abilities with your company.

Since the interview, I have given our discussion a great deal of thought and would like to make the following points:

- While working on the school newspaper, I gained interviewing experience that should make me better at completing the surveys you mentioned would be required as part of the position's responsibilities.
- I have earned over 50 percent of my college expenses and in the process have established a solid employment record over the past four years. I have proved my reliability in this position and hope you will call Mr. Jones at 212-555-1212 to hear his opinions of the contributions that I have made.

Again, thank you for your consideration. If there is any additional information I might be able to supply, please let me know. I am eager to hear from you.

Sincerely yours,

Your Name

The Followup Letter

PicTorial 3

Basic Formatting

After completing this PicTorial, you will be able to:

▶ Explain the differences between character and paragraph formats

▶ Change font faces, styles, and sizes

▶ Align text with margins

▶ Change line and paragraph spacing

▶ Control page breaks

▶ Set and use tab stops

▶ Indent paragraphs

▶ Number and bullet lists

As a document is being prepared, you can format it to improve its appearance and readability. Until very recently most typed documents looked pretty much alike. They were all typed on typewriters that had the same limited number of choices, some of which took a great deal of skill to use. Today, with word processing programs rivaling the power of desktop publishing programs, it's easy to format documents so they look as if they were prepared by a professional printer. In this PicTorial we explore some of the many formatting options you have at your disposal. We'll look at fonts, text alignment, line and paragraph spacing, bulleted lists, tabs, and indents. As you use these features, you'll also become more aware of how useful Word's WYSIWYG (pronounced "wizzy-wig") display is, because the screen shows you what the formats will look like in the final printout.

Word's preset formats automatically print a document single-spaced in 10 point Times New Roman type on an 8 ½-by-11-inch page with 1-inch top and bottom margins and 1 ¼-inch left and right margins. When you want to change these and other default settings, you do so by formatting either characters, paragraphs, or pages. In this PicTorial we concentrate on character and paragraph formatting, and in the next PicTorial we cover page formats such as margins and page numbers.

3-1. TYPES OF FORMATS

When formatting a document it's important to understand the difference between character and paragraph formats and how you apply, remove, and identify them. Taking the time now to understand these differences will make things a great deal easier for you later on.

▶ *Character formats* affect individual characters or groups of selected characters and include such things as boldfacing, italicizing, or superscripting.

▶ *Paragraph formats* affect selected paragraphs and include such things as text alignment and indents, line spacing, spacing between paragraphs, and tab stops. In Word the term *paragraph* means any line or lines that ends with a paragraph mark (¶) entered when you press [Enter ↵]. Therefore, a paragraph can be as short as a blank line without any text or as long as the complete document.

The way you format text with character and paragraph formats depends on whether the text is new or already exists.

APPLYING FORMATS TO NEW TEXT

To change character or paragraph formats for new text that you are about to type, position the insertion point where you want the change to take affect and then execute the formatting command. Any text you enter from that point on will have the new formats until you change them or turn them off. For example, to italicize a book title in a report, you could click the **Italic** button to turn italic on, type the title, and then click the **Italic** button again to turn italic off.

When typing new text in or near formatted text, the position of the insertion point determines the format of the new text. For example, let's say you have italicized the phrase *remember the Maine*:

▶ The new text will be italic if you position the insertion point anywhere in the phrase *remember the Maine*, or at the left side of the space following the word *Maine*.

▶ The new text will not be italic if you position the insertion point at the right side of the space following the word *Maine*, or you press [Ctrl]+[Spacebar] before typing it.

If you change a paragraph's format, and then press [Enter ↵] at the end of it, the new paragraph will have the same formats as the one you created it from. You could say that the paragraph formats of the new paragraph are inherited from the paragraph from which it was created.

APPLYING FORMATS TO EXISTING TEXT

To change formats in existing text, you first select the characters or paragraphs to be formatted and then use formatting commands to format them. For example, to italicize a book title in a report, you could type it, select it, and click the **Italic** button on the toolbar. Or, to align paragraphs, position the insertion point anywhere in the paragraph if you are formatting a single paragraph, or select all or part of two or more adjacent paragraphs. Selecting part of a paragraph is the same as selecting it all. For example, if you select the last word in one paragraph and the first word in the next, it's the same as selecting both paragraphs in their entirety.

TIP: FORMATTING PARAGRAPHS WITH SHORT LINES

When you specify a paragraph format, it affects all text up to the next hard return or paragraph mark. To format multiple lines with one command, such as those used in addresses, tables, or lists, do not end each line by pressing [Enter ↵]. Instead, press [⇧ Shift]+[Enter ↵] to enter a new-line character (↵) that ends the line without ending the paragraph. This way a paragraph format applied to one line affects all lines up to where you press [Enter ↵] to enter a hard return.

When you select text for formatting, its current formats are displayed on the toolbar and in related dialog boxes. However, when you select text that has more than one format, buttons and dialog box elements related to the command may be affected as follows:

▶ Text boxes are empty

▶ Check boxes are dimmed

▶ List boxes have no choice selected

▶ Toolbar buttons are not highlighted

If you enter a choice in one of these check boxes or click one of the toolbar buttons, you override previous formats, and all the selected text is affected. If you do not make a choice, the previous formats remain unaffected.

TIP: THE REPEAT COMMAND

The **Repeat** command is especially useful when formatting existing text. You format the first item, immediately select the next one, and then press F4 to repeat the format.

TIP: USING AUTOFORMAT

Word has an **AutoFormat** command that will quickly format an entire document for you. This command recognizes common elements such as headings, bulleted lists, and quotation marks and formats them as such. When Word recognizes an element, it applies a formatting style to it. Styles are beyond the scope of this book but are simply stored formats that can be applied to text by selecting their name from a menu. You can see the names of the styles in any document by clicking the **Style** drop-down arrow (⬇) on the toolbar. To use AutoFormat, pull down the **Format** menu and click the **AutoFormat** command to display a dialog box telling you the document will be automatically formatted. (Click the **Options** command button to specify formatting options.) Click the **OK** command button to begin and the status bar keeps you informed of the command's progress. When finished, a dialog box appears offering you the chance to review the changes, accept the changes, or reject the changes.

REMOVING CHARACTER AND PARAGRAPH FORMATS

Sometimes, when you apply a character or paragraph format to text and then press Spacebar or Enter↵, the format continues to affect the text you type when you don't want it to. At other times you format text and then change your mind. In either case, it's easy to return the text to Word's original preset formats. To begin, position the insertion point where you want the change to take affect, or select text you want changed. Then:

▶ To remove character formats, press Ctrl+Spacebar.

▶ To remove paragraph formats, press Ctrl+Q.

LOOKING BACK: DELETING PARAGRAPH MARKS

Word stores all paragraph formatting information in the paragraph mark (¶) at the paragraph's end, so when you delete the paragraph mark you lose the information. Deleting the paragraph mark makes the contents of the paragraph become part of the following paragraph, and it takes on the formatting of that paragraph. Since paragraph marks are so important, you should always have them displayed when you edit a document. To display them, click the **Show/Hide ¶** button on the toolbar.

KNOWING WHAT FORMATS ARE IN EFFECT

Current formats are indicated on the Formatting toolbar. For example, if the selected text is centered, the **Center** button on the toolbar will be highlighted. (If you select text with more than one format, the affected buttons will not be highlighted.) If you have not selected text, the toolbar shows you what formats will be used for any text you type at the insertion point's position.

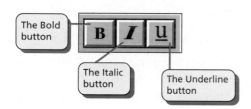

Clicking the Style drop-down arrow displays a list of predefined styles you can use.

The easiest way to determine formats is to click the **Help** button on the toolbar to add a question mark to the mouse pointer. Click the text whose formats you want to check. Each time you do so, the clicked text's style and direct formats are listed in a Reveal Styles box. Style formats, usually *Normal*, are applied by picking a stored format from a list. (Styles are beyond the scope of this text; however, you can see currently available styles by clicking the drop-down arrow (⬇) next to the **Style** box on the toolbar—see the margin illustration.) Direct formats are those you apply by using menu commands or buttons. When finished checking formats, press [Esc] or click the **Help** button on the toolbar again.

TUTORIAL

In this tutorial you explore applying, identifying, and removing character and paragraph formats.

Getting Started

1. Open the *formats.doc* document stored in the *tutorial* directory on the *Word Student Resource Disk (Part 1)* and enter your name where shown. Then click anywhere in the date and press [F9] to update it.

Applying Character Formats to Existing Text

The Bold button

The Italic button

The Underline button

2. Click in the selection bar next to the heading *Formatting Characters in Existing Text* to select it, and then click the **Bold** button on the toolbar—see the margin illustration. The line is boldfaced and the **Bold** button on the toolbar is highlighted. This indicates this format has been used for the selected text. Also, the Font box indicates that it is formatted as Times New Roman and the Font Size box indicates the font size is 12 (points).

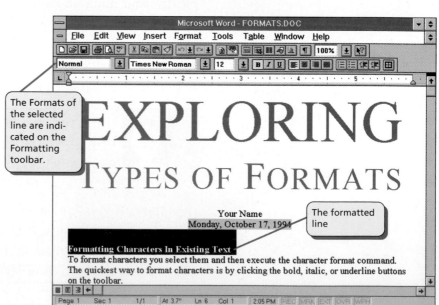

The Formats of the selected line are indicated on the Formatting toolbar.

The formatted line

3. Repeat Step 2 to format the other three headings: *Formatting Characters in New Text*, *Formatting a Single Paragraph*, and *Formatting Groups of Paragraphs*.

4. Double-click the word *bold* to select it in the sentence under the heading *Formatting Characters in Existing Text* and then click the **Bold** button on the toolbar.

5. Repeat Step 4 but select first *italic* and then *underline*, and for each click the button of the same name on the toolbar.

Applying Character Formats to New Text

6. Click on the line below the heading *Formatting Characters in New Text* to move the insertion point there.

7. Type the following sentence and as you do so, click the **Bold**, **Italic**, and **Underline** buttons on the toolbar before you type the words shown in those formats—where you click is indicated by the mice icons (🖱).Click the same buttons again immediately after typing the word in that format to turn the format off for the following text.

You can 🖱**boldface**🖱, 🖱*italicize*🖱, or 🖱<u>underline</u>🖱 text as you enter it.

Formatting a Single Paragraph

8. Position the insertion point anywhere in the paragraph under the heading *Formatting a Single Paragraph*, then click the **Center** button on the toolbar to center it between the margins. The entire paragraph is centered although you didn't select it.

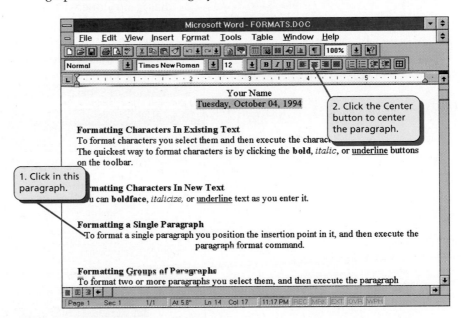

Formatting Groups of Paragraphs

9. Click the **Show/Hide ¶** button on the toolbar to show paragraph marks.

10. Click just to the left of the paragraph mark (¶) at the end of the first paragraph under the heading *Formatting Groups of Paragraphs*,

then hold down ⇧Shift and click just the to right of the letter *A* at the beginning on the last paragraph in the document. This selects all text between those two points.

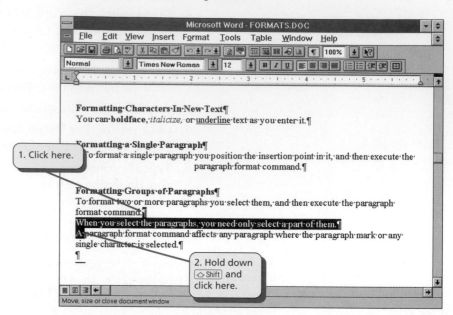

11. Click the **Center** button on the toolbar to center the selected paragraphs. All three paragraphs are centered, although you selected only part of the first and last paragraph.

Identifying Formats With the Help Button

12. Click the **Help** button on the toolbar once to add a question mark to the mouse pointer, then click any of the text you formatted. A dialog box opens listing the formats that have been applied to it. Practice clicking various elements to see their formats. Those listed under *Styles* are the program's preset formats. Those listed under *Direct* are the formats you have applied yourself.

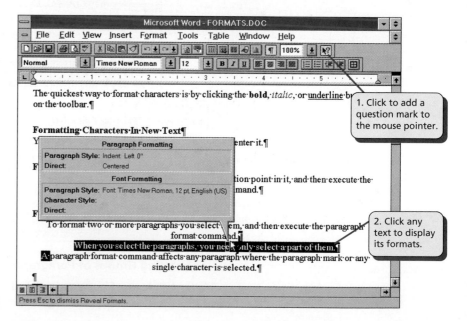

13. Click the **Help** button on the toolbar again to remove the question mark from the mouse pointer.

14. Save and print the document.

Removing Formats

15. Hold down Ctrl and press the 5 in the middle of the numeric keypad to select the entire document. (Or point to the selection bar and triple-click.)

16. Press Ctrl+Spacebar to remove all character formats from the text, then click the **Undo** button on the toolbar to restore them.

17. With the entire document still selected, press Ctrl+Q to remove all paragraph formats from the document, then click the **Undo** button on the toolbar to restore them.

Finishing Up

18. Close the document without saving your last changes.

3-2. CHANGING FONTS, FONT STYLES, AND FONT SIZES

One of the hallmarks of a professional looking document is the font used to print it. There are literally thousands of fonts from which to choose, and each has not only its own unique look but also a number of styles and sizes.

FONTS

A font, commonly called a *typeface*, has its own unique design that distinguishes it from all other fonts. Some fonts of a kind known as TrueType fonts are supplied with Windows. They include Arial, Courier New, and Times New Roman and are illustrated in the table "Fonts Supplied with Windows." In addition to these fonts, many others may be added to a system. Some of these fonts are called *serif* and others *sans serif*. Serif fonts, such as Times New Roman, have small cross bars on their bases. Sans serif fonts, such as Arial, do not. In fact, *sans* is French for "without."

FONT STYLES

Font style refers to variations on a basic font. Font styles supplied by Windows include regular, bold, italic, and bold italic. These styles are illustrated in the table "Windows Font Styles."

FONTS SUPPLIED WITH WINDOWS
Arial
Courier New
Times New Roman

WINDOWS FONT STYLES		
Arial	Courier New	Times New Roman
Arial Bold	**Courier New Bold**	**Times New Roman Bold**
Arial Italic	*Courier New Italic*	*Times New Roman Italic*
Arial Bold Italic	***Courier New Bold Italic***	***Times New Roman Bold Italic***

FONT SIZES

The size of a font is given in a unit of measurement called *points*. A point is about 1/72 of an inch, so 72-point type is 1 inch high, 36-point type is ½ inch high, and 18-point type is ¼ inch high. Normally, body text in books, magazines, and newspapers will be 10 to 12 points in size. The largest and smallest size fonts you can use depend on the capabilities of your printer. Typical sizes are illustrated in the table "Windows Font Sizes."

WINDOWS FONT SIZES

Arial 8 point
Arial 10 point
Arial 12 point
Arial 14 point
Arial 18 point
Arial 24 point

QUICKSTEPS: CHANGING FONT FACES, STYLES, AND SIZES
Fastest

1. Select the text to be formatted or position the insertion point where you want to type text with a new format.

2. Click the **Font** or **Font Size** drop-down arrows (▼) on the Formatting toolbar to display a list of fonts or font sizes, then click the one you want to use. Or click the **Bold**, **Italic**, or **Underline** buttons on the Formatting toolbar to select a font style.

Menus

1. Select the text to be formatted or position the insertion point where you want to type text with a new format.

2. Pull down the **Format** menu and click the **Font** command to display the Font Dialog box.

3. On the **Font** tab, specify the font and its characteristics using the dialog box options described in the box "Understanding The Font Dialog Box," and then click the **OK** command button.

UNDERSTANDING THE FONT DIALOG BOX

When you display the Font dialog box's Font tab, you have a number of options to choose from. As you select from these options, a preview of the resulting font is displayed in the lower-right corner of the screen along with a description.

Font lists the fonts from which you can choose.

Font Style lists the styles available for the selected font.

Size lists the sizes available for the selected font.

Underline drop-down arrow (⬇) displays a list of underlining styles including none, single, words only, double, and dotted.

Color drop-down arrow (⬇) displays a list of colors you can apply to the selected text.

Effects check boxes allow you to specify styles for the selected font. You can turn on or off any or all of the check boxes.

▶ **Strikethrough** strikes through text so you can indicate text proposed for deletion.

▶ **Superscript** prints characters in a smaller size type, raised above the line.

▶ **Subscript** prints characters in a smaller type, sunk below the line.

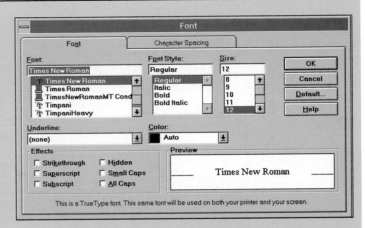

▶ **Hidden** hides text so it won't be seen on the screen or printed. (To control whether it is displayed or printed, pull down the **Tools** menu and click the **Options** command to display the Options dialog box. Click the **View** or **Print** tabs and click the **Hidden Text** check box on or off.)

▶ **Small Caps** displays and prints lowercase letters in uppercase but in a smaller font.

▶ **All Caps** displays and prints lowercase letters as uppercase.

Default command button makes the currently specified font the default font for all subsequent documents.

TIP: CHANGING THE DEFAULT FONT

If you want to change the font for most of your new documents, just select the font in the Font dialog box and then click the **Default** command button. When a dialog box appears asking if you want to change the default font, click the **Yes** command button. All new documents that you open will use the new font.

TIP: CHANGING CHARACTER SPACING

When the Font dialog box is displayed, you can click the **Character Spacing** tab and use its settings to expand or condense the spaces between selected characters. Normally you use expanded spacing in all-caps headings or special text. You condense it to fit more characters in a given space. You can also use this tab to raise or lower text above or below other text on the line.

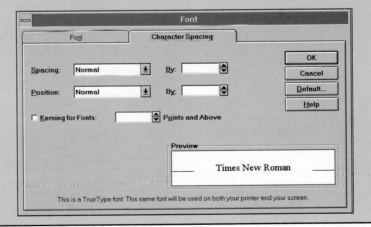

TUTORIAL

There is no way to change the appearance of a document faster than changing the font used to print it. In this tutorial you explore changing fonts, styles, and sizes using a document you have seen before in finished form.

Getting Started

1. Open the *educom.doc* document stored in the *tutorial* directory on the *Word Student Resource Disk (Part 1)*.

Changing Font Styles with the Toolbar

2. Scroll through the document, select all uppercase (all-caps) headings, and click the **Bold** button on the toolbar. (The headings include those on lines by themselves, as well as those that begin a paragraph. They are listed in the accompanying figure.)

USING SOFTWARE:

A GUIDE TO THE ETHICAL AND LEGAL USE OF SOFTWARE

FOR MEMBERS OF THE ACADEMIC COMMUNITY

HERE ARE SOME RELEVANT FACTS:

1. UNAUTHORIZED

2. UNAUTHORIZED

3. UNAUTHORIZED

RESPECT

THEREFORE

SOFTWARE AND INTELLECTUAL RIGHTS

QUESTIONS YOU MAY HAVE ABOUT USING SOFTWARE

ALTERNATIVES TO EXPLORE

A FINAL NOTE

3. Select the two paragraphs that follow the heading *SOFTWARE AND INTELLECTUAL RIGHTS* and click the **Italic** button on the toolbar.

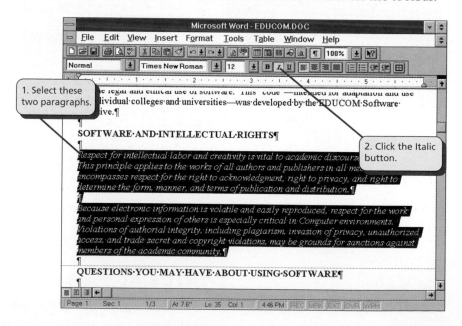

4. Under the heading *QUESTIONS YOU MAY HAVE ABOUT USING SOFTWARE*, there are a series of lettered questions (a-e). Each question is followed by a one-paragraph answer. Select each answer paragraph (but not the accompanying question paragraph), and click the **Italic** button on the toolbar.

Changing Font Styles with the Menu

5. Under the heading ALTERNATIVES TO EXPLORE, select the subheading *Site-Licensed and Bulk-Purchased Software*.

6. Pull down the **Format** menu, click the **Font** command to display the Font Dialog box, and click the *Font* tab to make it active.

7. Click the **Small Caps** check box to turn it on.

8. Click the **Underline** drop-down arrow (⬇) to display a list of underline styles, click the **Double** command to select it, and then click the **OK** command button to close the dialog box.

9. Select the subheadings *Shareware* and *Public Domain Software* one at a time and press F4 to repeat the previous formatting command.

Changing Font Sizes from the Toolbar

10. Select the entire document (hold down Ctrl and click in the selection bar), click the **Font Size** drop-down arrow (⬇) on the toolbar to display a list of sizes, and then click **10**.

11. Select the line with your name at the top of the document, click the **Font Size** drop-down arrow (⬇) on the toolbar to display a list of sizes, and then click **8**.

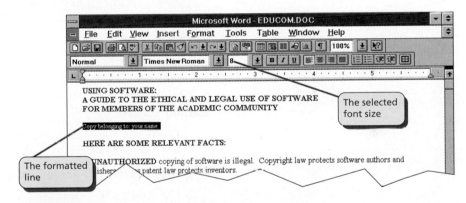

TIP: SLOW SYSTEM?

As you continue to format a document, you may begin to notice that your system slows down, especially when you scroll the screen. This is normal for all systems, although on more powerful systems the effect is less noticeable and less bothersome.

Finishing Up

12. Save the document, print the second page, and then close the document.

3-3. ALIGNING TEXT

When you first open a new document, text that you type is normally aligned just with the left margin, and the right margin is uneven. If you want, you can change the alignment of your lines and paragraphs so they align in any one of four ways.

▶ *Left Aligned* text is aligned with the left margin, and the right margin is uneven, or *ragged*. This is the default setting for new documents.

▶ *Centered* text is centered between the left and right margins.

▶ *Right Aligned* text is aligned with the right margin, and the left margin is uneven, or ragged.

▶ *Justified* text is aligned with both left and right margins. To make the line exactly fit the space between the margins, Word adds spaces between words. This alignment gives a finished appearance to a document and is therefore often used in publications. However, in short lines or lines with long words, the wide word spaces can make the paragraph harder to read.

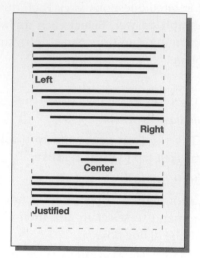

Paragraph alignments

 QUICKSTEPS: ALIGNING LINES
1. Position the insertion point in a paragraph or where you want to enter new text with the format, or select a group of paragraphs.
2. Click the **Align Left**, **Center**, **Align Right**, or **Justify** buttons on the toolbar, or pull down the **Format** menu, click the **Paragraph** command, and on the **Indents and Spacing** tab, use the **Alignment** drop-down arrow (▣) to choose an alignment.

TUTORIAL

Normally text is left-aligned, but it just takes a click of a button to align it another way. In this tutorial you practice aligning text in a document.

Getting Started

1. Open the *educom.doc* document stored in the *tutorial* directory on the *Word Student Resource Disk (Part 1)*.

Aligning Text with Both Margins (Justify)

2. Hold down [Ctrl] and click in the selection bar to select the entire document.

3. Click the **Justify** button on the toolbar, and all text in the document is justified.

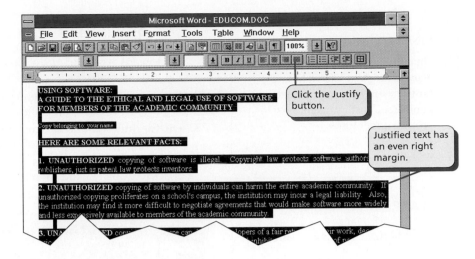

Centering Lines

4. Select the three-line heading at the top of the document and the line with your name and click the **Center** button on the toolbar to center the selected lines.

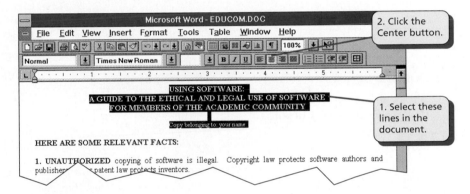

Finishing Up

5. Save the document, print the first page, and then close the document.

3-4. CHANGING LINE AND PARAGRAPH SPACING

The spacing between paragraphs and between lines within paragraphs determines how open or dense your document looks. Adding space makes it look more open and easier to read but also makes it longer. Removing space makes it more dense looking, but shorter. Whichever look you choose, you can easily implement it in Word.

CHANGING LINE SPACING

Most documents are single-spaced, but you can easily change this spacing when you want more space between lines of text within paragraphs, as shown in the margin art on the next page.

SINGLE SPACED

Unauthorized copying of software is illegal. Copyright law protects software authors and publishers, just as patent law protects inventors.

SPACE AND ONE-HALF

Unauthorized copying of software is illegal. Copyright law protects software authors and publishers, just as patent law protects inventors.

DOUBLE SPACED

Unauthorized copying of software is illegal. Copyright law protects software authors and publishers, just as patent law protects inventors.

Variations in line spacing

QUICKSTEPS: CHANGING LINE SPACING

1. Position the insertion point in a paragraph or where you want to enter new text with the format, or select a group of paragraphs.

2. Pull down the **Format** menu and click the **Paragraph** command to display the Paragraph dialog box.

3. On the **Indents and Spacing** tab click the **Line Spacing** drop-down arrow (⬇) to display a list of settings.

4. Choose any of the settings described in the box "Understanding Line Spacing Choices" and then click the **OK** command button.

UNDERSTANDING LINE SPACING CHOICES

When you click the **Line Spacing** drop-down arrow (⬇) on the **Indents and Spacing** tab of the Paragraph dialog box, a number of spacing choices are listed. Here is what each choice does.

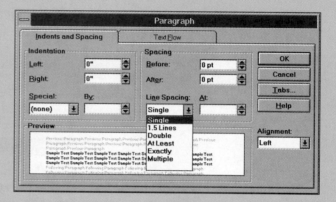

Single sets single spacing.

1.5 Lines sets one and one-half spacing.

Double sets double spacing.

At Least sets a minimal line spacing that Word can then adjust should you format some characters on the line with a larger font.

Exactly sets a fixed line spacing that will not be adjusted should you use larger type on a line.

Multiple is for fine-tuning line spacing. It allows lines to be increased by a specified percentage (or multiple). For example, if **Single** line spacing is too little spacing and **1.5 Lines** is too much, you can set line spacing to 1.2, 1.3, 1.4 or so on using this choice.

CHANGING PARAGRAPH SPACING

You can specify space above and below paragraphs to separate body paragraphs from one another without entering a blank line between them (see the margin art on the next page). You can also use it to add space above and below headings. Like fonts, paragraph spacing is specified in points. This is a useful command because you can set the space to fractions or multiples of a single line. For example, you can have 12 points above a heading and 6 below it to set it off.

6 POINTS

These paragraphs have 6 points of space below them.

These paragraphs have 6 points of space below them.

12 POINTS

These paragraphs have 12 points of space below them.

These paragraphs have 12 points of space below them.

24 POINTS

These paragraphs have 24 points of space below them.

These paragraphs have 24 points of space below them.

Variations in paragraph spacing

QUICKSTEPS: CHANGING PARAGRAPH SPACING

1. Position the insertion point in a paragraph or where you want to enter new text with the format, or select a group of paragraphs.
2. Pull down the **Format** menu and click the **Paragraph** command to display the Paragraph dialog box.
3. On the **Indents and Spacing** tab, click the **Before** or **After** spin buttons (⬍), or type a measurement into the text box.
4. Click the **OK** command button.

TUTORIAL

Increasing line and paragraph spacing makes a document look more open and inviting. In this tutorial you explore changing spacing to see the effects it has on a document's appearance.

Getting Started

1. Open the *educom.doc* document stored in the *tutorial* directory on the *Word Student Resource Disk (Part 1)*.

Changing Line Spacing

2. Hold down [Ctrl] and click in the selection bar to select the entire document.
3. Pull down the **Format** menu and click the **Paragraph** command to display the Paragraph dialog box.
4. Click the **Indents and Spacing** tab to make it the active tab.
5. Click the **Line Spacing** drop-down arrow (⬍) to display a list of settings.
6. Click the **1.5 Lines** command and then click the **OK** command button. The spacing in all paragraphs changes to one and one-half lines.

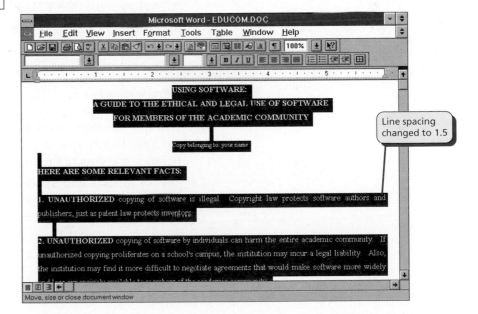

Restoring Line Spacing

7. Select the 3-line heading at the top of the document and the line with your name, then repeat Steps 3 through 6 but select the **Single** command instead of the **1.5 Lines** command.

8. Press Ctrl+End to move the insertion point to the end of the document, then select the last five lines of text beginning with the line reading *EDUCOM*. Repeat Steps 3 through 6 but select the **Single** command instead of the **1.5 Lines** command.

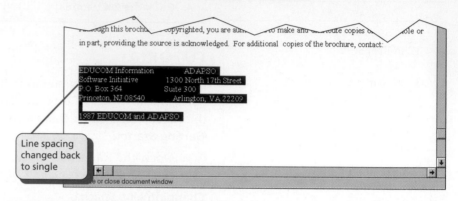

Adding Space Above and Below Paragraphs

9. Click the **Show/Hide ¶** button on the toolbar so you can see where paragraph marks are located.

10. Scroll through the document deleting blank lines—those that have only a ¶ symbol on them above and below the headings listed in the figure "Document Headings."

HERE ARE SOME RELEVANT FACTS:

SOFTWARE AND INTELLECTUAL RIGHTS

QUESTIONS YOU MAY HAVE ABOUT USING SOFTWARE

ALTERNATIVES TO EXPLORE

A FINAL NOTE

Document Headings

11. Position the insertion point in the first heading (*HERE ARE SOME RELEVANT FACTS:*), pull down the **Format** menu, and click the **Paragraph** command to display the Paragraph dialog box.

12. On the **Indents and Spacing** tab, click the up arrow on the **Before** spin button (⬍) to change the setting to 18pt (if you overshoot it, click the down arrow on the spin button).

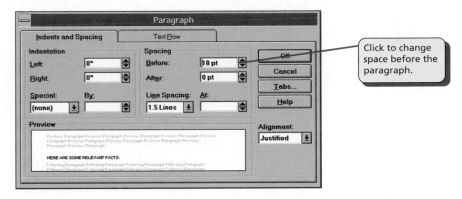

Click to change space before the paragraph.

13. Click the up arrow on the **After** spin button (⬍) to change the setting to 6pt, then click the **OK** command button.

14. Move the insertion point into each of the other headings listed in the figure "Document Headings" and then press F4 to repeat the format.

Finishing Up

15. Save the document, print the first page, and then close the document.

3-5. CONTROLLING PAGE BREAKS

A page break is the point at which the printer stops printing lines on the current sheet of paper and resumes printing on the next sheet. You can control where page breaks fall when you print a document. Doing so is important because there are certain places where you want to avoid page breaks and other places where you want them.

▶ Letters should not end with their closing alone at the top of a page.

▶ Tables should be kept together so that they do not break with one part on one page and the rest on the next page.

▶ In finished documents, the first line of a paragraph should not fall by itself at the bottom of a page and the last line of a paragraph should not fall by itself at the top.

▶ Reports, term papers, and other important documents should often have major sections begin at the top of a new page.

SOFT PAGE BREAKS

As you edit a document, Word automatically keeps track of how many lines of text will fit on each page when the document is printed. When it determines that a page is full, it inserts a *soft page break* where one page will end and the next will begin. In Page Layout view, a soft page break causes a new page to be displayed. In Normal view a soft page break is displayed as a thin dotted line across the screen. The only way to move one of these soft page breaks is to add or delete lines of text above it. However, there are times when soft page breaks fall at undesirable locations. For example, a soft page break may split a table or put a heading on one page and the paragraph that follows on another. When that happens, you enter a hard page break—see the margin illustration.

Types of page breaks

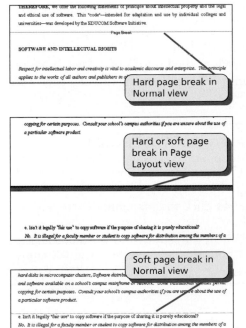

Hard page break in Normal view

Hard or soft page break in Page Layout view

Soft page break in Normal view

HARD PAGE BREAKS

To prevent unwanted page breaks, you enter *hard page breaks*. In Normal view a hard page break is displayed as a solid line across the document labeled *Page Break*. In Page Layout view, a hard page break looks just like soft page breaks—a new page is displayed. If you add or delete text above a hard page break, it doesn't adjust automatically as a soft page break does. As a result, the page before a hard page break may be too short. (To delete a hard page break, select it and press Del.)

QUICKSTEPS: ENTERING HARD PAGE BREAKS
Fastest
▶ With the insertion point where you want to start the new page, press Ctrl+Enter ↵.

Menus

1. Move the insertion point to the beginning of the line that you want to start the new page (or the end of the line you want to be the last on the previous page).

2. Pull down the **Insert** menu, click the **Break** command to display the Break dialog box, click to turn on the **Page Break** option button, and then click the **OK** command button.

KEEPING TEXT TOGETHER

You can prevent soft page breaks from occurring in undesirable places by using window/orphan control, keeping selected lines together, or keeping one paragraph with the next. These commands are extremely useful when you want to:

▶ Keep the lines of a table on the same page as the table headings

▶ Keep an illustration on the same page as the text that refers to it

▶ Keep a heading and at least the first two lines of the following text on the same page

▶ Avoid widows and orphans. In printing jargon, an orphan is the first line of a paragraph printed by itself at the bottom of a page. A widow is the last line of a paragraph printed by itself at the top of a page—see the margin illustration.

Widows and orphans

QUICKSTEPS: KEEPING TEXT TOGETHER

1. Position the insertion point in a paragraph or where you want to enter new text with the format, or select a group of paragraphs.

2. Pull down the **Format** menu and click the **Paragraph** command to display the Paragraph dialog box.

3. On the **Text Flow** tab choose any of the settings described in the box "Understanding Pagination Choices" and then click the **OK** command button.

UNDERSTANDING PAGINATION CHOICES

The **Text Flow** tab of the Paragraph dialog box offers three ways to protect sections of your text.

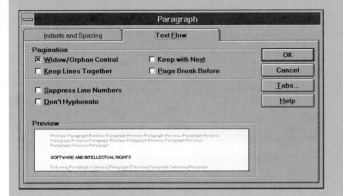

Widow/Orphan Control prevents widows and orphans. (The default setting is on.) If Word calculates that the first or last line of a paragraph will print at the bottom or top of a page by itself, it moves another line to accompany it. Since single lines are prevented, no three-line paragraphs will be split; the entire paragraph will move to the next page if it will not print on the current page.

Keep Lines Together keeps a paragraph from being split by a soft page break.

Keep with Next moves a paragraph to the next page if the paragraph that follows it is moved there. This command is ideal to keep a heading with the paragraph that follows it.

Page Break Before always keeps a paragraph at the top of a page because a page break is inserted before it.

TUTORIAL

Controlling page breaks is sometimes very important. In this tutorial you explore how you do so and see what effects various commands have.

Getting Started

1. Open the *educom.doc* document stored in the *tutorial* directory on the *Word Student Resource Disk (Part 1)*.

Entering a Hard Page Break

2. Move the insertion point to the beginning of the line that reads *SOFTWARE AND INTELLECTUAL RIGHTS* or *ALTERNATIVES TO EXPLORE* (whichever is closest to the bottom of a page) and press Ctrl + Enter⏎ to enter a hard page break. All text below the insertion point moves to the next page.

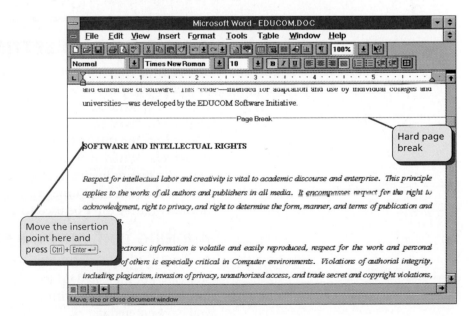

Protecting a Paragraph from a Page Break

3. Scroll through the entire document until you find a paragraph split by a soft page break. If you can't find one, select one just above and one just below a soft page break.

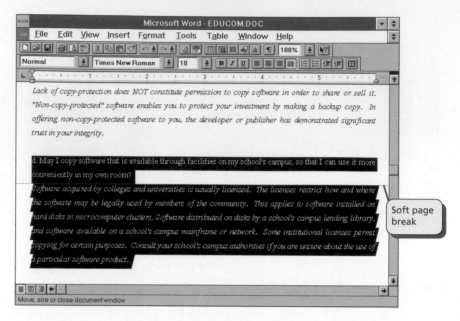

4. With the insertion point anywhere in the paragraph, pull down the **Format** menu, and click the **Paragraph** command to display the Paragraph menu. Click the **Text Flow** tab to make it the active page.

5. Click the **Keep Lines Together** command check box to turn it on and then click the **OK** command button. The entire paragraph moves to the next page if it was split by a soft page break.

Finishing Up

6. Close the document without saving your changes.

3-6. USING AND SETTING TAB STOPS

To indent the first line of a paragraph or get a column of figures to align properly, you use tab stops rather than regular spaces. Tab stops move text to a specific spot on the page, which is what you need for exact alignment. Pressing the spacebar does not accomplish the same thing. The reason for this is that Word handles spaces differently than other characters. When it wants to squeeze more characters onto a line or expand a line to justify it, it squeezes or expands the spaces on the line. Since spaces can have different widths depending on where they are in a document, they can't be used to align text properly.

ALIGNING TEXT WITH TAB STOPS

By default, Word sets left-aligned tab stops every 0.5 inches. (These tab stops are not indicated on the horizontal ruler when you display it.) You can left-align columns with these tab stops either as you enter it or after you have entered it.

- To align a column entry with a tab stop as you enter the text, press Tab⇆ until the insertion point is in the desired tab stop, and then type the text. (If you type enough text to reach past the right margin, the second and subsequent lines wrap back to and align with the left margin, not with the tab stop.)

- To align an entry with a tab stop after you have entered the text, position the insertion point to the left of the first character in the entry to be aligned. When you then press Tab⇆, the insertion point and all text to its right move to the next tab stop. You must be in insert mode to do this. If you are in overtype mode, pressing Tab⇆ will delete the character to its right.

CHANGING TAB STOPS

Although Word has left-aligned tab stops set every 0.5 inches, you can change tab stops at any point in the document, and the change affects all selected paragraphs. When you set a tab stop, it automatically turns off all of the default tabs stops set every 0.5 inches between it and the left margin. For example, without changing tab stops, each time you press Tab⇆ the insertion point moves 0.5 inches to the right. However, if you set a tab stop at 4 inches, pressing Tab⇆ the first time moves the insertion point 4 inches and then each time you press it, it moves only 0.5 inches.

When you set new tab stops, you have the choice of four possible alignments: left, centered, right, and decimal—see the margin illustration. You can specify a leader for a tab stop—a dotted, dashed, or solid line that fills the space between tabbed columns. Leaders make it easier for the eye to move from one column of text to the next without getting lost.

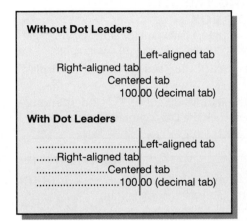

Types of tab stops

Types of tabs

- A left-aligned tab stop aligns columns flush left with the tab stop. Normally you use this type of tab stop to align text.

- A centered tab stop centers text on the tab stop's position. This alignment is frequently used for column headings in tables.

- A right-aligned tab stop aligns columns of text flush right with the tab stop. This alignment is widely used for numbers without decimal points.

- A decimal tab stop aligns columns of numbers containing decimal points. When you press Tab⇆ to move the insertion point to a decimal tab stop, characters you type align flush right with the stop until you type a decimal point. When you do so, the period remains fixed in the decimal column and additional characters that you type extend out to the right. You can also use decimal tab stops to right-align text with tab stops. Just enter the text without typing a period, or make the period the last character.

- Word also has a special kind of tab stop called a bar tab stop that sets a vertical line in the paragraph (see the illustration at the top of the next page). You might use this in a series of consecutive paragraphs to visually separate columns of text or numbers aligned with other tab stops.

Table 1. Major U.S. Dams and Reservoirs

Order	Dam Name	River	State	Height	Year
2	Hoover	Colorado	Nevada	725	1936
4	Glen Canyon	Colorado	Arizona	708	1966
5	New Bullards Bar	North Yuba	California	636	1970
8	Mossyrock	Cowlitz	Washington	607	1968
10	Hungry Horse	S Fork Flathead	Montana	564	1953
12	Ross	Skagit	Washington	541	1949
1	Oroville	Feather	California	754	1968
7	Swift	Lewis	Washington	610	1958
3	Dworshak	N Fork Clearwater	Idaho	718	1973
9	Shasta	Sacramento	California	600	1945
11	Grand Coulee	Columbia	Washington	551	1942
6	New Melones	Stanislaus	California	626	1979

Bar tabs

TAB STOP MARKERS

Marker	Description
L	Left aligned
⊥	Centered
⌐	Right aligned
⊥	Decimal

When you set tab stops, each type is represented on the horizontal ruler with a unique symbol. These symbols are illustrated in the table "Tab Stop Markers."

QUICKSTEPS: SETTING TAB STOPS USING THE TAB SET DIALOG BOX

1. Position the insertion point in a paragraph or at the point where you want to set a new tab stop, or select a group of paragraphs.

2. Pull down the **Format** menu and click the **Tabs** command to display the Tabs dialog box.

3. Specify tab stops using any of the settings described in "Understanding the Tab Set Dialog Box" and then click the **OK** command button.

UNDERSTANDING THE TAB SET DIALOG BOX

When you pull down the **Format** menu and click the **Tabs** command, the Tabs dialog box appears. You use this dialog box to specify the type and placement of tab stops.

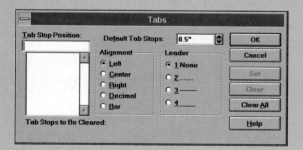

Tab Stop Position text box is where you enter the distance of the tab stop from the left margin. If the para-

graph already has any tab stops set, they are listed below the text box. To select one of them and list it in the text box (for example to clear it or add a leader), just click it. If there are some tabs stops that are set in one of the selected paragraphs but not in another, they are displayed dimmed on the ruler and are not shown on this list.

Alignment section contains option buttons where you specify whether the tab stop is **Left**, **Center**, **Right**, **Decimal**, or **Bar**.

Leader section specifies the type of leader, if any, for the tab currently displayed in the **Tab Stop Position** text box.

Command Buttons

Set sets a tab stop at the position currently displayed in the **Tab Stop Position** text box.

Clear clears any tab stop at the position indicated in the **Tab Stop Position** text box.

Clear All clears all existing tab stops, returning the paragraph to the default settings.

TIP: SELECTING TABBED COLUMNS

If you hold down [Alt] while dragging, you'll select a rectangular area within the document. You can use this procedure to format, copy, cut, delete, or drag and drop tabbed columns.

TUTORIAL

Many tables are arranged in columns with each column aligned with a tab stop. In this tutorial you set tab stops to correctly align the columns in a table listing the highest dams in the United States.

Getting Started

1. Open the *dams.doc* document stored in the *tutorial* directory on the *Word Student Resource Disk (Part 1)* and enter your name. Click anywhere in the date and press [F9] to update it. If the horizontal ruler is

not displayed, pull down the **View** menu and click the **Ruler** command to turn it on. Any tab stops you now set will be displayed on this ruler.

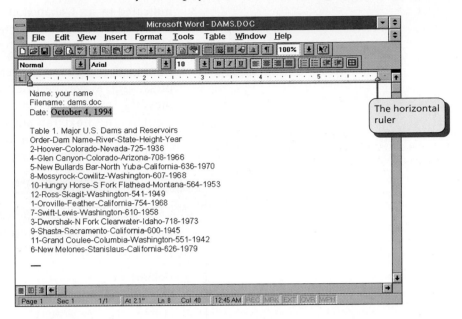

The horizontal ruler

Setting Tab Stops

2. Select the entire table beginning with the line that reads *Table 1. Major U. S. Dams and Reservoirs.*

3. Pull down the **Format** menu and click the **Tabs** command to display the Tabs dialog box.

4. Click the **Clear All** command button to clear any existing tab stops from the horizontal ruler.

5. With the insertion point in the **Tab Stop Position** text box, type **.5** (don't press Enter←), and click the **Set** command button to set a left-aligned tab stop .5" from the left margin.

6. With the previous entry still highlighted in the **Tab Stop Position** text box type **2** and click the **Set** command button.

7. With the previous entry still highlighted in the **Tab Stop Position** text box type **3.5** and click the **Set** command button.

8. With the previous entry still highlighted in the **Tab Stop Position** text box type **4.75**, click the **Right** option button in the *Alignment* section to turn it on, and then click the **Set** command button to set a right-aligned tab stop 4.75" from the left margin.

9. With the previous entry still highlighted in the **Tab Stop Position** text box type **5.5** (the **Right** option button in the *Alignment* section should still be on), and then click the **Set** command button. Your tab stop settings in the dialog box should now look like these.

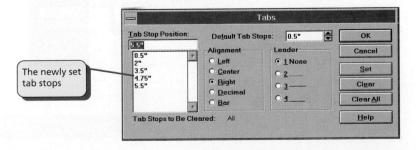

The newly set tab stops

10. Click the **OK** command button to close the Tabs dialog box and display the tabs on the horizontal ruler. The left-aligned tabs are indicated by an L-shaped character and the right-aligned tabs with a backward L-shaped character.

Tabbing Columns

11. Each hyphen in the document represents a place where you should press Tab⇆. Move the insertion point to the left of each hyphen, press Del to delete it, and then press Tab⇆ to tab the text to the right to the next tab stop. (Tip: It's a lot faster to search for hyphens and replace them with **Tab character**s listed on the **Special** button menu of the Replace dialog box.)

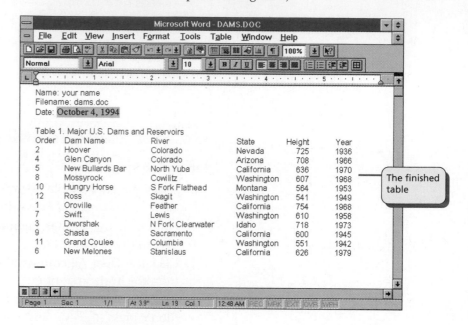

The finished table

Formatting a Single Column

12. Hold down Alt and point just to the left of the *H* in *Hoover* under the heading *Dam Name*. Hold down the left mouse button and drag the highlight so it just highlights entries in that column.

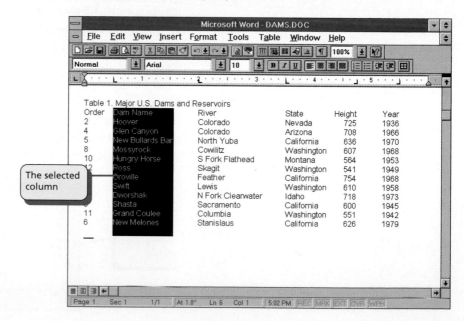

The selected column

13. Click the **Bold** button on the toolbar.

Finishing Up

14. Save, print, and close the document.

3-7. INDENTING PARAGRAPHS

Many times, when you want to indicate where a new paragraph starts, you press ⎆Tab to indent the first line. However, there are other indents you can use (see the top margin illustration), especially when you want to set off text in your document so it stands out.

▶ A paragraph with a *left* or *right indent* has all lines indented from the left or right margin, or from both margins.

▶ A paragraph with a *first line indent* has just the first line indented from the left margin.

▶ A paragraph with a *hanging indent* has the first line indented less than the other lines in the paragraph or not indented at all. This type of indent is frequently used for bibliographies. An enumerated list is a form of hanging indent (see the bottom margin illustration), but you press ⎆Tab between the number (or bullet) and the first word of the paragraph that follows it. This leaves the number (or bullet) hanging but the text in the paragraph is all aligned at the left indent marker.

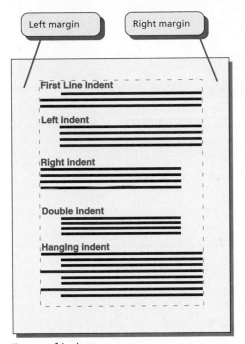

Types of indents

> **QUICKSTEPS: INDENTING PARAGRAPHS**
>
> **Fastest**
>
> ▶ To left-indent a paragraph, click the **Increase Indent** or **Decrease Indent** buttons on the toolbar. These commands indent the paragraphs to the next or previous tab stop.
>
> **Menus**
>
> **1.** Position the insertion point in a paragraph or where you want to enter new text with the format, or select a group of paragraphs.
>
> **2.** Pull down the **Format** menu, and click the **Paragraph** command to display the Paragraph dialog box, and on the **Indents and Spacing** tab use any of the settings in the *Indentation* section to indent the selected paragraphs. These settings are described in the box "Understanding Indentation Settings."
>
> **3.** Click the **OK** command to close the dialog box.

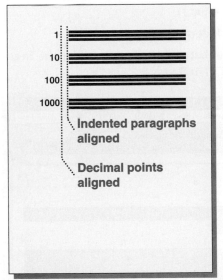

An enumerated list

UNDERSTANDING INDENTATION SETTINGS

When the Paragraph dialog box's **Indents and Spacing** tab is displayed, you can set indents with the commands listed in the *Indentation* section.

Left specifies the distance the whole paragraph is indented from the left margin.

Right specifies the distance the whole paragraph is indented from the right margin.

Special drop-down arrow (⬇) displays the choices **(none)**, **First Line**, and **Hanging** for shifting lines in selected paragraphs.

▶ **(none)** aligns the first line with the rest of the lines in the paragraph.

▶ **First Line** shifts to the right the first line by the distance you enter into the **By** text box.

▶ **Hanging** shifts to the right all lines but the first by the distance you enter into the **By** text box.

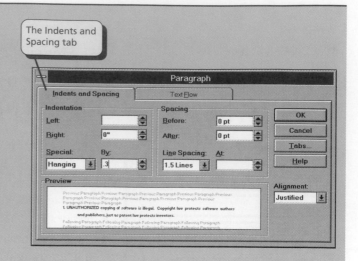

The Indents and Spacing tab

By specifies the indent distance for **First Line** and **Hanging** indents. You can type the distance into the text box or use the spin buttons (⬍).

TUTORIAL

Indents are a great way to give a professional look to a document. In this tutorial you use hanging indents and left indents to set off enumerated lists and answer paragraphs in the *educom.doc* document.

Getting Started

1. Open the *educom.doc* document stored in the *tutorial* directory on the *Word Student Resource Disk (Part 1)*.

Formatting Paragraphs as Hanging Indents

2. Select the three paragraphs numbered *1* through *3* under the heading *HERE ARE SOME RELEVANT FACTS*.

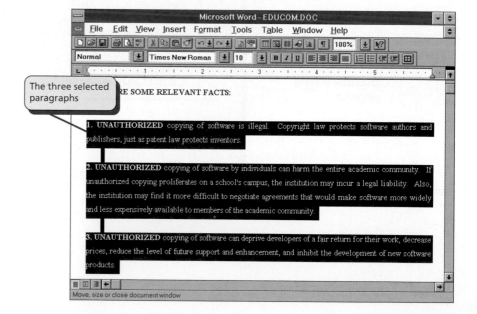

The three selected paragraphs

3. Pull down the **Format** menu and click the **Paragraph** command to display the Paragraph dialog box. Click the **Indents and Spacing** tab to make that the active tab.

4. Click the **Special** drop-down arrow (⬇) to display a list of choices and click **Hanging**. Double-click in the **By** text box to select the current entry, and then type **.3** to replace it.

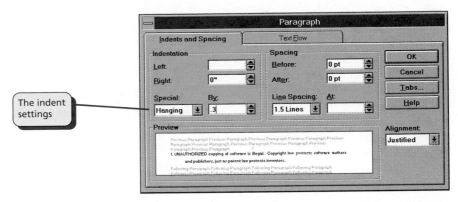

5. Click the **OK** command button to close the dialog box.

6. Following the periods after the numbers, delete the space and press `Tab⇄` to align the first line of text with those that follow.

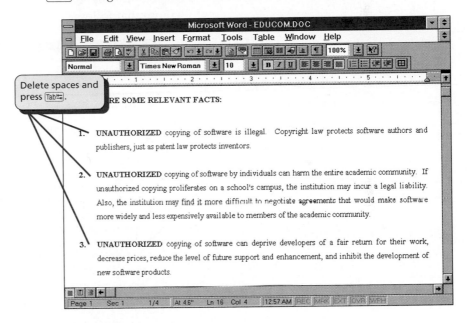

Formatting Questions as Hanging Indents

7. Move the insertion point anywhere in the question paragraph *a* that reads *What do I need to know about software and the U.S. Copyright Act?* under the heading *QUESTIONS YOU MAY HAVE ABOUT USING SOFTWARE.*

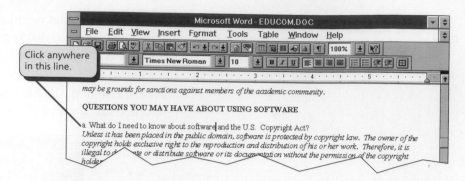

8. Pull down the **Format** menu and click the **Paragraph** command to display the Paragraph dialog box.

9. On the **Indents and Spacing** tab, click the **Special** drop-down arrow (⬇) to display a list of choices and click **Hanging**. Double-click in the **By** text box to select the current entry, type **.3** and then click the **OK** command button to close the dialog box.

10. Move the insertion point into each question paragraph lettered *b* through *e* and press F4 to repeat the pervious command and indent them.

11. Following the periods after the letters in each question paragraph, delete the space and press Tab⇆ to align the first line of text with those that follow.

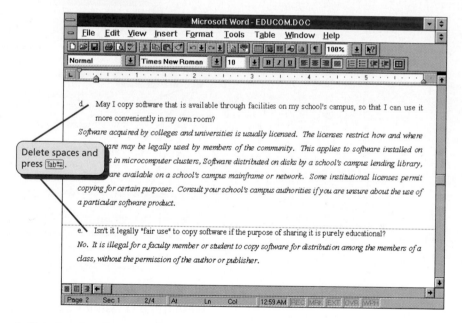

Left-Indenting Paragraphs

12. Move the insertion point anywhere in the answer paragraph following the question lettered *a* under the heading *QUESTIONS YOU MAY HAVE ABOUT USING SOFTWARE.*

13. Pull down the **Format** menu and click the **Paragraph** command to display the Paragraph dialog box.

14. On the **Indents and Spacing** tab, the **Left** text box should be selected. Type **.3** to replace the current entry, and the click the **OK** command button.

15. Click in each answer paragraph following the questions lettered *b* through *e* under the heading *QUESTIONS YOU MAY HAVE ABOUT USING SOFTWARE* and press `F4` to repeat the previous command and indent them.

Indenting the Addresses

16. Select the four address lines that begin with *EDUCOM* near the end of the document.

17. Pull down the **Format** menu and click the **Tabs** command to display the Tabs dialog box. With the insertion point in the **Tab Stop Position** text box, type **3** and then click the **OK** command button to close the Tabs dialog box and display the tabs on the horizontal ruler.

18. Delete the spaces separating the names and addresses of each organization and press `Tab⇆` to tab the *ADAPSO* information to the tab stop you just set.

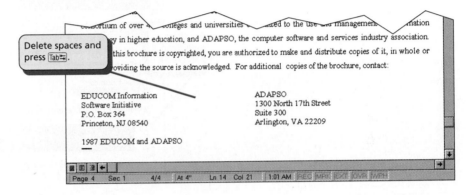

Finishing Up

19. Save the document, print the third page, and then close the document.

3-8. AUTOMATICALLY NUMBERING AND BULLETING LISTS

Many lists are set off from the rest of the text with numbers or bullets. Word makes it easy to create these lists. The command creates hanging indents—that is, lists in which bullets or numbers align to the left of the text that follows. To renumber a revised list, select the entire list again and repeat the command. The amount of indent is controlled by tab stops in the document.

>
> **QUICKSTEPS: NUMBERING AND BULLETING LISTS**
> 1. Position the insertion point in a paragraph or where you want to enter new text with the format, or select a group of paragraphs.
> 2. Click the **Numbering** or **Bullets** button on the Formatting toolbar or pull down the **Format** menu and click the **Bullets and Numbering** command to display the Bullets and Numbering dialog box.
> 3. On the **Bulleted**, **Numbered**, or **Multilevel** tab, select your choice and click the **OK** command button. (To have the bullets or numbers left hanging so they stand out, be sure the **Hanging Indent** check box is on (☒).)

A NUMBERED LIST
1. Arizona
2. California
3. Florida
4. New York
5. Ohio
6. Texas

A BULLETED LIST
• New York
• California
• Ohio
• Texas
• Florida
• Arizona

TUTORIAL

Many lists are either bulleted or numbered. Word makes it possible to do this with the click of a button, as you will see in this tutorial.

Getting Started

1. Open the *lists.doc* document stored in the *tutorial* directory on the *Word Student Resource Disk (Part 1)* and enter your name. Click anywhere in the date and press F9 to update it..

Numbering Paragraphs

2. Select the three paragraphs that follow the heading *Numbering and Bulleting Lists*.

3. Click the **Numbering** button on the toolbar to number the three paragraphs.

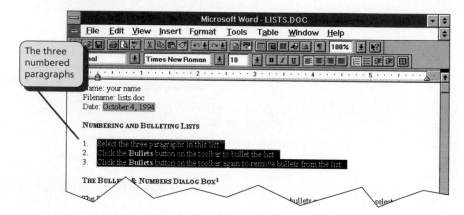

4. Select the last three paragraphs in the document (starting with **Styles** *specifies which ...*).

5. Click the **Numbering** button on the toolbar to number the three paragraphs.

Bulleting Paragraphs

6. With the last three paragraphs still selected, click the **Bullets** button on the toolbar to replace the numbers with bullets.

7. Print the document.

Removing Numbers and Bullets

8. Select the three paragraphs that follow the heading *Numbering and Bulleting Lists*and then click the **Numbering** button on the toolbar to remove the bullets.

9. Select the last three paragraphs in the document (the first begins **Styles** *specifies which ...*), then click the **Bullets** button on the toolbar to remove the bullets from the list.

Changing Bullet and Number Styles

10. Select the three paragraphs that follow the heading *Numbering and Bulleting Lists,* then pull down the **Format** menu and click the **Bullets and Numbering** command to display the Bullets and Numbering dialog box.

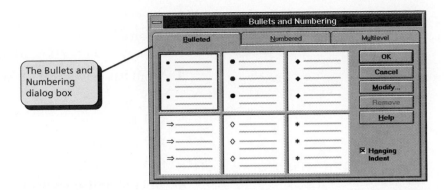

The Bullets and Numbering dialog box

11. Click the **Bulleted**, **Numbered**, or **Multilevel** tab to make that tab active, select your choice, and click the **OK** command button.

PAUSING FOR PRACTICE

Pause here to practice using the toolbar and the **Bullets and Numbering** command on the **Format** menu to number and bullet the two lists in this document.

Finishing Up

12. Close the document without saving it.

PicTorial 3 Review Questions

True-False

T F **1.** Word's screen shows you what the formats will look like in the final printout.

T F **2.** If you change a paragraph's format and then press Enter ↵ at the end of it, the new paragraph will not have the same formats as the one you created it from.

T F **3.** You cannot assign formats to existing text.

T F **4.** You can apply color to text.

T F **5.** Hidden text is not visible on the screen, but it will print.

T F **6.** Soft page breaks can be deleted.

T F **7.** By default, tab stops are set every 1/2 inch.

T F **8.** Lists in which bullets or numbers align to the left of the text create right indents.

T F **9.** Character formats cannot be turned off

T F **10.** The easiest way to determine existing formats is to click the **Help** button on the toolbar.

1. Word has preselected left and right margins set at _____ inch.

  a. 1

  b. 1 1/4

  c. 1 1/2

  d. 1 1/8

2. You can format an item, immediately select another one, and then press _____ to repeat the format.

  a. [F2]

  b. [F3]

  c. [F4]

  d. [F8]

3. To remove character formats, press _____.

  a. [Ctrl]+[Spacebar]

  b. [Ctrl]+[Del]

  c. [Alt]+[Del]

  d. [Ctrl]+[Q]

4. To remove paragraph formats, press _____.

  a. [Ctrl]+[Spacebar]

  b. [Ctrl]+[Del]

  c. [Alt]+[Del]

  d. [Ctrl]+[Q]

5. To insert a hard page break, press _____.

  a. [Enter ⏎]

  b. [Alt]+[Enter ⏎]

  c. [Ctrl]+[Enter ⏎]

  d. [⇧ Shift]+[Enter ⏎]

6. A paragraph with a _____ indent has the first line indented less than the other lines in the paragraph.

  a. Left

  b. Right

  c. First line

  d. Hanging

7. To select the entire document, hold down _____ and press the _____ on the numeric keypad.

  a. [Ctrl], [5]

  b. [Alt], [0]

  c. [Ctrl], [3]

  d. [Ctrl], [7]

8. Font sizes that you can use are dependent upon the _____.

   a. Printer

   b. Computer memory

   c. Document size

   d. Screen size

9. To keep a paragraph from being split by a soft page break, use the **Format, Paragraph, Text Flow** tab and choose _____.

   a. Widow/orphan control

   b. Keep lines together

   c. Keep with next

   d. Page Break Before

10. If you hold down _____ while dragging, you will select a rectangular area within the document.

    a. Ctrl

    b. ⇧ Shift

    c. Alt

    d. Ctrl + Alt

 Fill In the Blank

1. _____ formats affect individual characters or a group of selected characters.

2. To insert a newline character at the end of a line, press _____.

3. To display paragraph marks, click the _____ button on the toolbar.

4. Another name for a font is a(n) _____.

5. _____ fonts do not have small crossbars on their bases.

6. Arial Bold is an example of a(n) _____.

7. A point is about _____ of an inch.

8. _____ text is aligned with both left and right margins.

9. A(n) _____ is the last line of a paragraph printed by itself at the top of a page.

10. _____ formats include such things as text alignment and indents.

PicTorial 3 Lab Activities

▶▶ **COMPUTER-BASED TUTORIALS**

We suggest you complete the following computer-based lessons to learn more about the features discussed in this PicTorial. To do so, pull down the **Help** menu and click the **Examples and Demos** command, click the

Topic listed in the table "Suggested Examples and Demos to Complete," and then click the *Subtopic* listed in that same table. (If you need more help on using the system, see the "Computer-Based Tutorials" section at the end of PicTorial 2.)

Suggested Examples and Demos to Complete		
Done	**Topic**	**Subtopic**
☐	Formatting Text	Overview of Formatting Text Characters
☐	Formatting Text	Applying and removing character formats
☐	Formatting Paragraphs	Overview of Formatting Paragraphs
☐	Formatting Paragraphs	Centering or aligning text
☐	Formatting Paragraphs	Changing line spacing
☐	Formatting Paragraphs	Adjusting paragraph spacing
☐	Formatting Paragraphs	Setting or clearing tab stops
☐	Formatting Paragraphs	Indenting Paragraphs
☐	Formatting Paragraphs	Adding or removing bullets and numbers in a list
☐	Formatting Paragraphs	Converting bullets to numbers, or vice versa
☐	Formatting Paragraphs	Modifying bullet formats

▶▶ QUICKSTEP DRILLS

3-1. Types of Formats

As you have seen, there are character and paragraph formats. In this drill you explore applying and removing these two levels of formatting.

1. Open the *formats.doc* document stored in the *drill* directory of the *Word Student Resource Disk (Part 1)*.

2. Click the **Help** button on the toolbar to add a question mark to the mouse pointer, then click each of the numbered lines in the document anywhere but on the number to display the line's formatting. Summarize the direct formats in effect for each line in the table "Document Formats" on the next page, then click the **Help** button on the toolbar to remove the question mark from the mouse pointer.

3. With the insertion point anywhere on the heading line that reads *"Exploring Character and Paragraph Formats"* press Ctrl+Q to remove direct paragraph formats. Click the **Help** button on the Standard toolbar to add a question mark to the mouse pointer, then click the line to see that direct paragraph formats are no longer listed. Click the **Help** button on the Standard toolbar to remove the question mark from the mouse pointer. Then click the **Undo** button on the Standard toolbar to restore the line's paragraph formats.

4. Select the entire line that reads *"Exploring Character and Paragraph Formats,"* and press Ctrl+Spacebar to remove direct character formats. Click the **Help** button on the toolbar to add a question mark to the mouse pointer, then click the line to see that direct character for-

mats are no longer listed. Click the **Help** button on the toolbar to remove the question mark from the mouse pointer. Then click the **Undo** button on the Standard toolbar to restore the line's character formats.

5. Close the document without saving your changes.

Document Formats	
Number	**Description**
①	_____
②	_____
③	_____
④	_____
⑤	_____
⑥	_____
⑦	_____
⑧	_____

3-2A. Changing Font Faces, Styles, and Sizes

There are some places where the use of italics is encouraged. In this drill you format a document that explains some of those places.

1. Open the *italic.doc* document stored in the *drill* directory of the *Word Student Resource Disk (Part 1)* and enter your name, then click anywhere in the date and press F9 to update it.

2. Use the **Italic** button on the toolbar to italicize each of the red words and characters. (The color is just to allow you to identify where to use italic.)

3. Save, print, and close the document.

3-2B. Changing Font Faces, Styles, and Sizes

Ambrose Bierce (1842-1914), American journalist and author of short stories, wrote that his "*Devil's Dictionary* was begun in a weekly paper in 1881, and was continued in a desultory way and at long intervals until 1906. In that year a large part of it was published in covers with the title *The Cynic's Word Book*, a name which the author had not the power to reject or the happiness to approve."

1. Open the *devildic.doc* document stored in the *drill* directory of the *Word Student Resource Disk (Part 1)* and enter your name. Click anywhere in the date and press F9 to update it.

2. Use the **Bold** button on the toolbar to boldface the first word(s) in each entry. There are almost 30 entries, so to build speed skills, format the first, then double-click each of the others and press F4. (Clicking the **Show/Hide ¶** button on the toolbar makes it easier to see where paragraphs begin.)

3. Save the document, print the first page, and then close the document.

3-2C. Changing Font Faces, Styles, and Sizes

Since almost all modern fonts are specified in points, you have to be able to think in points or at least have an idea of what various point sizes look like. In this drill you format a document with a range of point sizes. You can then use this document as a reference when selecting type sizes for your own documents.

1. Open the *fontsize.doc* document stored in the *drill* directory of the *Word Student Resource Disk (Part 1)* and enter your name, then click anywhere in the date and press F9 to update it.

2. Double-click in the selection bar to select each of the paragraphs, then:

   ▶ For the 4- and 6-point paragraphs, type the point size into the **Font Size** text box on the Formatting toolbar and press Enter ⏎ to format them with the size mentioned at the beginning of the paragraph.

   ▶ For all other paragraphs, select the font size using the **Font Size** drop-down arrow (⬇) on the Formatting toolbar.

3. Save, print, and close the document.

3-2D. Changing Font Faces, Styles, and Sizes

Windows comes with a set of fonts included and you can almost be certain that these fonts are available on any system you use. Here you format a document so you have a sample of each font. You can use this as a reference when selecting fonts to use with your documents.

1. Open the *fonts.doc* document stored in the *drill* directory of the *Word Student Resource Disk (Part 1)* and enter your name, then click anywhere in the date and press F9 to update it.

2. Select each of the lines under the *Fonts Supplied with Windows* heading and format it with the matching font. You can use the **Font** drop-down arrow (⬇) to do this quickly. If there is any font listed in the document that is not listed on the drop-down list, add a note to its name to indicate that it doesn't exist on your system. (You'll see that the Arial line is already formatted and when you format the Wingdings and Symbol lines, the letters change to special characters.)

3. Save, print, and close the document.

3-2E. Changing Font Faces, Styles, and Sizes

In this drill you format a document with each of Word's font effects, styles, and underlines. You can then use this document as a reference when selecting font formats for your own documents.

1. Open the *fontstyl.doc* document stored in the *drill* directory of the *Word Student Resource Disk (Part 1)* and enter your name, then click anywhere in the date and press F9 to update it.

2. Select each of the lines one at a time and use the **Format**, **Font** command to display the Font dialog box. On the **Font** tab, format them with the effect, style, or underline mentioned on the line. (Formats in the "Font Style Section" can be applied using buttons

on the Formatting toolbar.) When formatting *Superscript 10oF*, superscript only the *o* in front of the letter *F*. When formatting *Subscript H20*, subscript only the number *2*.

3. Save, print, and close the document.

3-2F. Changing the Font for the Entire Document

It's not at all unusual to want to change the font for an entire document. To do so, you select the entire document and then use the font commands as you would normally.

1. Open the *fontstyl.doc* document stored in the *drill* directory of the *Word Student Resource Disk (Part 1)*.

2. Select the entire document and use the **Font** and **Font Size** drop-down arrows (⬇) to change the font to each of the fonts and font sizes listed in the table "Exploring Fonts." Click anywhere after changing to each font to see how it looks. Make a printout of any that you especially like.

3. Close the document without saving it.

3-3. Aligning Text

Aligning and justifying paragraphs is as easy as selecting them and clicking a button on the toolbar. In this drill you explore all of the alignments that you can use in your documents.

1. Open the *align.doc* document stored in the *drill* directory of the *Word Student Resource Disk (Part 1)* and enter your name, then click anywhere in the date and press ⟨F9⟩ to update it.

2. With the insertion point in each of the boxed paragraphs, use one of the buttons on the toolbar to align it as described in numbered paragraph above it.

3. Save, print, and close the document.

3-4. Changing Line and Paragraph Spacing

Most documents are single-spaced, but short documents, and documents you want to edit or write comments on, are better double-spaced. Also, you may want to add space between paragraphs or above and below headings without inserting a blank line to do so. In this drill you practice the procedures you use to change line and paragraph spacing.

1. Open the *devildic.doc* document stored in the *drill* directory of the *Word Student Resource Disk (Part 1)*.

2. Select all paragraphs below the heading. Then use the **Format**, **Paragraph** command to display the Paragraph dialog box, and on the **Indents and Spacing** tab, first change the line spacing to 1.5 Lines, then add 6 points of spacing **After** each paragraph. Click the **OK** command button to see the changes.

3. Save the document, print the first page, and then close the document.

EXPLORING FONTS	
Font	**Font Size**
Arial	10
Arial	12
Arial	14
Times New Roman	10
Times New Roman	12
Times New Roman	14
Courier New	12

3-5. Controlling Page Breaks

The program automatically inserts soft page breaks wherever a page is filled. However, there are times when you want to specify where pages should break. In this drill you add hard page breaks to a document so each major heading begins on a new page.

1. Open the *clouds.doc* document stored in the *tutorial* (not the *drill*) directory on the *Word Student Resource Disk (Part 1)* and enter your name.

2. Position the insertion point at the beginning of each of the following headings and press Ctrl + Enter ↵ to enter a hard page break.

> IDENTIFICATION
> HIGH CLOUDS
> MIDDLE CLOUDS
> LOW CLOUDS
> CLOUDS WITH EXTENSIVE VERTICAL DEVELOPMENT

3. Click the **Print Preview** button on the toolbar to see how the document will print. Then click the **Multiple Pages** button on the Print Preview toolbar and click the lower-right icon to display six pages. You can now see at a glance how the hard page breaks start new pages.

4. Click the **Close** button Print Preview toolbar, then remove the hard page breaks by selecting them and pressing Del.

5. Scroll down the document looking for a paragraph split by a page break or a heading split by a page break from the paragraph that follows. If you find one, move the insertion point anywhere in the split paragraph or heading, use the **Format**, **Paragraph** command to display the Paragraph dialog box, and display the **Text Flow** tab. Then:

   ▸ For a paragraph split by a page break, turn on the **Keep Lines Together** check box and then click the **OK** command button.

   ▸ For a heading separated from the paragraph that follows it, turn on the **Keep with Next** check box and then click the **OK** command button.

6. Close the document without saving it.

3-6. Using and Setting Tab Stops

All computer keyboards have special characters besides the number and letter keys with which you are familiar. These keys are used for a number of purposes when working with the computer. Here you format a table that names each of these special keys.

1. Open the *keyboard.doc* document stored in the *drill* directory on the *Word Student Resource Disk (Part 1)* and enter your name, then click anywhere in the date and press F9 to update it.

2. Select the line that reads *Key Name*, and use the **Format**, **Tabs** command to clear all existing tab stops. Then set a left-aligned tab stop 1 inch from the left margin.

3. Delete the space between *Key* and *Name* and press ⌨Tab⇥ to move *Name* to the next column.

4. Select the *Key* and *Name* line and click the **Bold** button on the Formatting toolbar to boldface it.

5. Select all lines in the table under the line that reads *Key Name*, and use the **Format**, **Tabs** command to clear all existing tab stops. Then set a left-aligned tab stop 1 inch from the left margin and specify a **2**........ leader.

6. On the lines that follow the column headings, delete the spaces between each character and its name and then press ⌨Tab⇥ to move the name to the *NAME* column.

7. Save, print, and close the document.

3-7. Indenting Paragraphs

You use hanging indents to format enumerated lists and bibliographies. In this drill you format a bibliography so you can use the document as a reference when you format bibliographies in your own papers.

1. Open the *bibliog.doc* document stored in the *drill* directory on the *Word Student Resource Disk (Part 1)* and enter your name, then click anywhere in the date and press ⌨F9 to update it.

2. Use the **Format**, **Paragraph** command and on the **Indents and Spacing** tab format all bibliography entries—beginning with the one under the heading "Book with One Author"—as double-spaced with hanging indents of 0.5". (Tip: After formatting one, you can click in each of the others and press ⌨F4 to repeat the formatting command.)

3. Save, print, and close the document.

3-8A. Automatically Numbering and Bulleting Lists

Bullets are frequently used to set off the items in a list. Here you add bullets to each of the entries in *The Devil's Dictionary* so you can easily tell where each definition begins.

1. Open the *devildic.doc* document stored in the *drill* directory of the *Word Student Resource Disk (Part 1)*.

2. Select the entire document beginning with the first paragraph below the heading.

3. Click the **Bullets** button on the toolbar to add round bullets to the selected paragraphs.

4. Select the two-line poem beginning *A cube of cheese no larger than a die* and then:
   ▶ Click the **Bullets** button on the toolbar to remove the bullets.
   ▶ Click the **Italic** button on the Formatting toolbar to italicize both lines so they stand out.
   ▶ Click the **Increase Indent** button on the Formatting toolbar to indent the lines.

5. Save the document, print the first page, and then close the document.

3-8B. Automatically Numbering and Bulleting Lists

Here you use the **Bullets** button on the toolbar to add bullets and numbers to each of the rules for freshman woman in a document you edited in PicTorial 3.

1. Open the *freshman.doc* document stored in the *drill* directory of the *Word Student Resource Disk (Part 1)*. Click anywhere in the date and press F9 to update it.

2. Select all of the paragraphs that begin with the word "Freshman" and use the **Bullets** button on the toolbar to add bullets to them.

3. Select the same paragraphs and use the **Numbering** button on the toolbar to replace the bullets with numbers.

4. Select the same paragraphs and use the **Numbering** button on the toolbar to remove the numbers so the document looks just as it was when you opened it.

5. Select the same paragraphs and use the **Format**, **Bullets and Numbering** command to add various types of bullets and numbers. Print the one that you especially like.

6. Save and close the document.

 ▶▶ **SKILL-BUILDING EXERCISES**

3-1. Formatting a Description of Memo Formats

The format for interoffice memorandums varies in details, but the standard parts include a heading with a TO:, FROM:, DATE:, and SUBJECT:. This heading is then followed by the body text, and then by identification. Additional memo parts such as enclosure notations, attachment notations, and copy notations are included when necessary.

1. Open the *memrules.doc* document stored in the *exercise* directory on the *Word Student Resource Disk (Part 2)* and enter your name, then click anywhere in the date and press F9 to update it.

2. Select the entire document and use the **Font Size** button on the Formatting toolbar to change the font size to 10 points.

3. Select each of the headings *Margins*, *Heading*, *Body Text*, *Identification*, and *Page Numbers* and use the **Format**, **Font** command to format them as bold with small caps. After formatting the first you can use F4 to repeat the format for the others.

4. Select all paragraphs except the 3-line heading and use the **Format**, **Paragraph** command to change their **Line Spacing** on the **Indents and Spacing** tab to a **Multiple** of 1.25.

5. Select all paragraphs except the 3-line heading and use the **Justify** button on the toolbar to change their alignment.

6. Use the **Bullets** button on the toolbar to add bullets to each of the entries under the headings. (The bullets will be the same kind that were last selected with the **Format**, **Bullets and Numbering** command).

7. Select the last four indented entries in the document and click the **Increase Indent** button on the Formatting toolbar to indent them under the bullet above.

8. Select all paragraphs except the 3-line heading. Use the **Format, Paragraph** command, and on the **Indents and Spacing** tab add 6 points **After**.

9. Save, print, and close the document.

3-2. Formatting a Description of Block-Style Letter Formats

Most business firms have prepared strict guidelines that specify the way business letters should be formatted. Company employees are expected to follow these guidelines so that the firm presents a unified style to all people receiving letters. Letter formats vary from firm to firm; however, many use the block-style format or a variation of it.

1. Open the *ltrrules.doc* document stored in the *exercise* directory on the *Word Student Resource Disk (Part 2)* and enter your name, then click anywhere in the date and press ⌷F9⌷ to update it.

2. Select the entire document and use the **Font** and **Font Size** buttons on the Formatting toolbar to change the font to Arial 10 point.

3. Select each of the headings *Margins, Letterhead, Dateline, Letter Address, Salutation, Body Text, Closing, Signature Line, Identification, Page Numbers, and Open versus Mixed Punctuation* and use the **Format, Font** command to format them as bold, with small caps, and dotted underlines. After formatting the first you can use ⌷F4⌷ to repeat the format for the others.

4. Select all paragraphs except the 3-line heading and use the **Format, Paragraph** command to change their and **Line Spacing** on the **Indents and Spacing** tab to a **Multiple** of 1.1.

5. Select all paragraphs except the 3-line heading and use the **Justify** button on the toolbar to change their alignment.

6. Use the **Format, Bullets and Numbering** command to add diamond-shaped bullets to each of the entries under the headings.

7. Select the last four entries under the *Page Numbers* heading and click the **Increase Indent** button on the Formatting toolbar to indent them under the bullet above. Then use the **Format, Bullets and Numbering** command to change the diamond-shaped bullets to circles.

8. Select all paragraphs except the 3-line heading. Use the **Format, Paragraph** command, and on the **Indents and Spacing** tab add 12 points **After**.

9. Click the **Show/Hide ¶** button on the toolbar to display paragraph marks and delete all blank lines except the one below the 3-line heading at the top of the document.

10. Save the document, print the first page, and then close the document.

3-3. Formatting the Job-Guide Document

In this exercise you begin to format a report on how to prepare a successful job-search kit.

1. Open the *jobs.doc* document stored in the *exercise* directory on the *Word Student Resource Disk (Part 2)*.

2. Select all body paragraphs below the letterhead and use the **Format**, **Tabs** command to clear all tabs and set a new tab stop .25" from the left margin. Notice how the indents for all of the paragraphs change.

3. Select all body paragraphs and use the **Justify** button on the toolbar to change their alignments.

4. Select all paragraphs except the heading and use the **Format**, **Paragraph** command to change their and **Line Spacing** on the **Indents and Spacing** tab to a **Multiple** of 1.2.

5. Select all paragraphs except the letterhead and use the **Font Size** button on the Formatting toolbar to change the font to 10 points.

6. Select each of the headings *The Cover Letter*, *The Resume*, and *The Followup Letter* and use the **Format**, **Font** command to format them as bold with small caps. After formatting the first you can use F4 to repeat the format for the others.

7. Select each of the headings *The Cover Letter*, *The Resume*, and *The Followup Letter* and use the **Format**, **Paragraph** command to set spacing on the **Indents and Spacing** tab to 18 points **Before** and 2 points **After**. After formatting the first you can use F4 to repeat the format for the others.

8. Select each of the run-in heads (the first word in a paragraph) *Salutation*, *Opening*, *Body*, and *Closing* and use the **Bold** button on the Formatting toolbar to boldface them.

9. There are three lists located throughout the document that use hyphens to set off the paragraphs in the lists. Select each list and use the **Bullets** button on the Formatting toolbar to add bullets to them. Then delete each hyphen and the space that follows it.

10. Select each of the three bulleted lists and use the **Format**, **Paragraph** command to set a **Right** indent of 0.5" on the **Indents and Spacing** tab. Then use the **Increase Indent** button on the toolbar to increase the left indent.

11. Use the **Edit**, **Replace** command to replace each occurrence of the word *resume* with *résumé*. To type the *é* in the **Replace With** box, hold down Ctrl and press ', then release both and press E. (See the Tip box "Inserting Symbols.")

12. Click the **Show/Hide ¶** button on the toolbar to display paragraph marks and delete all blank lines except the one below the letterhead at the top of the document.

13. Save the document, print the first page, then close the document.

TIP: INSERTING SYMBOLS

Word lets you insert characters that are not on the keyboard, such as the *é* in the word *résumé*. To do so, pull down the **Insert** menu and click the **Symbol** command. On the **Symbols** tab choose **(normal text)** in the **Font** drop-down list, click the symbol you want to insert, and then click the **Insert** button. Or click the symbol you want to insert and make a note of the **Shortcut Key** you can use to insert it manually. (For *é* it is **Ctrl+', e.**)

3-4. Formatting the Careers Document

In this exercise, you format the document on careers in the computer field. As you do so, you make it more attractive and more inviting to read.

1. Open the *careers.doc* document stored in the *exercise* directory on the *Word Student Resource Disk (Part 2)*.

2. Select each body paragraph (not the headings) and use the **F**ormat, **P**aragraph command to change their first line indent to .25".

3. Select the heading *Careers in Information Processing* and the line below it with your name and use the **Center** button on the Formatting toolbar to align it.

4. Select all body paragraphs and use the **Justify** button on the toolbar to change their alignments.

5. Select all body paragraphs and use the **F**ormat, **P**aragraph command to change their **Li**n**e Spacing** on the **I**ndents and Spacing tab to a **Multiple** of 1.1.

6. Select the heading *Careers in Information Processing* and use the **F**ormat, **F**ont command to format it as 14 points with small caps.

7. Select the line with your name on it and use the **Italic** button on the Formatting toolbar to format it.

8. Select the entire document below the heading and use the **Font Size** button on the Formatting toolbar to change the font to 10 points.

9. Boldface all uppercase headings using the **Bold** button on the toolbar. After formatting the first you can use F4 to repeat the format for the others.

10. Select the subheads *Formal Training* and *Informal Training* under the heading *TRAINING AND SUPPORT* and use the **F**ormat, **F**ont command to format them as small caps. After formatting the first you can use F4 to repeat the format for the other.

11. Under the heading *PROCESSOR POSITIONS*, there is an introductory paragraph and then three paragraphs describing specific positions. Use the **Bullets** button on the Formatting toolbar to add bullets to these three paragraphs and then delete the blank lines between them.

12. Under the heading *SPECIALIST POSITIONS*, there is an introductory paragraph and then a series of paragraphs describing specific positions. Use the **Bullets** button on the Formatting toolbar to add bullets to these later paragraphs and then delete the blank lines between them. You may have to insert spaces following each of the bullets.

13. Select the first uppercase heading, ORIGINATOR POSITIONS. Use the **F**ormat, **P**aragraph command, and on the **I**ndents and Spacing tab add 12 points **B**efore. Immediately use F4 to repeat the command for all other headings, including the *Formal Training* and *Informal Training* subheads.

14. Select the first body paragraph (it begins *The increased computerization of the workplace...*) and use the **F**ormat, **P**aragraph command to add 6 points **Aft**e**r** on the **I**ndents and Spacing tab. Immediately use F4 to repeat the command for all other body paragraphs but not headings or bulleted lists.

15. Select the last paragraph in the first bulleted list. Then use the **F**ormat, **P**aragraph command, and on the **I**ndents and Spacing tab, add 6 points **Aft**e**r**. Immediately use F4 to repeat the command for the last paragraphs in the other bulleted list.

TIP: EN AND EM DASHES

Dashes are used to separate phrases—often to indicate an interruption in thought. Typists indicate dashes with two hyphens, but in desktop publishing a long dash called an *em dash* performs this function. Desktop publishing also uses the *en dash*, which is shorter than the em dash, to join ranges of numbers such as *13–151* or to join single words to phrases that contain two or more words, such as *London–New York*. To insert em or en dashes, pull down the **Insert** menu, click the **Symbol** command, and on the **Special Characters** tab click the symbol you want to insert.

16. Use the **Edit**, **Find** command to locate the first occurrence of the words *originators* and *processors*, and boldface them.

17. Use the **Edit**, **Find** command to locate double hyphens (--) and replace any you find with em dashes. (See the Tip box "En and Em Dashes.")

18. Click the **Show/Hide ¶** button on the toolbar to display paragraph marks and delete all blank lines except the one below the letterhead at the top of the document.

19. Save the document, print the first page, and close the document.

3-5. Formatting the Bill of Rights Document

In this exercise you format the Bill of Rights so it looks as if it has been desktop published.

1. Open the *rights.doc* document stored in the *exercise* directory on the *Word Student Resource Disk (Part 2)*. Click anywhere in the date and press F9 to update it.

2. Insert a blank line above the first amendment, click the **Center** button on the toolbar, type the heading **Bill of Rights** and press Enter ↵.

3. Each of the ten amendments has a 2-line heading with the number and title of the amendment. Select each heading and use the **Center** button on the toolbar to center it.

4. Select the entire document except the 3-line heading and use the **Font Size** button on the Formatting toolbar to change the font to 18 points.

5. Select the centered heading and use the **Font Size** button on the Formatting toolbar to change the font to 48 points.

6. Scroll down the document looking for an amendment split by a page break or a heading split by a page break from the amendment that follows. If you find one, move the insertion point anywhere in the split paragraph or heading, use the **Format**, **Paragraph** command to display the Paragraph dialog box, and display the **Text Flow** tab. Then:

   ▶ For a paragraph split by a page break, turn on the **Keep Lines Together** check box and then click the **OK** command button.

   ▶ For a heading separated from the paragraph that follows it, turn on the **Keep with Next** check box and then click the **OK** command button.

7. Save the document, print the first page, and then close the document.

3-6. Formatting the Newsletter Document

In this exercise you format a newsletter so it looks as if it has been desktop published.

1. Open the *newsltr.doc* document stored in the *exercise* directory on the *Word Student Resource Disk (Part 2)* and enter your name following *Publisher* in the masthead at the top of the document.

2. Select all body paragraphs below the *Volume 1 Number 1* line and use the **Format**, **Tabs** command to set a new tab stop .25" from the left margin. Notice how the indents for all of the paragraphs change.

3. With the insertion point on the line that gives the volume and number, use the **Format**, **Tabs** command to clear all tab stops, and set a right-aligned tab stop at the right margin. (You can tell where the right margin is by looking at the ruler.) Delete the space that separates *Number 1* from *Volume I*, and press ⎄Tab⎇ to separate the columns. The number should become right-aligned with the right margin.

4. Select the title *THE END USER'S NEWSLETTER*, and use the **Format**, **Font** command to change **Spacing** on the **Character Spacing** tab to **Expanded** and set **By** to 10 pts. The title should now almost fill the width of the page. If it wraps to a second line, repeat the command setting **By** to 9, 8, 7 and so on until it just fits. When it's right, click the **Center** button on the toolbar to center it.

5. Select all body paragraphs below the *ERGONOMICS AND HEALTH* heading and use the **Justify** button on the Formatting toolbar to change their alignments.

6. Select all body paragraphs below the title and use the **Font Size** button on the toolbar to change their size to 10 points.

7. Select each of the four headings in the body that are all caps and use the **Bold** button on the toolbar to boldface them.

8. Select each of the two headings that begin *Checklist* and use the **Format**, **Font** command to format them on the **Fonts** tab as small caps. After formatting the first you can use ⎡F4⎤ to repeat the format for the other.

9. Under the heading *END-USER SURVEY REPORT* use the **Italic** button on the toolbar to italicize the two run-in heads that read *Microcomputer Applications Survey* and *Benefits of Microcomputer Use*.

10. There are two lists in the document where each item begins with a hyphen. Use the **Bullets** button on the Formatting toolbar to add bullets to the lists, then delete the hyphens and the spaces that follow them.

11. There are two lists in the document below headings that begin *Checklist* where each item begins with an asterisk. Use the **Bullets** button on the Formatting toolbar to add bullets to the lists, then delete the asterisks and the spaces that follow them.

12. Use the **Edit**, **Find** command to locate double hyphens (--) and replace any you find with em dashes. (See the Tip box "En and Em Dashes" on page 138.)

13. Save the document, print the first page, and close the document.

3-7. Formatting the Desktop Publishing Document

In this exercise, you desktop-publish the article on desktop publishing.

1. Open the *dtp.doc* document stored in the *exercise* directory on the *Word Student Resource Disk (Part 2)* and enter your name following *By* below the title.

2. Select the title *Desktop Publishing* and use the **Center** button on the Formatting toolbar to center it. Then use the **Font Size** drop-down arrow (▣) on the Formatting toolbar to change it to 48 points.

3. Select the line with your name, use the **Center** button on the Formatting toolbar to center it, then use the **Format, Font** command to format it as 14-point italic.

4. Select all body paragraphs below the 2-line title and then:
   ▶ Use the **Format, Paragraph** command to change their first line indent on the **Indents and Spacing** tab to .25" and **Line Spacing** to a **Multiple** of 1.1.
   ▶ Use the **Justify** button on the toolbar to change their alignments.
   ▶ Use the **Font Size** button on the toolbar to change the font size to 10 points.

5. Use the **Edit, Find** command to locate the first occurrence of the phrase *desktop publishing* in the body of the document, change it to *desktop publishing (DTP)*, and use the **Bold** button on the toolbar to boldface it.

6. Use the **Bold** button on the toolbar to boldface the following headings:
   ▶ *The Creation Phase*
   ▶ *The Production Phase*
   ▶ *The Manufacturing Phase*

7. Use the **Italic** button on the toolbar to italicize the following headings:
   ▶ *Design*
   ▶ *Copyediting*
   ▶ *Typemarking*
   ▶ *Art Preparation*
   ▶ *Typesetting*
   ▶ *Proofreading*
   ▶ *Pasteup*
   ▶ *Printing and Binding*

8. Save the document, print the first page, and close the document.

3-8. Formatting the Menu from Alyce's Restaurant

In this exercise you format a menu so it looks as if it has been desktop published.

1. Open the *alyces.doc* document stored in the *exercise* directory on the *Word Student Resource Disk (Part 2)* and enter your name, then click anywhere in the date and press [F9] to update it.

2. With all lines selected starting with the line that reads *Alyce's Restaurant*, use the **Format, Tabs** command to clear all existing tab stops and set new center tab stops 1.5", 3.5", and 5.5" from the left margin.

3. Columns are now separated by one or two spaces indicated by asterisks. Delete those asterisks and press [Tab⇆] in place of each one that you delete. (Tip: To do this quickly, press [Ins] so *OVR* is dis-

played on the status bar. Then click to the left of an asterisk and press ⎡Tab⇥⎤. This inserts a tab stop and deletes the asterisk at the same time. When finished, be sure to press ⎡Ins⎤ so *OVR* is no longer displayed on the status bar.)

4. Format *Alyce's Restaurant* as 18 point type, small caps, bold.

5. Format *Famous Homemade Ice Cream* as 14 point type.

6. Format *Flavors* as 18 point.

7. Format all text beginning with the line *Open All Year* as 18 point type. Your document should now look like the illustration below.

8. Save, print, and close the document.

Name: your name
Filename: ALYCES.DOC
Date: October 4, 1994

ALYCE'S RESTAURANT
Famous Homemade Ice Cream

| Sundaes | Ice Cream Sandwiches (any flavor) | Frappes |
| Ice Cream Sodas | Milk Shakes | Floats & Malteds |

Flavors

Vanilla	Rocky Road	Pistachio
Chocolate	Chocolate Chip	Coffee Almond
Coffee	Chocolate Chocolate Chip	Oreo
Strawberry	Mint Chip	Butter Crunch
Chocolate Almond Fudge	Mocha Chip	Reeses
Banana	Grape Nut	M & M
Bubble Gum	Maple Walnut	Almond Joy
Peppermint Stick	Black Raspberry	Strawberry Cheese
Frozen Pudding	Milky Way	Snickers
Almond Joy	Coffee Almond Fudge	Orange Sherbet
Raspberry Sherbet	Watermelon	Rainbow

Open All Year

Serving You For Over 60 Years
Indoor Seating Available
SEE OUR FOOD MENU ON REVERSE SIDE

▶▶ **REAL-WORLD PROJECTS**

3-1. The Research Paper

Many courses in college require the preparation of a research paper. To prepare such a paper, you must select a topic, research it, and then prepare a written document. The computer can greatly ease the process of writing, editing, and formatting the paper. You may also find computers in the library that allow you to search for information on specific subjects, easing the research task as well. In this project, you'll be glad to know we have done the research for you. All you have to do is format the document.

As Lynn Quitman Troyka puts it in *Simon & Schuster Handbook for Writers* (Englewood Cliffs: Prentice, 1987, pp. 618-19): "Because of the differences among disciplines, different formats are expected in each for presentation of material. These special formats have evolved to communicate a writer's purpose, to emphasize contents by eliminating distracting variations in format, and to make the reader's work easier. Writing in the humanities is less often subject to set formats although your writing is expected to be well organized, and accepted documentation formats are expected. Writing in the social sciences and natural sciences often calls for using fixed special formats for specific types of writing. For example, if you are writing a case study or a laboratory report, you are expected to use the formats always used for such writings."

The paper on which you work in this project is based on the style of the Modern Language Association.

1. Open the *respaper.doc* document stored in the *project* directory on the *Word Student Resource Disk (Part 2)*.

2. Enter your name, your instructor's name, the course number, and today's date where indicated.

3. Change the font for the entire document to 10 points.

4. Change line spacing to double for all paragraphs below the title.

5. Format the headings *Microcomputer Hardware: The Early Years* and *Microcomputer Software: The Early Years* as follows:

   ▶ Boldface them.

   ▶ Change paragraph spacing before them to 18 points and space after to 6 points.

6. Underline the titles <u>IBM's Early Computers</u> and <u>Popular Electronics</u> in the text. (Use the **Find** command to locate them.)

7. The two paragraphs above the heading *Microcomputer Software: The Early Years* are direct quotations. Indent them a half-inch from the left and right margins.

8. Format the table that begins with the heading *Key Dates in the History of Microcomputers* as follows:

   ▶ Clear all tab stops and set a new left-aligned tab stop at 1".

   ▶ Delete the blank line between the table's title and the column headings.

   ▶ Boldface the table's title and column headings.

   ▶ Set the line spacing to single.

9. Enter a hard page break above the *Works Cited* heading, and center the heading on the first line of the new page.

10. Underline the book titles in the *Works Cited* section.

11. Format the list of titles in the *Works Cited* section so they have a hanging indent of 0.5".

12. Save the document, print the first page, then close the document.

3-2. The Flier's Rights Booklet

It feels at times that we are a herd of cattle as we head for the boarding gate at the airport. However, every air traveler has rights, and the U.S. Department of Transportation has published a guide to inform you of them when flying on an American airline in the United States. (The rules are different in other countries.) In this project, you begin formatting this document as a booklet.

1. Open the *flyright.doc* document stored in the *projects* directory on the *Word Student Resource Disk (Part 2)* and enter your name.

2. Format the entire document as follows:
   ‣ Change the font to 8 points.
   ‣ Change the alignment to justified.
   ‣ Change line spacing to 1.1.
   ‣ Set a tab stop at .25".

3. Format all headings as follows:
   ‣ Select all uppercase headings, and format them as 10 points, bold.
   ‣ Select all headings with only the first character uppercased, and format them as 10 points, italic.
   ‣ Change space before all headings to 12 points before and 2 points after.

4. Format all body paragraphs other than headings and lists so they have 6 points after.

5. Format all lists that currently are formatted as paragraphs with beginning asterisks:
   ‣ Add bullets to the list and then remove the asterisk.
   ‣ Indent both the left and right sides.

6. Format all body paragraphs other than headings and lists so they have a .25" first line indent.

7. Delete all blank lines in the document.

8. Format the title so it looks as much like the figure "The Fly-Rights Title" as you can make it.

9. Save the document, print the first page, then close the document.

Fly-Rights
A Guide to Air Travel in the U.S.

U.S. Department of Transportation
your name

The Fly-Rights Title

PicTorial 4

Advanced Formatting

After completing this PicTorial, you will be able to:

▸ Format text using the horizontal ruler
▸ Copy formats and find and replace them
▸ Add headers, footers, and page numbers
▸ Add footnotes and endnotes
▸ Change, margins, paper size, and page orientation
▸ Enter section breaks
▸ Sort documents

Once you have learned how to enter, edit, and format a document, you are ready to move onto more advanced formatting procedures. In this PicTorial you are introduced to many of these procedures, including formatting text from the ruler; adding headers, footers, page numbers, and footnotes; changing paper size, margins, and orientation; breaking your document into sections; and sorting paragraphs and tabbed material. Mastering these procedures will allow you to prepare almost any kind of document.

4-1. FORMATTING FROM THE RULER

Word's rulers not only show you margins and a paragraph's tab stops and indents—they allow you to change them by dragging markers with the mouse.

DISPLAYING THE RULERS

The vertical and horizontal rulers reflect settings in the paragraph containing the insertion point. You can change the selected paragraph's margins by dragging margin boundaries, set tab stops by clicking, and set indents by dragging markers.

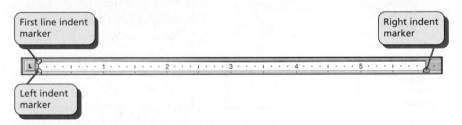

First line indent marker

Right indent marker

Left indent marker

QUICKSTEPS: DISPLAYING AND HIDING THE RULERS

▸ To display or hide the horizontal ruler, pull down the **View** menu and click the **Ruler** command to turn it on or off.

▸ To display the vertical ruler, click the **Page Layout View** button in the lower-left corner of the window.

CHANGING MARGINS

You change left or right margins for selected paragraphs or top and bottom margins for the document by dragging the margin boundaries on the rulers. These boundaries are the gray part of the ruler just to the left or right of the white area on the horizontal ruler or above or below the white area on the vertical ruler. When you point to this boundary area in Page Layout View or in Print Preview, the mouse pointer turns into a double-headed arrow. (↔). You cannot drag these margin boundaries in Normal view.

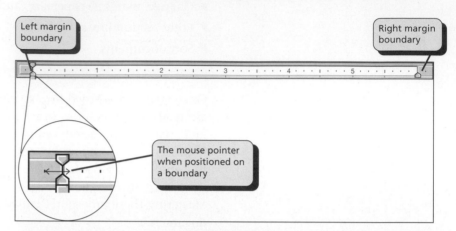

TIP: POSITIONING MARKERS ACCURATELY

As you drag markers or margin boundaries, hold down Alt so their current position is displayed on the ruler at the right end of the status bar. Keep your eye on this readout when you want to position a marker accurately.

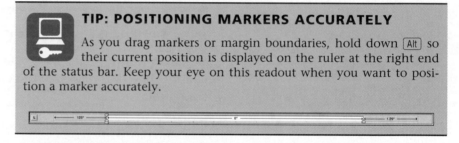

CHANGING INDENTS

To change indents, you can drag any one of the three paragraph indent markers. The way you arrange them determines whether you get a first line indent, an entire paragraph indent, or a hanging indent. Dragging the right indent marker is straightforward. However, when dragging the left, there is a little trick involved. If you drag it by either triangle, the markers move independently. If you drag it by the square bottom half, the two indent markers move together.

To indent the first line of a paragraph, drag the first line indent marker (the upper triangle) to the right of the left indent marker.

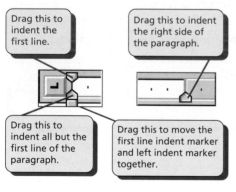

Changing indents

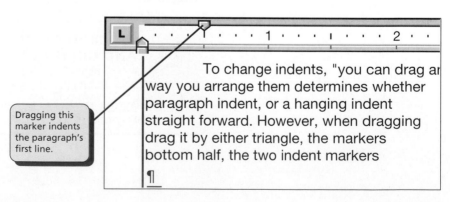

To indent the entire paragraph, drag the square left indent marker or the right indent marker.

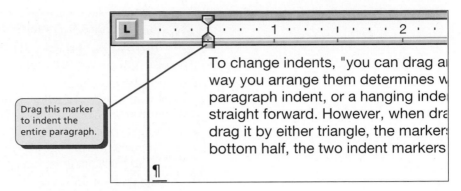

Drag this marker to indent the entire paragraph.

To create a hanging indent, drag the triangular left indent marker to the right of the first line indent marker.

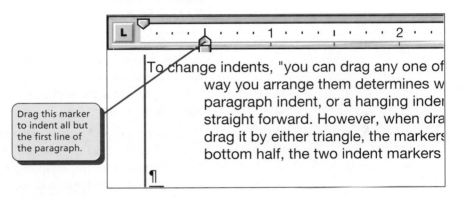

Drag this marker to indent all but the first line of the paragraph.

CHANGING TAB STOPS

To change tab stops, you just point and click on the horizontal ruler to insert new tab stops, or drag existing tab stops to new positions.

▶ To move a tab stop, drag its marker to a new position and release it. To display the current position as you do so, hold down [Alt] while you drag.

▶ To set a new tab stop of the type displayed on the **Tab Alignment** button, click on the ruler.

The Tab Alignment button

▶ To set a new tab stop of a different type, click the **Tab Alignment** button until the type is displayed. Each time you click it, a new tab type is displayed. With the correct type displayed, click on the ruler.

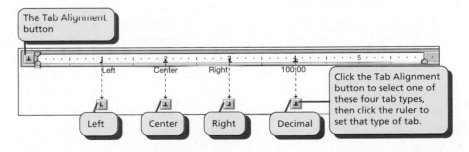

The Tab Alignment button

Left   Center   Right   100:00

Left   Center   Right   Decimal

Click the Tab Alignment button to select one of these four tab types, then click the ruler to set that type of tab.

TIP: SELECTING PARAGRAPHS

Changing indents and tabs affects only selected paragraphs. If there are some tabs stops that are not common to all of the selected paragraphs, they are displayed dimmed on the ruler.

▶ To delete a tab stop, drag its marker off the top or bottom of the ruler and release it.

TIP: DISPLAYING DIALOG BOXES

You can display appropriate dialog boxes by clicking on the horizontal ruler.

▶ To display the Page Setup menu double-click the margin boundaries when the mouse pointer is displayed as a double-headed arrow. This allows you to change margins, page size, or orientation,

▶ To display the Paragraph dialog box at any point, double-click any indent marker. This allows you to change paragraph indents, alignments, and spacing.

▶ To display the Tabs dialog box, double-click any tab stop. This allows you to change tab stops or add leaders in the usual way.

TUTORIAL

In this tutorial you drag markers on the ruler to format a document designed to illustrate the results you can expect to get. As you do so, you hold down **Alt** so measurements are displayed on the ruler. You use these measurements to format the text.

Getting Started

1. Open the *indents.doc* document stored in the *tutorial* directory on the *Word Student Resource Disk (Part 1)* and enter your name. Click anywhere in the date and press **F9** to update it. If the horizontal ruler is not displayed, pull down the **View** menu and click the **Ruler** command to turn it on.

2. Click the **Page Layout View** button at the bottom of the screen. (You have to use this view to change margins on the ruler.)

3. Click the Zoom Control drop-down arrow (⬇) on the Standard toolbar, and click the **Page Width** command to enlarge the document as much as possible.

Changing Margins

4. Hold down **Ctrl** and click in the selection bar to select the entire document.

5. Point to the space on the horizontal ruler between the left indent markers (the margin boundary), and the mouse pointer turns into a double-headed arrow.

The double-headed arrow

6. Hold down **Alt** and drag the left margin boundary to 1.75" on the horizontal ruler. As you do so, keep your eye on the measurements displayed on the ruler, since they always give the current position.

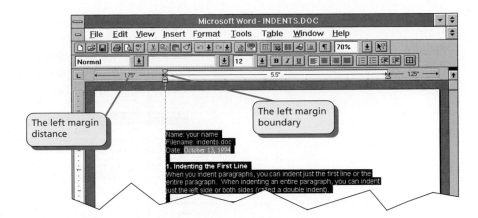

7. Hold down Alt and drag the right margin boundary to 1.75" on the horizontal ruler. (The text area will be 5" wide.)

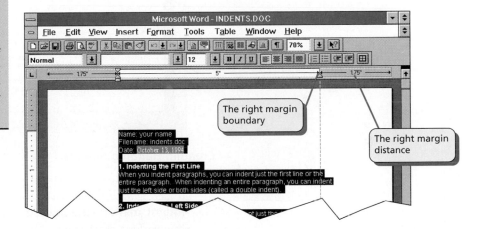

Indenting the First Line of a Paragraph

8. Click anywhere in the paragraph below the heading *1. Indenting the First Line*, hold down Alt, and drag the first line indent marker (the upper triangle) 0.5 inches to the right.

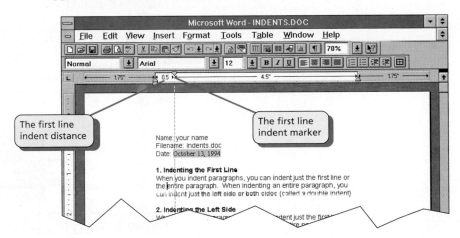

Indenting the Entire Paragraph

9. Click anywhere in the paragraph below the heading *2. Indenting the Left Side*, hold down Alt, and drag the square bottom part of the left indent marker 0.5 inches to the right (all indent markers move together).

10. Click anywhere in the paragraph below the heading *3. Indenting both the Left and Right Sides*, hold down [Alt], and drag the square left indent marker 0.5 inches to the right, then hold down [Alt] and drag the right indent marker (the right triangle) 0.5 inches to the left (the text area measurement will read 4).

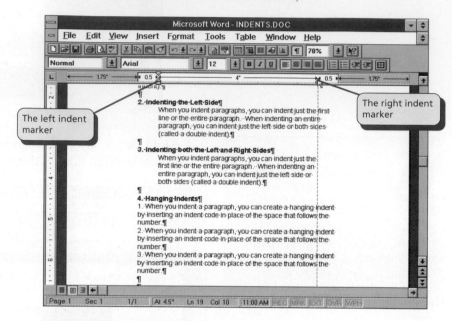

Creating Hanging Indents

11. Select the three paragraphs numbered *1* through *3* under the heading *4. Hanging Indents*, hold down [Alt], and drag the triangular left indent marker (the lower triangle) 0.5 inches to the right (the first line indent marker won't move with it).

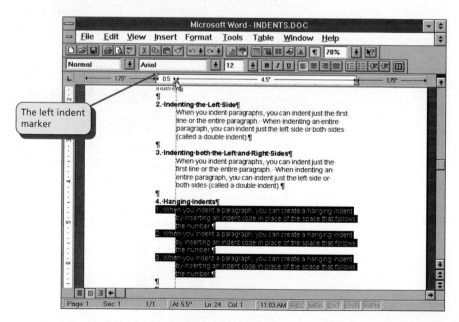

12. Following the periods after the numbers *1* through *3* at the beginning of the paragraphs, delete the spaces and press [Tab↹] to align the paragraphs following the numbers.

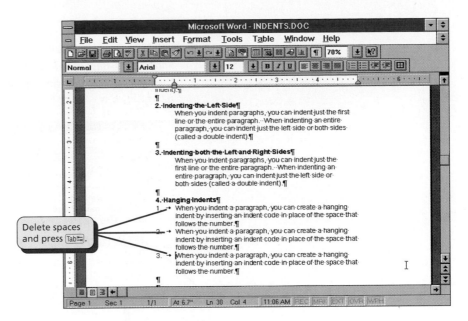

Finishing Up

13. Save, print, and close the document.

4-2. COPYING FORMATS

Click the Format Painter button to copy the format of the selected text.

Once you have formatted some text in a document, there is no reason to use commands and dialog boxes to format something else just like it. Word's Format Painter allows you to quickly copy the format from one place to another (see the margin illustration).

QUICKSTEPS: COPYING FORMATS

1. Select the text that has the format you want to copy. If copying paragraph formats, be sure the paragraph mark at the end of the paragraph is included in the selection.

2. Click the **Format Painter** button on the Standard toolbar, and a paintbrush appears on the mouse pointer. (Double-click it if you want to copy the formats to a number of places.)

3. Select the text you want to apply the copied format to. When you release the mouse button, the paintbrush disappears from the mouse pointer. (If you double-clicked the **Format Painter** button on the toolbar, click it again to turn it off when finished copying the formats.)

TUTORIAL

In this tutorial, you copy formats from one place to another in a document.

Getting Started

1. Open the *painter.doc* document stored in the *tutorial* directory on the *Word Student Resource Disk (Part 1)* and enter your name, then click anywhere in the date and press F9 to update it.

COPYING FORMATS

2. Clicking in the selection bar, select the line that reads *Text with Formats to Be Copied*, and then click the **Format Painter** button on the toolbar. The mouse pointer now has a paintbrush attached to it.

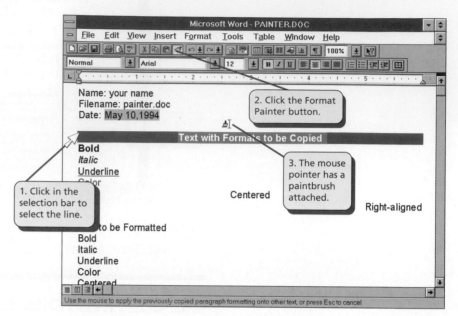

3. Clicking in the selection bar, select the line that reads *Text to be Formatted*, and it is immediately formatted like the line above.

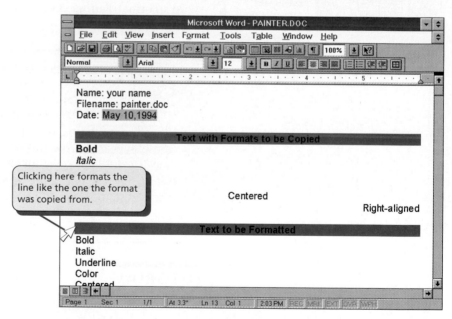

4. Repeat Steps 2 and 3 to copy formats from each line in the section headed *Text with Formats to Be Copied* to the matching line in the section headed *Text to Be Formatted*.

Finishing Up

5. Save, print, and then close the document.

4-3. FINDING AND REPLACING FORMATS

Just as you can Find and Replace text in a document, you can Find and Replace formats. This speeds up formatting when you want to make changes. For example, you can quickly change boldfaced book titles to italic, or find key terms that you have italicized, underlined, or bold-faced.

QUICKSTEPS: FINDING AND REPLACING FORMATS

1. Pull down the **Edit** menu and click the **Find** or **Replace** command to display the Find or Replace dialog box. (If replacing, move the insertion point into the **Find What** or **Replace With** text boxes.)

2. Click the **Format** command button to display a list of formats. (Or click the **No Formatting** command button to remove previously specified formats.)

3. Click the **Font** or **Paragraph** command to display the Font or Paragraph dialog box.

4. Select formats to find or replace just as you would apply them when formatting text, and then click the **OK** command button.

5. Proceed with the operation just as you would normally.

TUTORIAL

In this tutorial you are introduced to finding and replacing formats.

Getting Started

1. Open the *findfont.doc* document stored in the *tutorial* directory on the *Word Student Resource Disk (Part 1)* and enter your name, then click anywhere in the date and press F9 to update it.

Finding a Font Style

2. Pull down the **Edit** menu and click the **Find** command to display the Find dialog box.

3. Click the **Format** command button to pull down a menu, and click the **Font** command to display the Find Font dialog box. Click the Font tab if necessary.

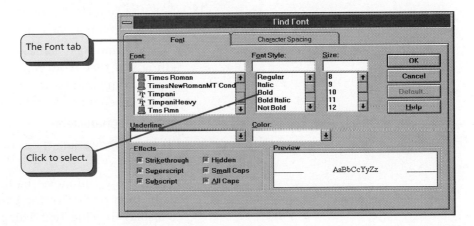

4. Click *Bold* on the **Font Style** list and then click the **OK** command button to return to the Find dialog box.

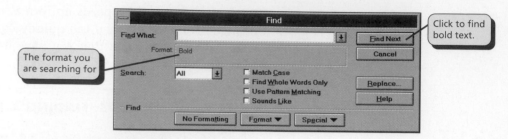

5. Click the **Find Next** command button, and the procedure finds the first boldfaced word.

6. Click the **Find Next** command button again until a message appears telling you that Word has finished searching the document. Click the **OK** command button to close the message box, and then click the **Cancel** command button to close the Find Text dialog box.

Finding Text of a Specific Font and Size

7. Pull down the **Edit** menu and click the **Find** command to display the Find dialog box.

8. Click the **No Formatting** button to remove *Bold* from the dialog box below the **Find** text box.

9. Click the **Format** command button to pull down a menu, and click the **Font** command to display the Find Font dialog box.

10. Specify *Arial* as the **Font** and *10* as the **Size** (leave the **Font Style** empty), and then click the **OK** command button to return to the Find dialog box.

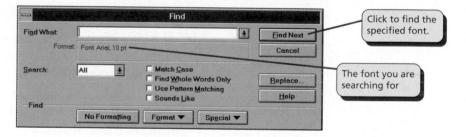

11. Click the **Find Next** command button, and the procedure finds the word *Arial* on the line that reads *Arial 10-point*.

12. Click the **Find Next** command button again, and a message appears telling you that Word has finished searching the document. Click the **OK** command button to close the message box, and then click the **Cancel** command button to close the Find Text dialog box.

Finding Special Characters

13. Click the **Show/Hide ¶** button on the toolbar to display paragraph marks.

14. Press [Ctrl]+[Home] to move the insertion point to the top of the document, then pull down the **Edit** menu and click the **Find** command to display the Find Text dialog box.

15. Click the **No Formatting** button to remove *Arial, 10pt* from the dialog box below the **Find** text box.

16. Click the **Spe̲cial** command button to display a list of special characters, and click **Pa̲ragraph Mark** to select it and list its code ^p in the **Fi̲nd** text box.

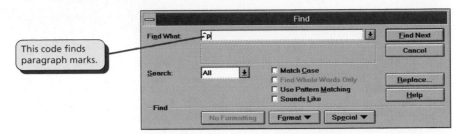

This code finds paragraph marks.

Find
Find What: ^p

17. Click the **Fi̲nd Next** command button repeatedly to jump from one paragraph mark to the next. At any point, click the **Cancel** command button to quit looking and close the Find Text dialog box.

Finishing Up

18. Save the document and then close it.

4-4. ADDING HEADERS AND FOOTERS

Headers are lines of text that print in the top margin of pages, and *footers* are lines of text that print in the bottom margin (see the margin illustration). If they print on more than one page in a sequence, they are called running heads and running feet. They frequently include dates, names, and chapter or part titles that indicate a page's position in a document. To see them on the screen when you aren't entering or editing them, you must be in Page Layout View.

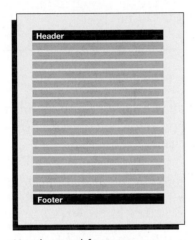

Headers and footers

> **QUICKSTEPS: CREATING AND EDITING HEADERS AND FOOTERS**
>
> 1. Pull down the **V̲iew** menu and click the **Header and Footer** command to display the insertion point in the header area (a nonprinting dashed-line box labeled *Header* at the top of the page). The Header and Footer toolbar is also displayed. Text in the document is dimmed. (To edit an existing header or footer in Page Layout View you can also double-click it.)
>
> 2. Type the header or footer text, edit and format it using any of the commands you use to format your document, or use any of the commands described in the box "Understanding the Header and Footer Toolbar."
>
> 3. Click the Header and Footer toolbar's **Close** command button to remove the toolbar and return to the document.

UNDERSTANDING THE HEADER AND FOOTER TOOLBAR

When you use the command to enter a header or footer in a document, the Header and Footer toolbar is displayed. Here is a brief description of each of the buttons on the toolbar.

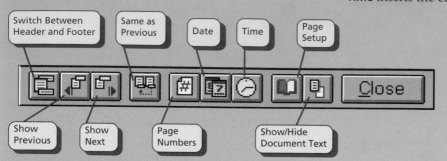

Switch Between Header and Footer switches the insertion point between the boxes at the top and bottom of the document.

Show Previous displays the previous header or footer, if any.

Show Next displays the next header or footer, if any.

Same as Previous is used when you want to print different headers or footers in the same document. To do so, you must add sections as described in Section 4-8.

Page Numbers inserts page numbers in the header and footer.

Date inserts the current date into the header and footer.

Time inserts the current time into the header and footer.

Page Setup displays the page setup dialog box. On the **Margins** tab you can set the distance between the edge of the page and the header or footer in the **Header** and **Footer** text boxes. On the **Layout** tab you can then turn on or off the **Different Odd and Even** and **Different First Page** commands.

▶ **Different Odd and Even** specifies if you want different headers or footers on odd and even pages.

▶ **Different First Page** specifies if you want a different header or footer on the first page.

Show/Hide Document Text displays or hides the document text (which is displayed dim when shown).

Close returns you to the document and removes the toolbar.

TUTORIAL

Headers and footers are used in almost all published documents and college research papers. In this tutorial you explore entering headers and footers into the *educom.doc* document.

Getting Started

1. Open the *educom.doc* document stored in the *tutorial* directory on the *Word Student Resource Disk (Part 1)*.

Adding a Header

2. Pull down the **View** menu and click the **Header and Footer** command to display the insertion point in a nonprinting dashed-line box labeled *Header* at the top of the page. The Header and Footer toolbar is also displayed, and text in the document is dimmed.

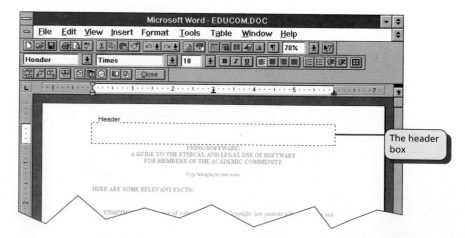

3. Click the **Align Right** button on the Formatting toolbar to move the insertion point flush with the document's right margin.

4. Type your last name in all capital letters.

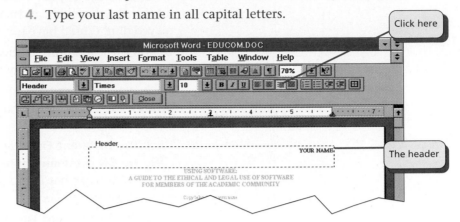

5. Click the **Close** command button on the Header and Footer toolbar to return to the document.

Adding a Footer

6. Pull down the **View** menu and click the **Header and Footer** command to display the insertion point in a nonprinting dashed-line box labeled *Header* at the top of the page.

7. Click the **Switch Between Header and Footer** button on the toolbar to move the insertion point to the dashed-line box labeled *Footer*.

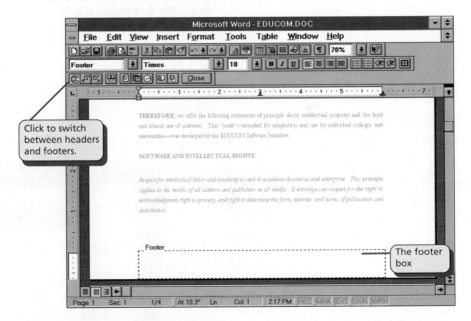

8. Click the **Align Right** button on the Formatting toolbar to move the insertion point flush with the document's right margin.

9. Type **Page** and press Spacebar, then click the **Page Numbers** button on the toolbar to insert the page number in the footer.

10. Click the **Close** command button on the Header and Footer toolbar to return to the document.

Turning Off a Header on the First Page

11. Click the **Page Layout View** button at the bottom of the page to display the document in that view. The headers and footer are displayed dim. (You'll have to scroll to see them.)

12. Double-click the dimmed header displayed at the top of the document to select it and display the Header and Footer toolbar.

13. Click the **Page Setup** button on the Header and Footer toolbar to display the Page Setup dialog box. The dialog box's **Layout** tab should be displayed.

14. Click the **Different First Page** check box to turn it on, and then click the **OK** command button. The header is no longer displayed on the first page, but if you look at the top of the second page you will see it is still there.

15. Click the Header and Footer toolbar's **Close** command button to return to the document.

16. Click the **Page Up** and **Page Down** buttons below the scroll bar to scroll through the document checking the header on each page.

Finishing Up

17. Save the document, print the first two pages, and then close the document.

4-5. ADDING AND REMOVING PAGE NUMBERS

Word does not normally print page numbers, but you can have them automatically printed on any or all pages. You can also specify that they be printed as Arabic numbers (1, 2, 3), Roman numerals (i, ii, iii or I, II, III), or letters (a, b, c or A, B, C), and print them in a variety of positions on the page.

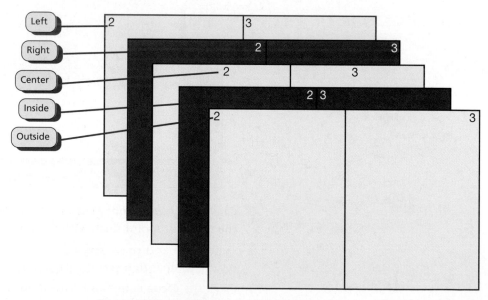

Page number positions

ADDING PAGE NUMBERS

To add page numbers, you select their position and alignment from drop-down lists in a dialog box. The page numbers are added to the headers and footers. You can display headers and footers at any point to change the format or alignment of the page numbers.

QUICKSTEPS: ADDING PAGE NUMBERS
1. Pull down the **Insert** menu and click the **Page Numbers** command to display the Page Numbers dialog box.
2. Make any of the choices described in the box "Understanding the Page Numbers Dialog Box."
3. Click the **OK** command button.

UNDERSTANDING THE PAGE NUMBERS DIALOG BOX

When you use the **Insert**, **Page Numbers** command, the Page Numbers dialog box is displayed. When you make changes in this dialog box, the results of those changes are shown in the Preview area so you can preview your choices before clicking the **OK** command button.

Position drop-down list (⬇) lets you specify if page numbers are printed at the top or bottom of the page.

Alignment drop-down list (⬇) lets you specify one of the following positions:

▸ **Left**, **Center**, **Right** aligns the page number relative to the left and right margins.

▸ **Inside** or **Outside** prints the page numbers on alternating left and right pages so they appear aligned with the inside or outside margins when pages are printed or copied back to back and bound.

Show Number on First Page check box prints a page number on the first page when on, and doesn't when off.

Format command button displays a dialog box you use to specify a **Number Format** (1,2, 3; a, b, c; i, ii, iii, and so on), include chapter numbers, or specify how numbering continues from the previous section (see Section 4-8).

REMOVING PAGE NUMBERS

Once you have inserted page numbers, you can delete them if you no longer want them.

QUICKSTEPS: REMOVING PAGE NUMBERS
1. Pull down the **View** menu and click the **Header and Footer** command to display the header area of the document. If the page number is in a footer, click the **Switch Between Header and Footer** button on the Header and Footer toolbar.
2. Select the page number and then press ⌈Del⌉ to delete it.
3. Click Header and Footer toolbar's **OK** command button to close the toolbar.

TUTORIAL

In this tutorial you remove existing page numbers from the footer of the *overview.doc* document and then insert new ones in the header.

Getting Started

1. Open the *overview.doc* document stored in the *tutorial* directory on the *Word Student Resource Disk (Part 1)*. The document already contains page numbers in the footer.

Removing Page Numbers

2. Pull down the **View** menu and click the **Header and Footer** command to display the header area of the document. Click the **Switch Between Header and Footer** button on the Header and Footer toolbar.

3. Select the page number and press Del to delete it.

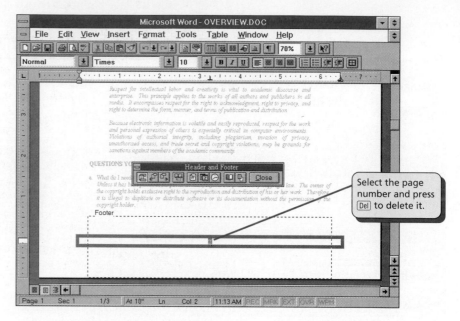

4. Click the Header and Footer toolbar's **OK** command button to close the toolbar.

Specifying Page Numbers

5. Pull down the **Insert** menu and click the **Page Numbers** command to display the Page Numbers dialog box. It is currently set to print page numbers at the bottom of the page aligned with the right margin.

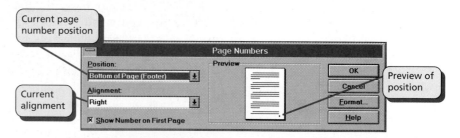

6. Click the **Position** drop-down arrow (⬇) to display a list of choices, and click **Top of Page (Header)**. The choice is illustrated in the *Preview* area of the dialog box.

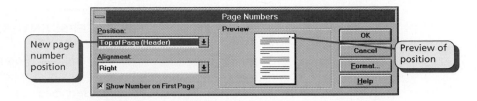

7. Click the **Format** command button to display the Page Number Format dialog box.

8. Click the **Number Format** drop-down arrow (⬇) to display a list of choices, and click **i, ii, iii.**

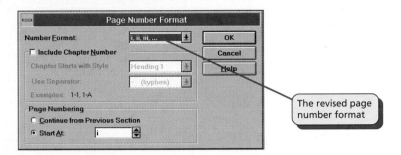

The revised page number format

9. Click the **OK** command button to close the Page Number Format dialog box.

10. Click the **OK** command button to close the Page Numbers dialog box.

11. Click the **Page Layout View** button in the lower-left corner of the window. The page number is displayed dim in the upper-right corner of the page.

Finishing Up

12. Click the **Page Up** and **Page Down** buttons below the scroll bar to scroll through the document checking the page number on each page.

13. Save the document, print the first two pages, and then close the document.

4-6. ENTERING FOOTNOTES AND ENDNOTES

Word automates the insertion of footnotes and endnotes into a document. Footnotes are notes or comments or references placed at the foot (bottom) of a page and keyed to the body text with a reference mark (see the margin illustration). Endnotes are like footnotes, but they appear at the end of the document. Most academic disciplines have conventional practices for the use of footnotes and endnotes in research papers, and it is there that you will probably make the greatest use of this Word feature. A major benefit of the feature is that whenever you add or delete a note it automatically renumbers the notes that follow.

ENTERING FOOTNOTES AND ENDNOTES

You can enter a footnote or endnote anywhere in a document and view the result in Page Layout View.

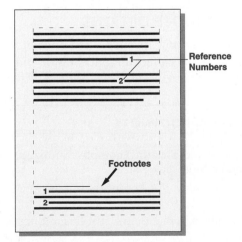

Reference Numbers

Footnotes

Footnotes

QUICKSTEPS: ENTERING A FOOTNOTE OR ENDNOTE

1. Position the insertion point where you want to enter a footnote or endnote reference number.

2. Pull down the **Insert** menu and click the **Footnote** command to display the Footnote and Endnote dialog box.

3. Click the **AutoNumber** option button if you want notes numbered (the default) or click the **Symbol** command button and select a symbol instead. When you click a symbol and then click the **OK** command button, the symbol is displayed in the **Custom Mark** text box and that command's option button is on.

4. Click the **Footnote** or **Endnote** option button to turn it on (◉) and then click the **OK** command button. The insertion point moves to the end of the page or document. If there are any footnotes or endnotes already entered, they are listed. If you move the insertion point into one of them to edit it, the document scrolls so you can see the reference number and its context.

5. Type in the text of the footnote or endnote or edit and format it.

6. Click back in the document to return there.

EDITING FOOTNOTES AND ENDNOTES

After entering footnotes or endnotes, you can edit them. During editing, they are displayed the same way as when you enter them.

QUICKSTEPS: EDITING A FOOTNOTE OR ENDNOTE

1. With the insertion point anywhere in the document, pull down the **View** menu and click the **Footnotes** command to display existing footnotes or endnotes. (In Normal View all are shown in their own window. In Page Layout View only those on the same page are shown in position on the page.)

2. When you move the insertion point into one of them to edit it, the document scrolls so you can see the reference number and its context.

3. Edit the footnote or endnote and then click back in the document to return there.

CHANGING FOOTNOTE AND ENDNOTE OPTIONS

Word gives you a great deal of control over how footnotes and endnotes print. The changes you make in these settings affect all footnotes or endnotes in the document.

QUICKSTEPS: CHANGING FOOTNOTE AND ENDNOTE OPTIONS

1. Pull down the **Insert** menu and click the **Footnote** command to display the Footnote and Endnote dialog box.

2. Click the **Options** command to display the Footnote or Endnote Options dialog box.

3. Change any of the settings described in the boxes "Understanding the Note Options Dialog Box."

4. Click the **OK** command button twice.

UNDERSTANDING THE NOTE OPTIONS DIALOG BOX

When you display the Footnote or Endnote dialog box, you can click the **Options** command button to display the Note Options dialog box. The changes you make in these settings affect all endnotes or footnotes in the document. The commands for them are the same except Endnotes doesn't have the option to restart numbering each page.

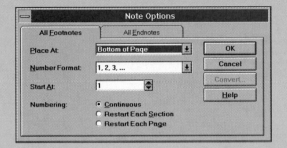

Place At displays a list of positions where footnotes or endnotes can be printed.

Number Format displays a list of number formats you can choose from.

Start At is where you can enter a number that you want the first footnote or endnote to start at.

Numbering section allows you to specify how number sequences run through the document.

▶ **Continuous** numbers footnotes or endnotes continuously through the document.

▶ **Restart Each Section** restarts footnote or endnote numbering for each section. Sections are discussed in Section 4-8.

▶ **Restart Each Page** (footnotes only) restarts footnote numbering on every page.

Convert command button converts endnotes to footnotes or vice versa.

TUTORIAL

In this tutorial you explore adding footnotes to the *educom.doc* document.

Getting Started

1. Open the *educom.doc* document stored in the *tutorial* directory on the *Word Student Resource Disk (Part 1)*.

2. If the document isn't displayed in Page Layout View, click the **Page Layout View** button in the lower-left corner of the window.

Entering a Footnote

3. Use the **Find** command to find the first occurrence of the term *ADAPSO*, and move the insertion point to the right of the comma that follows it. (The word is near the end of the document under the heading *A FINAL NOTE.*)

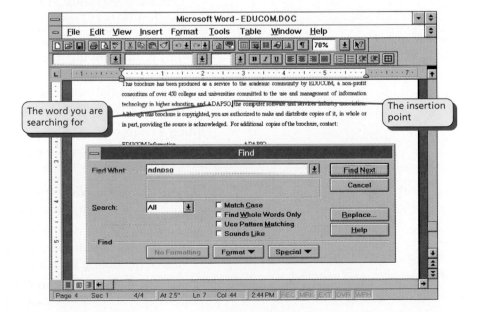

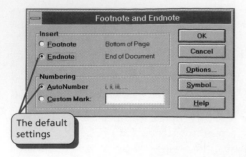

The default settings

4. Pull down the **Insert** menu and click the **Footnote** command to display the Footnote and Endnote dialog box (see the margin illustration). All of the default settings are what you want to use.

5. Click the **OK** command button, and the insertion point moves to the end of the page.

6. Type **Now called the Information Technology Association of America.** (including the period).

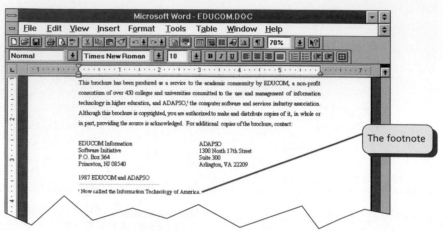

The footnote

7. Click back in the document and notice the number *1* at the previous position of the insertion point. This is the footnote reference number. (To quickly locate it, you can press `⇧ Shift`+`F5` to return to previous edits.)

Entering a Second Footnote

8. Move the insertion point up to the end of the paragraph that follows the heading *Shareware*.

9. Pull down the **Insert** menu and click the **Footnote** command to display the Footnote and Endnote dialog box, and click the **OK** command button.

10. Type **A good source of this type of software is Public Brand Software, P.O. Box 51315, Indianapolis, IN 46251.** (including the period).

11. Click back in the document and notice the number *1* at the previous position of the insertion point. Scroll to the bottom of the document, and you'll see that the previous number 1 footnote has been automatically renumbered 2. (To quickly locate them, you can press `⇧ Shift`+`F5` to return to previous edits.)

Editing a Footnote

12. Click the **Normal View** button at the bottom of the screen to return to Normal view.

13. Pull down the **View** menu and click the **Footnotes** command to display all existing footnotes.

14. Position the insertion point at the end of the footnote numbered *1*, press `← Bksp` to delete the period, and type , **phone 1-800-426-3475.** (including the comma and the period).

15. Click the **Close** command button on the footnote window.

Changing Options

16. Position the insertion point to the left of footnote reference number *1*, hold down ⟨⇧ Shift⟩, and press ⟨→⟩ to select the footnote number.

17. Pull down the **Insert** menu and click the **Foot<u>n</u>ote** command to display the Footnote and Endnote dialog box.

18. Click the **Options** command to display the Note Options dialog box. Then click the **All <u>F</u>ootnotes** tab to make it active.

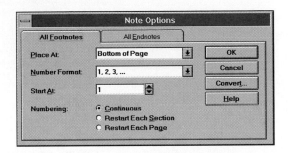

19. Click the **<u>N</u>umber Format** drop-down arrow (⬇), click the ***, †, ‡, §, ...** command to select it, and then click the **OK** command button to return to the Footnote and Endnote dialog box.

20. Click the **OK** command button to close the Footnote and Endnote dialog box. All footnotes are now referenced with symbols instead of numbers.

Finishing Up

21. Save, print, and close the document. Each footnote is printed at the bottom of the page containing its reference character.

4-7. CHANGING PAGE SETUP

You've seen how to change margins by dragging the margin boundaries on the rulers. However, you can also change them with the Page Setup menu. This not only gives you a few more options but also allows you to change the orientation of the page on the paper from vertical to horizontal.

MARGINS

Margins are the white area on the page around the printed block of text on the page (see the margin illustration). Word is preset to print documents with 1" top and bottom margins and 1.25" left and right margins. You can change one or all of these margin settings. For example, you may want more room on the left edge so you can punch pages for a binder. A change in margin settings affects the entire document.

When you change margins, you can specify gutter margins. The gutter is the area on the inside or binding edge of a document that is printed on both sides of the page. On page 2, it would be the right margin and on page 3 the left (see the illustration at the top of the following page).

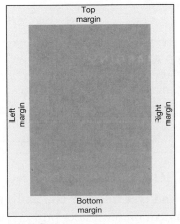

Margins

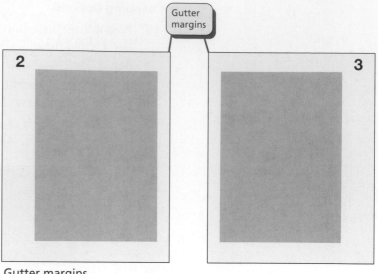

Gutter margins

Finally, you can also mirror margins. When you do so, you can have matching inside and outside margins.

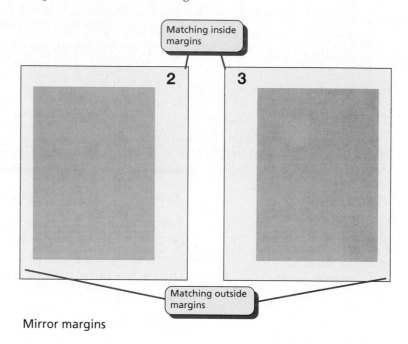

Mirror margins

QUICKSTEPS: CHANGING MARGINS
1. Pull down the **File** menu and click the **Page Setup** command to display the Page Setup dialog box.

2. On the **Margins** tab, click the up or down arrow in the **Top, Bottom, Left, Right**, or **Gutter** text box, or double-click in the text box and type a new number, and then click the **OK** command button.

PAPER SIZE AND PAGE ORIENTATION

With Word it's easy to change the size and type of paper you are printing on. For example, if you print a document on most laser printers, you can print text across the width or length of the page. The direction is

Portrait and landscape orientations

called the orientation or mode, and it can be either portrait mode or landscape mode. *Portrait* is the orientation of a normal document, that is, text is printed across the width of the page. *Landscape* orientation rotates the image 90 degrees so that it is printed along the length of the page. This mode is useful when you are printing wide tables, charts, and illustrations that are more horizontal than vertical (see the margin illustration).

TUTORIAL

In this tutorial, you change margins and then change a document to landscape orientation and back again using menu commands.

1. Open the *educom.doc* document stored in the *tutorial* directory on the *Word Student Resource Disk (Part 1)*.

Changing Margins

2. Pull down the **File** menu, click the **Page Setup** command to display the Page Setup dialog box, and click the *Margins* tab to make it active.

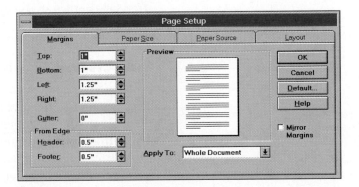

3. Change all four margins to 2 inches. To do so, either click the up arrow in each text box or double-click in each text box to select the current entry and then type **2**.

4. Click the **OK** command button to close the dialog box, and the margins of the document change on the screen.

5. Click the **Page Layout View** button at the bottom of the window and scroll through the document to see the changes.

Changing to Landscape Orientation

6. Pull down the **File** menu, click the **Page Setup** command to display the Page Setup dialog box, and click the **Paper Size** tab to make it active.

7. Click the **Landscape** option button to turn it on, and then click the **OK** command button to return to the document. The document is

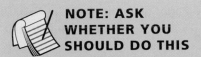

NOTE: ASK WHETHER YOU SHOULD DO THIS

Some printers are not capable of printing in landscape orientation or take so long to do so that you wouldn't want to bother. Ask your lab assistant if you should complete this tutorial on printing in landscape mode.

now displayed on your screen in landscape orientation, with a text width of 7 inches.

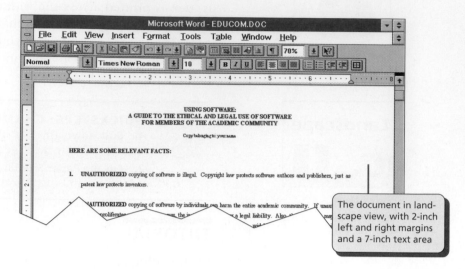

The document in land-scape view, with 2-inch left and right margins and a 7-inch text area

8. Print the first page of the document.

9. Pull down the **File** menu, click the **Page Setup** command to display the Page Setup dialog box, on the **Paper Size** tab click the **Portrait** option button to turn it on, and then click the **OK** command button to return to the document. The document should be again displayed on your screen in portrait orientation.

Finishing Up

10. Save and close the document.

4-8. ENTERING SECTION BREAKS

When you open a new document, it is all one section. *Section formats* such as margins, headers and footers, page numbers, and columns affect all pages in the document. To change section formats, for example to switch from Roman numeral to Arabic page numbers, or to change headers and footers, you have to create a new section where you want the section formats to change. To do so, you move the insertion point to the point at which you want the new section to begin and use the **Insert**, **Break** command. This inserts a dotted double line labeled *End of Section*. This line is simply a visual indicator of where you changed section formats. Until you make any changes, both sections have the same formats. However, when you now change section formats they only apply to the section in which the insertion point is positioned.

Section breaks are similar to paragraph marks in that they store all section formatting information. You can delete a section break by selecting it and pressing Del. When you do so, the formats from the lower section are automatically applied to the top section also.

When dividing a document into more than one section, here are some things to keep in mind:

▶ When you enter a header or footer in a document with more than one section, it will print on all pages of all sections. If you revise it in one section, it will be revised in all sections. To change a header or footer in only one section, you break the link between sections. To do so, you click the **Same As Previous** button on the Header and Footer toolbar to turn it off. Then when you delete or revise the new header or footer the change affects only the current section.

▶ To specify pages when using the **Go To** or **Print** commands, you indicate the section number as well as the section number. For example, to go to or print the first page in the second section, you would specify the page as 1s2. To print pages 1 through 3 of the second section, you would specify 1s2-3s2.

▶ To use more than one type of page numbering in a document, create a new section and change its number format. For example, to use Roman numerals for the table of contents and Arabic numbers for the rest of the document, enter a section break following the table of contents.

▶ When you change margins or switch from portrait to landscape or back again, you can have the change affect the entire document, just the section, or from the insertion point forward in the document.

QUICKSTEPS: CREATING A NEW SECTION

1. With the insertion point where you want the new section to begin, pull down the **Insert** menu and click the **Break** command to display the Break dialog box.

2. Make any of the choices described in the box "Understanding Section Break Choices" and click the **OK** button.

UNDERSTANDING SECTION BREAK CHOICES

When you display the Break dialog box, the section headed *Section Breaks* contains four option buttons from which to choose.

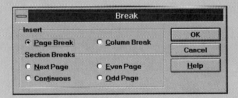

Next Page starts the new section at the top of a new page. The section break acts like a hard page break.

Continuous starts the new section on the same page as the old without inserting its own page break. Some section formats may apply to the top of the page and others at the bottom. For example, margins could be changed to accommodate a table.

Even Page starts the new section on the next even-numbered page, and inserts a blank page if needed.

Odd Page starts the new section on the next odd-numbered page, and inserts a blank page if needed.

TUTORIAL

In this tutorial you insert a section break into a document to separate the title page and body text. You then use this section break to add different headers and footers.

Getting Started

1. Open the *clouds.doc* document stored in the *tutorial* directory on the *Word Student Resource Disk (Part 1)*.

Inserting a Section Break

2. Move the insertion point to the beginning of the first body paragraph that begins *Clouds, to almost everyone,...*

3. Pull down the **Insert** menu and click the **Break** command to display the Break dialog box.

4. Click the **Next Page** option button under the *Section Breaks* heading to turn it on, then click the **OK** button. A dotted line labeled *End of Section* appears on the screen.

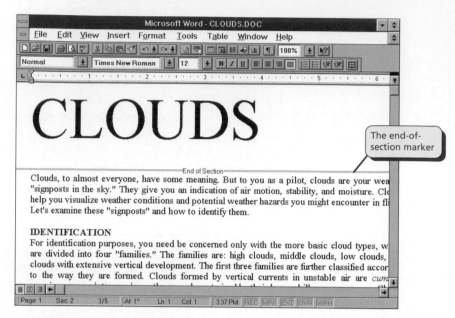

Moving Between Sections

5. Press F5 to display the Go To dialog box, type **2S2** into the **Enter Page Number** text box, and click the **Go To** command button. You immediately jump to the second page in the second section, and the status bar reads *Page 2 Sec 2*.

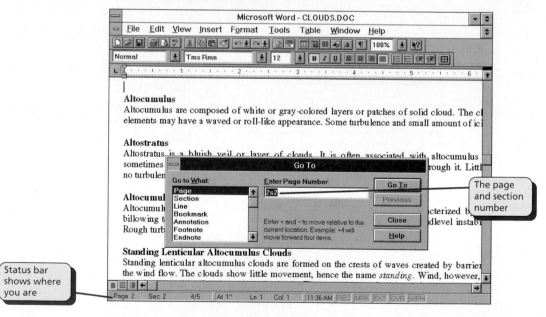

6. Type **1** into the **Enter Page Number** text box and click the **Go To** command button. You immediately jump to the first page in the document and the status bar reads *Page 1 Sec 1*.

7. Type **1S2** into the **Enter Page Number** text box and click the **Go To** command button. You immediately jump to the first page in the second section and the status bar reads *Page 1 Sec 2*.

8. Click the **Close** command button to close the Go To dialog box.

Inserting a Header

9. With the insertion point anywhere in the document, pull down the **View** menu and click the **Header and Footer** command to display the insertion point in a nonprinting dashed-line box labeled *Header* at the top of the page. The Header and Footer toolbar is also displayed, and text in the document is dimmed.

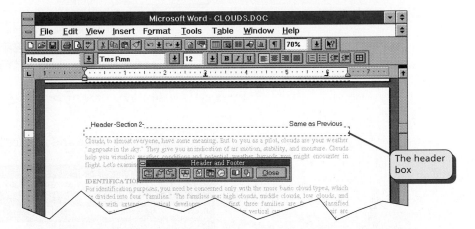

The header box

10. Click the **Align Right** button on the Formatting toolbar to move the insertion point flush with the document's right margin.

11. Type your last name in all capital letters.

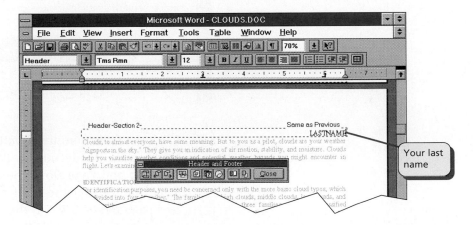

Your last name

12. Click the **Close** command button on the Header and Footer toolbar to return to the document.

13. Click the **Page Layout View** button to see the document in Page Layout view and page through it using the **Page Up** and **Page Down** buttons at the bottom of the scroll bar. You'll notice that the same header is on all pages.

Changing the Header

14. With the insertion point anywhere in the second section, pull down the **View** menu and click the **Header and Footer** command

to display the header you just entered. The **Same as Previous** button should be highlighted to indicate that it is on. Click it to turn it off.

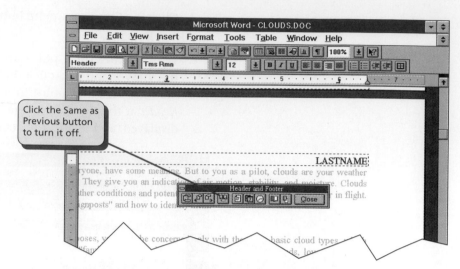

Click the Same as Previous button to turn it off.

LASTNAME

15. Delete your name and replace it with the header **CLOUDS**.

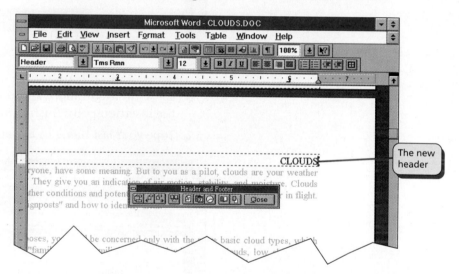

CLOUDS

The new header

16. Click the **Close** command button on the Header and Footer toolbar to return to the document. Page through the document using the **Page Up** and **Page Down** buttons at the bottom of the scroll bar. You'll notice that the header shows your name at the top of the first page and *CLOUDS* at the top of all pages in the second.

Printing Pages

17. Pull down the **File** menu and click the **Print** command to display the Print dialog box.

18. In the **Pages** text box, type **1s1** and click the **OK** command button. Only the first page of the first section is printed.

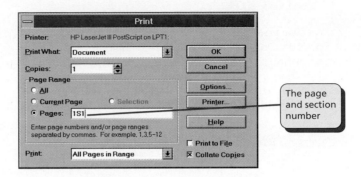

The page and section number

Finishing Up

19. Save the document and then close it.

4-9. SORTING DOCUMENTS

Word allows you to sort all or part of a document into ascending or descending order. All you have to do is make a few choices from a dialog box and the job is done.

When you sort, you can do so by paragraphs or by fields. Paragraphs are any lines that end with paragraph marks. Fields are tabbed columns, or text separated by commas or other characters, and are counted from left to right. When you sort using fields, you must specify which fields are to be used as the basis of the sort. For example, if you want to sort a table that has three columns—name, department, and extension—you can sort it by any column—called a field. Perhaps you want the names in alphabetic order to use as a phone directory or the phone extensions in numeric order for the maintenance department. When you sort, you must tell the program which field you want to sort by. When you specify a field and sort the document, the sort is based on that field, and all lines are rearranged, not just the column you specified.

QUICKSTEPS: SORTING DOCUMENTS

1. Select the data that you want to sort.

2. Pull down the **Table** menu and click the **Sort Text** command to display the Sort Text dialog box.

3. Make any of the settings described in the box "Understanding the Sort Text Dialog Box."

4. Click the **OK** command button.

UNDERSTANDING THE SORT TEXT DIALOG BOX

When you pull down the **Table** menu and click the **Sort Text** command, the Sort Text dialog box is displayed. It contains three identical sections, **Sort By**, **Then By**, and **Then By**. The choices in each of these sections work exactly the same but the last two work only when sorting by fields and not paragraphs.

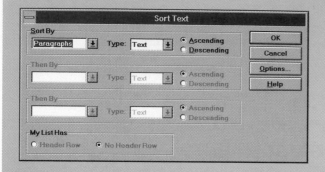

Sort By specifies whether the selected text is to be sorted by **Paragraphs** or **Fields**. Fields are specified when sorting tabbed columns of data or when sorting data separated by commas or other characters.

▶ **Type** specifies whether the data in the field is text, numbers, or dates.

▶ **Ascending** and **Descending** specify the order of the sort. If you specify an ascending sort, the file is arranged so that numbers go from 0 to the highest number, followed by words beginning with letters from *A* to *Z*. Any special characters are sorted to the bottom of the document. If you specify a descending sort, the order of the file is reversed.

Then By and **Then By** allow you to break ties in the original sort when sorting by fields. For example, should you sort tabbed columns by last names, you can use the first one of these sections to sort then by first names so they are also in order. The **Type**, **Ascending**, and **Descending** options work the same here as they do in the **Sort By** section.

Header Row and **No Header Row** specifies if the selected text includes a header such as column headings. Turning on the **Header Row** keeps this header row from being sorted along with the rows that follow it.

Options command button lets you specify if fields (columns) are separated by tabs, commas, or other characters. It also allows you to make the sort case sensitive and to sort a column by itself without including other entries on the row.

TUTORIAL

In this tutorial you sort a document based both on paragraphs and fields.

Getting Started

1. Open the *firms.doc* document stored in the *tutorial* directory on the *Word Student Resource Disk (Part1)* and enter your name following *Sorted by:* in the heading.

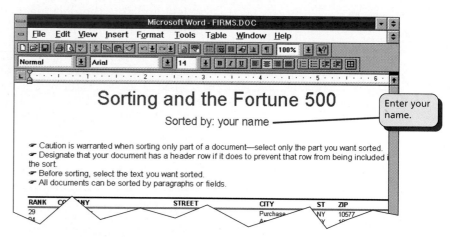

Sorting Paragraphs

2. Select the four paragraphs below the heading. Each begins with a pointing hand (☞).

3. Pull down the **Table** menu and click the **Sort Text** command to display the Sort Text dialog box. All of the default settings are as you want them.

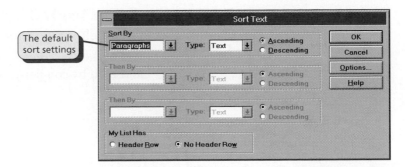

The default sort settings

4. Click the **OK** command button to sort the paragraphs into ascending order.

Sorting the List of Companies in Ascending Order

5. Select all of the lines of data beginning with the heading row that identifies the contents of the table columns (RANK, COMPANY, STREET, and so on).

6. Pull down the **Table** menu and click the **Sort Text** command to display the Sort Text dialog box.

7. Click the **Sort By** drop-down arrow (⬇), click **RANK** to select it, and click the **Header Row** option button to turn it on.

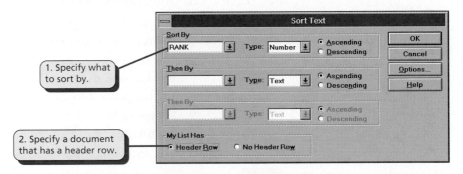

1. Specify what to sort by.

2. Specify a document that has a header row.

8. Click the **OK** command button to sort the file in ascending order based on the numbers in the first column.

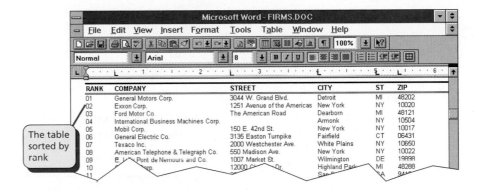

The table sorted by rank

Sorting the List By State and Then By Rank

9. Select all of the lines of data beginning with the heading row that identifies the contents of the table columns (RANK, COMPANY, STREET, and so on).

10. Pull down the **Table** menu and click the **Sort Text** command to display the Sort Text dialog box.

11. Click the **Sort By** drop-down arrow () and click **ST** to select it.

12. Click the **Then By** drop-down arrow (⬇) and click **RANK** to select it.

13. Click the **OK** command button. The table is sorted first by state and then by company rank within the state.

Finishing Up

14. Save, print, and close the document.

PicTorial 4 Review Questions

True-False

T F **1.** You cannot drag margin boundaries when the document is displayed in the Print Preview mode.

T F **2.** Changing indents and tabs affects the entire document.

T F **3.** You can copy formats.

T F **4.** By default, Word prints page numbers.

T F **5.** Footnotes are visible in the Normal view.

T F **6.** All printers are capable of printing in landscape mode.

T F **7.** In addition to a horizontal ruler, there is also a vertical ruler.

T F **8.** The way you arrange the paragraph indent markers determines if you create a first line indent, an entire paragraph indent, or a hanging indent.

T F **9.** Dragging the margin boundaries changes the margins for the entire document.

T F **10.** You can Find and Replace formats.

Multiple Choice

1. When you sort, you sort by paragraphs or by _____.
   a. Lines
   b. Fields
   c. Records
   d. Ranges

2. When you point to a boundary area on the horizontal ruler, the mouse pointer turns into a(n) _____.
   a. Double-headed arrow
   b. I-beam
   c. Left-pointing arrow
   d. Right-pointing arrow

3. There are _____ paragraph indent markers.
   a. 2
   b. 3
   c. 4

d. 5

4. Headers that print on more than one page in a sequence are called _____ heads.

   a. Sequential

   b. Continuous

   c. Repeating

   d. Running

5. To add page numbers to a document, use the _____ menu.

   a. Format

   b. Insert

   c. Edit

   d. File

6. To add footnotes to a document, use the _____ menu.

   a. Format

   b. Insert

   c. Edit

   d. File

7. To change margins, use the **File,** _____ command.

   a. **Margins**

   b. **Page Setup**

   c. **Page View**

   d. **Print Preview**

8. Landscape mode rotates the image _____ degrees.

   a. 90

   b. 80

   c. 120

   d. 360

9. Another name for columns is _____.

   a. Records

   b. Fields

   c. Cells

   d. Files

10. To remove page numbers, select the _____ menu.

    a. Edit

    b. View

    c. Format

    d. Insert

Fill In the Blank

1. The _____ displays markers that reflect settings in the paragraph containing the insertion point.

2. As you drag markers or margin boundaries, hold down _____ so their current position is displayed on the ruler.

3. To indent the first line of a paragraph, drag the _____ marker to the right of the left indent marker.

4. Use the _____ to copy formats.

5. Headers are lines of text that print in the _____.

6. To see headers and footers on the screen, you must be in the _____ view.

7. _____ mode is the orientation of a normal document.

8. If you specify a(n) _____ sort, the file is arranged so that numbers go from 0 to the highest number.

9. To display or hide the horizontal ruler, pull down the _____ menu and click the _____ command.

10. To change margins on the ruler, you must be in the _____ view.

PicTorial 4 Lab Activities

 ▶▶ **COMPUTER-BASED TUTORIALS**

We suggest you complete the following computer-based lessons to learn more about the features discussed in this PicTorial. To do so, pull down the **Help** menu and click the **Examples and Demos** command, click the *Topic* listed in the table "Suggested Examples and Demos to Complete," and then click the *Subtopic* listed in that same table. (If you need more help on using the system, see the "Computer-Based Tutorials" section at the end of PicTorial 2.)

Suggested Examples and Demos to Complete		
Done	**Topic**	**Subtopic**
☐	Typing and Editing	Finding text and formatting
☐	Formatting Text	Copying character formats
☐	Page Design and Layout	Creating a header or footer
☐	Working with Long Documents	Overview of Footnotes and Endnotes
☐	Working with Long Documents	Inserting footnotes and endnotes
☐	Page Design and Layout	Setting Margins
☐	Typing and Editing	Going to a page, bookmark, footnote, table, annotation, graphic or other location
☐	Working with Long Documents	Moving, copying, or deleting a footnote or endnote

▶▶ QUICKSTEP DRILLS

4-1. Formatting from the Ruler

Dragging markers on the ruler is the fastest way to change margins, indents, and tab stops. It's also the most visual way to do it since you can see the changes immediately. In this drill you practice making changes using the ruler.

1. Open the *rulerbar.doc* document stored in the *drill* directory on the *Word Student Resource Disk (Part 1)* and enter your name in the *From:* line, then click anywhere in the date and press F9 to update it.

2. Click the **Page Layout View** button at the bottom of the screen to display the document in that view.

3. Hold down Alt to display measurements and drag the left ruler boundary (with the mouse pointer displayed as a double-headed arrow) to set the left margin to 2".

4. Select the two lines in the letterhead with the address and phone numbers and drag the tab marker now at 6" on the ruler to 5.25" where it overlaps the right margin.

5. With the insertion point on the blank line below the last body paragraph in the document, click the **Tab Alignment** button at the left end of the ruler twice to display a right-aligned tab stop symbol, and then click on the ruler to set right-aligned tab stops at 1.5, 2, 2.5, and 3 inches. After setting a tab stop, you can hold down Alt and drag it into the exact position.

6. Press Enter⏎ and enter the two tables shown in the figure "System Board Price Tables." Boldface the table titles and the column headings.

7. Save, print, and close the document.

TABLE 1 Shark System Board Costs

CPU	Q1	Q2	Q3	Q4
Pentium/60	550	500	475	450
Pentium/66	600	550	525	500
Pentium/100	650	600	575	525

TABLE 2 Microprocessor Pricing

CPU	Q1	Q2	Q3	Q4
Pentium/60	250	250	225	200
Pentium/66	300	275	250	225
Pentium/100	350	325	300	250

System Board Price Tables

4-2. Copying Formats

Once you have formatted an element the way you like it, you can easily copy the format to other elements in the document. In this drill you practice using Word's Format Painter to do so.

1. Open the *copyform.doc* document stored in the *drill* directory on the *Word Student Resource Disk (Part 1)* and enter your name, then click anywhere in the date and press F9 to update it.

2. To copy character formats, click in any of the entries under the heading "Character Formats to Copy From," click the **Format Painter** button on the toolbar, and drag the mouse pointer under the same word or phrase under the heading "Character Formats to Copy To." If you make any mistakes, click the **Undo** button on the toolbar to undo them.

3. To copy paragraph formats, select at least the paragraph mark at the end of the paragraph under the heading "Paragraph Formats to Copy From," click the **Format Painter** button on the toolbar, and then click anywhere in the same entry under the heading "Paragraph Formats to Copy To." If you make any mistakes, click the **Undo** button on the toolbar to undo them.

4. Print the document, then close it without saving your changes.

4-3. Finding and Replacing Formats

When you receive e-mail or other text files over electronic distribution networks such as the Internet or CompuServe, they are frequently in a very simple format called ASCII. These files have no bold, italic, or other familiar formats. In addition, all lines end in hard returns—making them very hard to edit or format. To make these file more editable, you have to remove these hard returns. Here is how many people convert ASCII text files to normal document files:

1. Open the *textfile.txt* document stored in the *drill* directory of the *Word Student Resource Disk (Part 1)*. (To do so, type ***.txt** into the Open dialog box's **File Name** text box and press Enter↵ to display files with the *.txt* extension.)

2. Select the whole document below the 8 lines of headings, and use the **Edit**, **Replace** command to display the Replace dialog box.

   ▶ With the insertion point in the **Find What** text box, click the **Special** command button and then click **Paragraph Mark** on the list to insert the code ^*p* in the text box. Repeat the command again so the **Find What** text box displays ^*p*^*p*.

   ▶ In the **Replace With** text box, type **[CR]** (including the square brackets). This term is used because it isn't likely to appear elsewhere in the document.

3. Click the **Replace All** command button, and all blank lines are removed from the document. When asked *Do you want to continue searching at the beginning*, click **No**.

4. With the Replace dialog box still displayed:

   ▶ Delete one of the ^*p* codes from the **Find What** text box so the text box displays ^*p*.

   ▶ Double-click in the **Replace With** text box and press Spacebar so you replace single paragraph marks with spaces.

5. Click the **Replace All** command button, and the document closes up into one long paragraph. When asked *Do you want to continue searching at the beginning*, click **No**.

6. With the Replace dialog box still displayed:

  ▶ Delete the ^p from the **Fi̲nd What** text box and type **[CR]**.

    ▶ In the **Re̲place With** text box, delete the space, click the **Sp̲ecial** command button, and then click **P̲aragraph Mark** on the list to insert the code ^p in the text box. Repeat the command again so the **Re̲place With** text box displays ^p^p.

7. Click the **Replace A̲ll** command button, and the document is broken back up into its original paragraphs. When asked *Do you want to continue searching at the beginning*, click **N̲o**. Close the Replace dialog box.

8. Save the document, print the first page, and then close the document.

4-4. Adding Headers and Footers

Headers and footers can be used to list names, page numbers, chapter or part titles, or anything else that would help you know where you are in a document. In this drill you add headers and footers to a document that discusses when to use headers and footers and what to put in them.

1. Open the *headfoot.doc* document stored in the *drill* directory on the *Word Student Resource Disk (Part 1)* and enter your name, then click anywhere in the date and press [F9] to update it.

2. Use the **V̲iew**, **Header and Footer** command to display the header and footer boxes.

  ▶ Enter a flush right header that reads **HEADERS & FOOTERS**.

  ▶ Click the **Switch Between Header and Footer** button on the Headers and Footers toolbar, enter a flush right footer that reads **PAGE**, press [Spacebar], and click the **Page Numbers** button on the Headers and Footers toolbar.

3. Click the **C̲lose** button on the Headers and Footers toolbar and use the **Print Preview** button on the Standard toolbar to preview your results.

4. Save, print, and close the document.

4-5. Adding and Removing Page Numbers

Unless you specify otherwise, none of your documents will be printed with page numbers. This isn't a problem with very short documents, but it is with longer documents. In this drill you practice the procedures you use to add page numbers to a document and change their format.

1. Open the *pagenumb.doc* document stored in the *drill* directory on the *Word Student Resource Disk (Part 1)* and enter your name, then click anywhere in the date and press [F9] to update it.

2. Click the **Page Layout View** button so you can see the results of your changes on screen.

3. Use the **I̲nsert**, **Page N̲umbers** command to add page numbers to the bottom right corner of every page.

4. Use the **I̲nsert**, **Page N̲umbers** command to change the page numbers from Arabic numbers to lowercase Roman numerals.

5. Save, print, and close the document.

4-6. Entering Footnotes and Endnotes

In college papers or business reports, footnote references to cited works are often required. In this drill you enter the form of various footnotes so you will have a reference you can later use when entering your own. These forms indicate what information should be provided, how it should be arranged, and how it should be formatted.

1. Open the *footform.doc* document stored in the *drill* directory on the *Word Student Resource Disk (Part 1)* and enter your name, then click anywhere in the date and press F9 to update it.

2. Click the **Normal View** button and use the **Insert**, **Footnote** command to enter the first five footnotes shown in the table "Footnote Forms" at the end of the line in the document with the matching number.

3. Click the **Page Layout View** button and use the **Insert**, **Footnote** command to enter the last five footnotes shown in the table "Footnote Forms."

4. Save, print, and close the document.

	FOOTNOTE FORMS
Number	**Footnote to Enter**
1	First Last, *Title* (City, State: Publisher, copyright date), pages.
2	First Last, First Last, and First Last, *Title* (City, State: Publisher, copyright date), pages.
3	Name of Corporation, *Title* (City, State: Publisher, copyright date), pages.
4	First Last, *Title,* Volume or Part (City, State: Publisher, copyright date), pages.
5	First Last, "Title of Article," in *Title of Publication,* ed. First Last (City, State: Publisher, copyright date), pages.
6	"Title of Section," *Title of Book,* copyright or edition date.
7	First Last, "Title of Article," *Name of Periodical,* date, section, page, column.
8	First Last, "Title of Article," *Name of Newspaper,* date of issue, page.
9	First Last, dir., *Film Title,* with Major Actor, Studio, date of release.
10	Personal interview with First Last, date.

4-7A. Changing Page Setup

Often, tables and other documents print better in landscape orientation than in portrait orientation. In this exercise, you change the orientation of an existing document and then preview or print it. As you have seen, some printers are not capable of printing in landscape orientation. If you are using such a printer, preview the document but don't print it.

1. Open the *landscap.doc* document stored in the *drill* directory on the *Word Student Resource Disk (Part 1)* and enter your name.

2. Use the **Print Preview** button on the toolbar to display the document on the screen. You'll notice that the table extends off the right side of the page.

3. Use the **File**, **Page Setup** command to change landscape orientation on the **Paper Size** tab.

4. Save, print, and close the document.

4-7B. Changing Margins

Changing margins is one of the easiest things you can do with a word processor. Although it's easy, it can have a dramatic impact on how a document looks. In this drill you change the margins on a document that discusses the concepts behind changing margins.

1. Open the *margins.doc* document stored in the *drill* directory of the *Word Student Resource Disk (Part 1)* and enter your name, then click anywhere in the date and press F9 to update it.

2. Click the **Page Layout View** button at the bottom of the window to display the document in Page Layout view so you can see the header at the very top of the document (*MARGINS*) and footer at the very bottom (*PAGE* followed by the page number).

3. Use the **File**, **Page Setup** command to change the left and right margins to 2" on the **Margins** tab.

4. Use the **Print Preview** button on the toolbar to preview the results, then print the first page of the document. Notice how the margins for the header and footer changed automatically when you changed those for the page.

5. Use the **File**, **Page Setup** command to change the left and right margins back to 1.25".

6. Close the document without saving it.

4-8. Entering Section Breaks

In this drill you enter a section break in a document.

1. Open the *pagenumb.doc* document stored in the *drill* directory on the *Word Student Resource Disk (Part 1)*. Click anywhere in the date and press F9 to update it

2. With the insertion point at the beginning of the heading that reads *Page Number Positions*, use the **Insert**, **Break** command to insert a **Next Page** section break.

3. With the insertion point at the beginning of the heading that reads *Page Number Styles*, use the **Insert**, **Break** command to insert a **Continuous** section break.

4. Click at the top of the document, then under the headings *Page Number Positions* and *Page Number Styles*. As you do so, watch the section number change on the status bar.

5. Use the **Edit**, **Go To** command to display the Go To dialog box, then:

   ▶ With **Go To What** set to *Page*, enter **1S1**, **1S2**, and then **1S3** in the **Enter Page Number** text box and click the **Go To** command button for each. As you do so, notice where you go and what the status bar says about the section.

   ▶ With **Go To What** set to *Section*, enter **1**, **2**, and then **3** in the **Enter Page Number** text box and click the **Go To** command button for each. As you do so, notice where you go and what the status bar says about the section.

6. Display the document in Page Layout View or use Print Preview to see the page numbers at the bottom of each page. They will be Arabic numbers or Roman numerals running consecutively through the document.

7. With the insertion point anywhere in the second section, use the **Insert**, **Page Numbers**, **Format** command to change the **Number Format** to the opposite of what it currently is.

8. Display the document in Page Layout View or use Print Preview to see the page numbers at the bottom of each page. They will be different in different sections.

9. Use the **File**, **Print** command to print **Pages** 1S2, then close the document without saving your changes.

4-9. Sorting Documents

In this drill you sort of long list of films in which Bugs Bunny starred. This allows you to quickly see films grouped by director and studio, and arranged in the order in which they were released.

1. Open the *bugs.doc* document stored in the *drill* directory on the *Word Student Resource Disk (Part 1)*. Click anywhere in the date and press F9 to update it.

2. Select the entire table beginning with the row below the column headings. Then use the **Table**, **Sort Text** command to **Sort By** *Field 4* in **Ascending** order. This sorts the table by *Director* from A to Z— the fourth column. Print the first page.

3. With the table still selected, use the **Table**, **Sort Text** command to **Sort By** *Field 4* in **Descending** order. This sorts the table by *Director* from Z to A. Print the first page.

4. With the table still selected, use the **Table**, **Sort Text** command to **Sort By** *Field 1* in **Ascending** order. This sorts the table by *Dates* from earliest to latest. Print the first page.

5. With the table still selected, use the **Table**, **Sort Text** command to **Sort By** *Field 1* in **Descending** order. This sorts the table by *Dates* from latest to earliest. Print the first page.

6. Close the document without saving your changes.

 ▶▶ **SKILL-BUILDING EXERCISES**

4-1. Formatting the Job-Guide Document

In this exercise you change indents and add footers and footnotes to the document describing how you prepare a job-search kit.

1. Open the *jobs.doc* document stored in the *exercise* directory on the *Word Student Resource Disk (Part 2)*.

2. Use the **File**, **Page Setup** command to change the left margin to 1.5" on the **Margins** tab.

3. Select the two lines in the letterhead with the address and phone numbers and drag the tab marker so it overlaps the right margin.

4. Use the **View**, **Header and Footer** command to display the Header and Footer toolbar.

   ▶ Click the **Switch Between Header and Footer** button on the Header and Footer toolbar to move the insertion point to the footer box.

   ▶ Click the **Page Setup** button on the Header and Footer toolbar, then click the **Different Odd and Even** check box to turn it on.

   ▶ Click the **Show Next** and **Show Previous** buttons on the Header and Footer toolbar to move between the *Even Page Footer* and *Odd Page Footer* boxes.

   ▶ In the *Odd Page Footer* box, enter a footer that prints your last name flush right in all uppercase letters.

   ▶ In the *Even Page Footer* box and a footer that prints your last name flush left in all uppercase letters.

5. Use the **Insert**, **Page Numbers** command to add page numbers that print in the top outside corner of every page but the first.

6. Use the **Insert**, **Footnote** command to enter a footnote at the end of the first body paragraph that reads **These recommendations have been adapted from a government publication.** (including the period).

7. At the end of the sentence that begins *Let's go through a typical letter point by point:* just above the *Salutation* section on the first page, use the **Insert**, **Footnote** command enter a footnote that reads **These letter formats are also discussed in the *ltrrules.doc* file in the *exercise* directory of the *Word Student Resource Disk (Part 2)*.** (including the period and using italics where shown).

8. Use Print Preview to see how page numbers, footers, and footnotes look. Your name should appear on the outside (right) edge of odd-numbered pages and on the inside (left) edge of even-numbered pages.

9. Save, print, and then close the document.

4-2. Formatting the Careers Document

In this exercise you indent body paragraphs, add headers and footers, and add a footnote to the document describing careers in the computer field.

1. Open the *careers.doc* document stored in the *exercise* directory on the *Word Student Resource Disk (Part 2)*.

2. Use the **File**, **Page Setup** command to change the left margin to 1.5 inches on the **Margins** tab.

3. Select the two lines in the letterhead with the address and phone numbers and drag the tab marker so it overlaps the right margin.

4. Use the **View**, **Header and Footer** command to add a flush-right header on every page but the first with your last name in uppercase letters.

5. Use the **View**, **Header and Footer** command to add a flush-right footer on every page but the first that prints today's date.

6. Immediately after the phrase *One major company* in the first paragraph, use the **Insert**, **Footnote** command to add the footnote **Federal Express Corporation**.

7. Use the **Insert**, **Page Numbers** command to add pages numbers so that they print in the bottom center of every page but the first.

8. Save, print, and then close the document.

4-3. Formatting the Bill of Rights Document

In this exercise you enter footers and footnotes in the Bill of Rights.

1. Open the *rights.doc* document stored in the *exercise* directory on the *Word Student Resource Disk (Part 2)* and click anywhere in the date and press `F9` to update it.

2. Use the **View**, **Header and Footer** command to display the Header and Footer toolbar.

   ▶ Click the **Page Setup** button on the Headers and Footers toolbar, then click the **Different Odd and Even** check box to turn it on.

   ▶ Click the **Show Next** and **Show Previous** buttons on the Headers and Footers toolbar to move between the *Even Page Footer* and *Odd Page Footer* boxes.

   ▶ In the *Odd Page Footer* box, enter a footer that prints *Bill of Rights* flush right.

   ▶ In the *Even Page Footer* box use the **Date** button on the Header and Footer toolbar to enter the date flush left.

3. Use the **Insert**, **Page Numbers** command to add page numbers that print in the upper-right corner of every page.

4. Following the centered heading at the top of the document, use the **Insert**, **Footnote** command to enter a footnote that states **All amendments passed unanimously** and use the **Options** command button to change the footnote numbering method to symbols.

5. Save and then print the document. Notice where the page numbers, footer, and footnote print.

4-4. Formatting the Newsletter Document

In this exercise you indent body paragraphs and add page numbers to the newsletter.

1. Open the *newsltr.doc* document stored in the *exercise* directory on the *Word Student Resource Disk (Part 2)*.

2. Use the **File**, **Page Setup** command to change all four margins to .75" on the **Margins** tab.

3. Use the **Insert**, **Page Numbers** command to add pages numbers so that they print centered at the bottom of every page but the first.

4. Save and then print the document.

4-5. Formatting the Desktop Publishing Document

In this exercise you indent body paragraphs and add headers, footers, and footnotes to the desktop publishing document.

1. Open the *dtp.doc* document stored in the *exercise* directory on the *Word Student Resource Disk (Part 2)*.

2. Use the **File**, **Page Setup** command to change all four margins to .75″ on the **Margins** tab.

3. Use the **View**, **Header and Footer** command to display the header box:

   ▸ Add a flush-right header on every page with your last name in uppercase letters followed by a space and then a page number entered by clicking the **Page Numbers** button on the Header and Footer toolbar.

   ▸ Add a flush-right footer on every page with today's date entered by clicking the **Date** button on the Header and Footer toolbar.

5. After the phrase *Desktop publishing* at the end of the first body paragraph use the **Insert**, **Footnote** command to enter the footnote **Including a more recent program, QuarkXpress.**

6. Use the **Insert**, **Page Numbers** command to add page numbers that print in the bottom center of every page.

7. Save the document, print the first page, and then close the document.

▶▶ REAL-WORLD PROJECTS

5-1. The Research Paper—Continued

In this project you continue working on the research paper about the history of computing.

1. Open the *respaper.doc* document stored in the *projects* directory on the *Word Student Resource Disk (Part 2)*.

2. Enter a right-aligned header that prints your last name flush-right in all uppercase letters.

3. Enter a right-aligned footer that prints PAGE followed by the page number.

4. At the end of the phrase *companies that supplied its components* enter the endnote shown here:

> Though the MITS system is no longer manufactured, its method for connecting peripherals and the main computer has become an industry standard. Within three years after it was introduced, Radio Shack, Apple, and Commodore had entered the market.

5. At the end of the phrase *VisiCalc did that for them* enter the endnote shown here:

> The introduction of VisiCalc is usually credited with making the Apple II the fastest selling computer of its time and with making the microcomputer acceptable in business offices.

6. Insert a hard page break at the end of the document. Then on the first line of the new page enter the heading **Notes**. Center the heading, and insert two blank lines below it so that the endnotes print starting on the third line.

7. Save, print, and close the document.

5-2. The Flier's Rights Booklet—Continued

In this project you continue formatting the *flyright* document as a booklet.

1. Open the *flyright.doc* document stored in the *projects* directory on the *Word Student Resource Disk (Part 2)*.

2. Enter the header FLIER'S RIGHTS so it's right-aligned on odd-numbered pages and left-aligned on even-numbered pages.

3. Enter the footer PAGE followed by the page number so it's right-aligned on odd-numbered pages and left-aligned on even-numbered pages.

4. After the heading **Introduction**, enter the following footnote:

> We're making every effort to keep Fly-Rights up to date, but during this period of deregulation, airlines are making many changes in the way they do business. So by the time you read this, a few rules we explain may be different. Contact the airline you plan to use if you have any questions.

5. Change all four margins to 0.5".

6. Insert a section break below your name on the title page that begins a new page.

7. Save the document, print page 2, then close the document.

PicTorial 5

AUTOMATING PROCEDURES

After completing this PicTorial, you will be able to:

▶ Describe the structure and function of main documents and data sources

▶ Merge main documents and data sources to print customized letters and labels

▶ Add input from the keyboard while merging documents

▶ Specify that only selected records are merged

▶ Record, play back, and edit macros

▶ Using AutoText and AutoCorrect to speed things up

The true power of a word processing program is best demonstrated when you begin to use it to automate your work. The two most common ways of doing this are with Mail Merge and macros. Mail Merge is a way to automatically print customized letters, labels, or other documents. Macros are a way to automate other procedures so you can execute them quickly. Word also has some automatic features built in. These include AutoText, which enters text you have previously saved, and AutoCorrect, which corrects common spelling mistakes as you make them.

5-1. INTRODUCTION TO MAIL MERGE

Most of us have received one of those mailers proclaiming something like **Mr. Steven Johnson of 100 Mill Street, you may have won $1-million dollars!** Ever wonder how they print your name on the copy you receive and each of your neighbors' names on the ones they receive? It's done with a process called mail merge. Instead of individually entering and editing tens, hundreds, or thousands of letters, envelopes, mailing labels, forms, or other documents, Mail Merge combines two documents: a *main document* containing the data that is to appear in each copy and a *data source* that contains the data that personalizes each copy. In our example, the mailer you received would be the main document because it is the same for everyone on your street, in your city, and in the country. The screaming headline that tries to make you think you have won something is from a data source because it personalizes the mailer for you and you alone. As you have seen from the volume of these customized mailers that arrive, Mail Merge can greatly increase your speed in preparing all kinds of documents which are essentially the same, except for minor changes, from copy to copy.

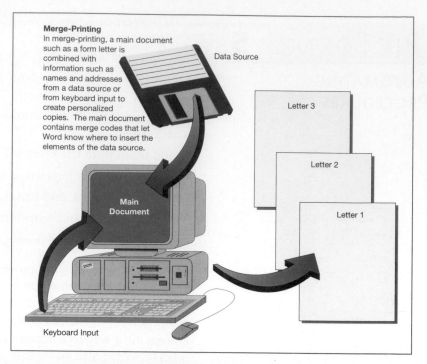

Merge-Printing
In merge-printing, a main document such as a form letter is combined with information such as names and addresses from a data source or from keyboard input to create personalized copies. The main document contains merge codes that let Word know where to insert the elements of the data source.

Data Source

Letter 3

Letter 2

Letter 1

Main Document

Keyboard Input

UNDERSTANDING DATA SOURCES

The information that customizes copies during merge-printing, such as names and addresses, is stored in a data source. A data source is a structured document that has three basic parts: a header row, fields, and records. Think of it as a table, like this:

Header row

Field

Record

Salutation	FirstName	LastName	Company	Address1	City	State	PostalCode
Mrs.	Suzanne	Steven	3D Graphics	1 Pierce Street	Saratoga	CA	95070
	Kim	Foley	Virtual Reality	60 Friend Street	Beverly	MA	1915
Mrs.	Debbie	Star		1 Oak Road	Marblehead	MA	1945

▶ The header row, the first row in the table, contains the names of all fields in the data source.

▶ The table's columns are fields, and each field contains a specific piece of information. For example, fields can store first and last names or postal codes.

▶ The table's rows are records, each divided into a number of fields. A typical record would contain a person's name, company, and address.

When merged, each record causes one new document to be printed. For example, the name and address in the first record are used to print the first envelope. Then the name and address in the second record are used to print the second envelope and so on.

The advantage of storing data in a data source is that the data can be used over and over again to automatically print documents such as letters, envelopes, and mailing labels.

UNDERSTANDING MAIN DOCUMENTS AND MERGE-PRINTING

The part of a mail-merged document that stays the same from copy to copy is stored in the main document. However, it also contains codes—called *merge fields*—that specify what and where data is to be inserted into each copy from the data source during merge-printing. For example, merge fields placed in the heading of the main document might specify where people's first and last names are to be inserted.

When the document is merge-printed, its merge fields are replaced with the names taken from the data source. The reason the correct information is inserted is that each merge field refers to a specific field in the data source. It's as if a link is established between a code and the field to which it refers. When merged, as the first copy is being printed, data is sent down that link from the first record in the data source. As the second copy is being printed, data is sent down that link from the second record in the data source. This process continues until a document has been printed for each record in the data source. Each copy of the final document contains all of the text from the main document and all of the specified fields from a single record in the data source. Therefore, if the data source contains 10 records, 10 different letters can be merged.

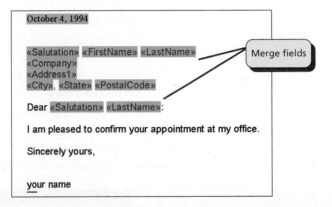

> **TIP: DISPLAYING MERGE FIELDS**
>
> When you enter merge fields in a document, they are enclosed in chevrons. This view is called "field results." To see them in their entirety, you can display them as "field codes." For example, the merge code «*name*» displayed as a field result becomes { *MERGEFIELD name* * *MERGEFORMAT* } when displayed as a field code. To change your view of the codes, pull down the **Tools** menu, click the **Options** command to display the Options dialog box, on the **View** tab click the **Field Codes** check box to turn it on (☒) or off (☐), and then click the **OK** command button to return to the document.

UNDERSTANDING MAIL MERGE HELPER

Word's built-in Mail Merge Helper guides you through the process of creating main documents and data sources and merging them. As you progress through the steps in the sequence, the variations depend on your previous responses. Just carefully read the instructions as you progress and you can create or open a main document and a data source and then merge them.

QUICKSTEPS: USING MAIL MERGE HELPER

1. Pull down the **Tools** menu and click the **Mail Merge** command to display the Mail Merge Helper dialog box.

2. Use the **Create** button under the section heading *1 Main Document* to open or create a main document—the document that contains the text that is to appear in each copy and merge fields that will be replaced with personalized data from the data source during merging. When you do so, select the type of document (Form Letters, Mailing Labels, Envelopes, or Catalog) and specify if you want to use the document in the **Active Window** or a **New Main Document**.

3. Use the **Get Data** button under the section heading *2 Data Source* to open or create a data source—the file that contains the data to be inserted into each copy of the main document during merging to personalize it. Once the two files have been opened or created and then saved, they are permanently linked. Whenever you open the main document, it is recognized by Word as a main document linked to the specific data source that you specified.

4. Use the **Merge** button under the section heading *3 Merge the Data with the Document* heading to merge the documents.

TUTORIAL

In this tutorial you are introduced to Mail Merge Helper using two existing documents. The main document contains merge fields that will print names and company information on name tags. The data source is a Word table that contains information on four individuals.

Getting Started

1. Open the *nametags.doc* document stored in the *tutorial* directory of the *Word Student Resource Disk (Part 1)*. This Mail Merge main document contains the four merge fields <<FirstName>>, <<LastName>>, <<Title>>, and <<Company>>.

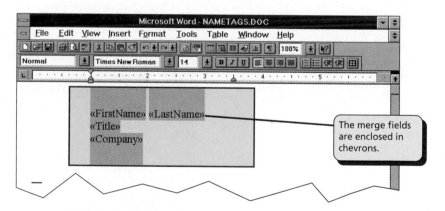

The merge fields are enclosed in chevrons.

Specifying the Main Document

2. Pull down the **Tools** menu and click the **Mail Merge** command to display the Mail Merge Helper dialog box.

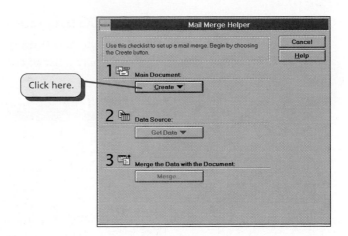

3. Click the **Create** button under the section heading *1 Main Document* to display a list of main document types you can create.

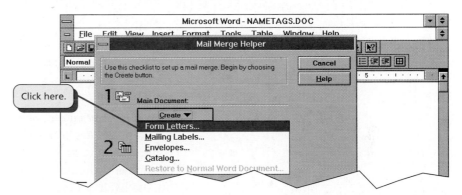

4. Click the **Form Letters** command to display a dialog box asking if you want to use the document in the **Active Window** or a **New Main Document**.

5. Click the **Active Window** button to work with the *nametags.doc* document in the active window and return to the Mail Merge Helper dialog box. Notice how the document's type and name are now listed below the **Create** button.

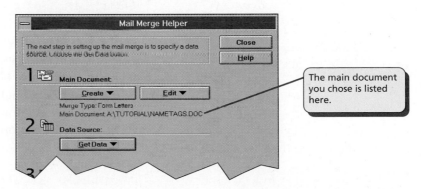

Specifying the Data Source

6. Click the **Get Data** button under the section heading *2 Data Source* to display a list of commands.

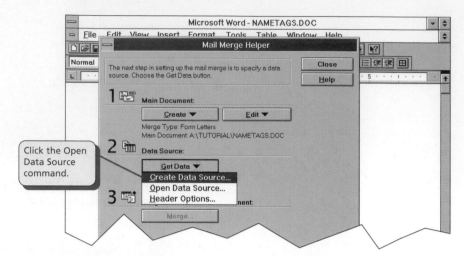

7. Click the **Open Data Source** command to display the Open Data Source dialog box, which works just like the dialog box you use to open documents.

8. Click the *names.doc* document stored in the *tutorial* directory of the *Word Student Resource Disk (Part 1)* to select it and then click the **OK** command button to return to the Mail Merge Helper. Notice how the name of the document is now listed below the **Get Data** button on the Mail Merge Helper dialog box. The Mail Merge toolbox opens below the Formatting toolbar.

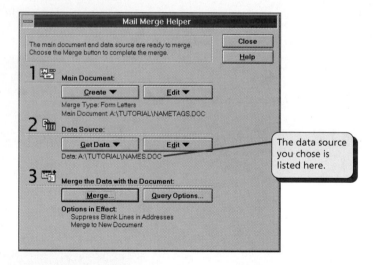

9. Click the **Edit** button under the section heading *2 Data Source* to display a list of data sources with only one listed, and click the *NAMES.DOC* name to display the Data Form dialog box.

10. Click the **Next Record** button (▶) in the **Record** section three times to scroll through the four records in this data source. When finished, click the **OK** button to return to the main document.

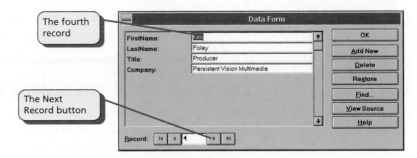

The fourth record

The Next Record button

11. Click the **View Merged Data** button on the Mail Merge toolbar to display the first record in the main document. This command allows you to see how data from the data source will look when inserted into the document in place of the merge fields.

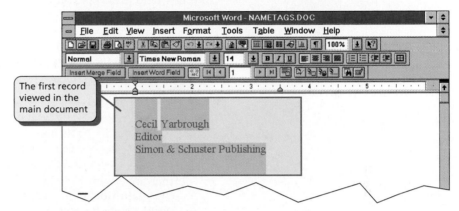

The first record viewed in the main document

Cecil Yarbrough
Editor
Simon & Schuster Publishing

12. Click the **Next Record** button (▶) on the Mail Merge toolbar to scroll through the four records to preview how each will appear when merged.

Mail-Merging the Documents

13. Click the **Merge to New Document** button on the Mail Merge toolbar to merge the main document (*nametags.doc*) and its data source (*names.doc*). Notice how each merge field in the main document has been replaced with specific data from the data source. Also, each label is on its own page separated from the next by a section break.

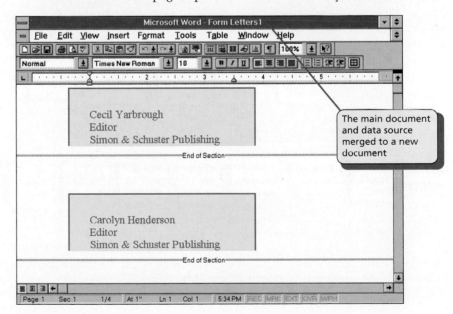

The main document and data source merged to a new document

14. Close all open documents without saving them.

5-2. MAIL-MERGING FORM LETTERS

One of the most common uses of Mail Merge is the printing of form letters. It's an easy process since Word's Mail Merge Helper is designed to lead you step by step through the preparation of a main document and a data source and then merging the two.

Not all data merged into the main document has to come from the data source. You can insert merge fields that display a prompt during merging that asks you to enter data from the keyboard. For example, the FILLIN field prompts you to type data that is then merged into the document at the place where the FILLIN field is entered.

QUICKSTEPS: MERGING YOUR OWN DOCUMENTS

1. Open a new document or open an existing document that you want to use as a main document for your form letter.

2. Pull down the **Tools** menu and click the **Mail Merge** command to display the Mail Merge Helper dialog box.

3. Complete each of the three steps in order and follow the instructions that appear on the screen during the procedure. When working on the main document, use the command buttons on the toolbar to insert merge fields or Word fields. These buttons are described in the box "Understanding the Main Document Toolbar."

4. Save the finished main document.

UNDERSTANDING THE MAIL MERGE TOOLBAR

When you are working on a main document, the Mail Merge toolbar is displayed. You use the buttons on this bar to enter merge fields into the main document, preview merged data, merge the documents, and find and edit records in the data source.

Insert Merge Field displays a list of the field names in the data source which you can insert into the main document. For example, if the data source has a field named *Company*, selecting that name from the list will insert a field <<*Company*>> in the main document, and data stored in the *Company* field of the data source will be inserted in that location in place of the merge field in each document that is merged.

Insert Word Field displays a list of other fields you can insert into the document. For example, inserting the **Fill-in** field in a main document will display a dialog box into which you can type the requested information which is then inserted into a single copy of the merged document.

View Merged Data replaces merge fields in the main document on screen with data from the first record in the data source. This allows you to preview your results before you merge the documents. You can also use the buttons described below to scroll through the data source record by record.

First Record, **Previous Record**, **Go to Record**, **Next Record**, and **Last Record** buttons scroll you through records in the data source when you are viewing merged data.

Mail Merge Helper displays the Mail Merge Helper dialog box.

(Continued)

Check for Errors checks to see if there are any errors in the merge fields and reports any that it finds.

Merge to New Document merges the main document and data source to a new document on the screen so you can check it before printing.

Merge to Printer merges the main document and data source directly to the printer.

Mail Merge displays the Merge dialog box where you can specify if the merge is to a new document or the printer, specify the records in the data source to be merged if you don't want to merge all of them, and specify whether blank lines are printed or not when a data field on a line by itself is empty.

Find record displays a dialog box in which you specify a field in the **In Field** drop-down list and its contents in the **Find What** text box so you can locate any matching records. The number of any found record is listed on the status bar, and you can click the **Edit Data Source** button on the Mail Merge toolbar to display it. (If you click the **Edit Data Source** button on the Mail Merge toolbar to display the data form, you can also click its **Find** button to locate records.

Edit Data Source displays the Data Form dialog box listing records in the data source so you can edit, add, or delete records.

TUTORIAL

In this tutorial you use Mail Merge Helper to create a data source with four records which you then merge with a form letter confirming appointment times and dates. Since the times and dates vary widely when sending confirmations, that data is not stored in the data source. Instead, merge fields are inserted into the main document that will prompt you to enter this information from the keyboard when merging the documents.

Getting Started

1. Open the *formltr.doc* document stored in the *tutorial* directory on *Word Student Resource Disk (Part 1)*.

Displaying the Maiil Merge Helper

NOTE: QUITTING

This tutorial is quite long, due to the nature of Word's Mail Merge Helper. If you have to quit, do so after Step 23.

2. Pull down the **Tools** menu and click the **Mail Merge** command to display the Mail Merge Helper dialog box.

Specifying the Main Document

3. Click the **Create** button under the section heading *1 Main Document* to display a list of main document types you can create.

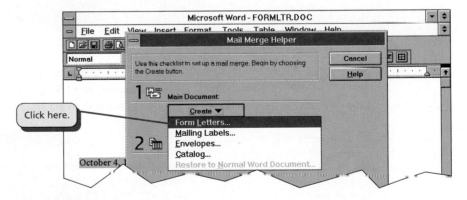

4. Click the **Form Letters** command to display a dialog box asking if you want to use the document in the **Active Window** or a **New Main Document**.

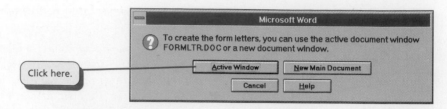

Click here.

5. Click the **Active Window** button to work with the new document you just opened and return to the Mail Merge Helper dialog box. Notice how the document's type and name are now listed below the **Create** button.

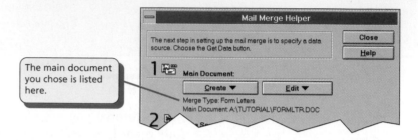

The main document you chose is listed here.

Creating the Data Source

6. Click the **Get Data** button under the section heading *2 Data Source* to display a list of commands.

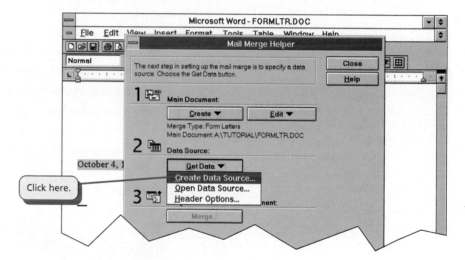

Click here.

7. Click the **Create Data Source** command to display the Create Data Source dialog box. A list of commonly used field names is listed on the **Field Names in Header Row** list.

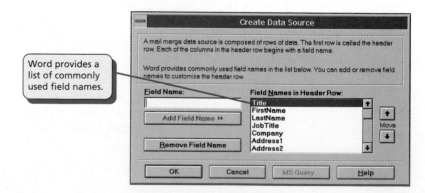

Word provides a list of commonly used field names.

8. Type **Salutation** into to the **Field Name** text box and then click the **Add Field Name** command button. The new field name is added to the bottom of the list in the **Field Names in Header Row** list. Click the down arrow button (⬇) in the *Move* section to wrap it back to the top of the list.

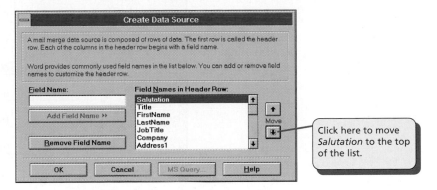

9. Click each of the names shown struck out in the figure "Field Names to Delete" and click the **Remove Field Name** command button to remove the selected name from the list. When finished, only the names shown in the figure "Field Names to Use" remain displayed in the list.

10. Click the **OK** command button to display the Save Data Source dialog box, which works just like any other Save box.

11. Save the data source as **namelist** in the *tutorial* directory of the *Word Student Resource Disk*. When you do so, a dialog box then tells you that you can edit either the data source or the main document.

12. Click the **Edit Data Source** button to edit the data source and display the Data Form dialog box.

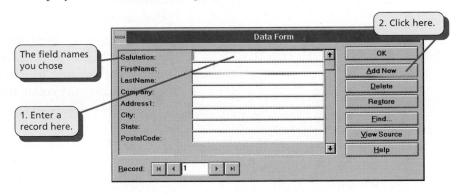

13. Enter each of the four records shown in the figure "Records to Enter" by typing in the fields in each of the four records (notice that one field is left blank). Proofread each record against the figure as you complete it. If you find an error, click back in the field to edit it. When the record is perfect, click the **Add New** button for all but the last record to display a new blank form. For the last record, enter your own name and address but don't press any button yet. (Also use a fake address if you want.)

Salutation
~~Title~~
FirstName
LastName
~~JobTitle~~
Company
Address1
~~Address2~~
City
State
PostalCode
~~Country~~
~~HomePhone~~
~~WorkPhone~~

Field Names to Delete

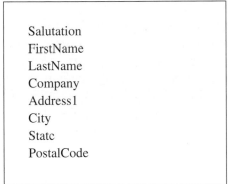

Salutation
FirstName
LastName
Company
Address1
City
State
PostalCode

Field Names to Use

Field Names	Record 1	Record 2	Record 3	Record 4
Salutation	Mrs.	Ms.	Mrs.	yours
FirstName	Suzanne	Kim	Debbie	yours
LastName	Steven	Foley	Star	yours
Company	3D Graphics	Virtual Reality		yours
Address1	1 Pierce Street	60 Friend Street	1 Oak Road	yours
City	Saratoga	Beverly	Marblehead	yours
State	CA	MA	MA	yours
PostalCode	95070	01915	01945	yours

Records to Enter

14. In the **Record** section in the lower-left corner of the dialog box, click the **Previous Record** (◀) and **Next Record** (▶) buttons to scroll through the four records, checking them again.

15. Click the **OK** command button to close the dialog box and return to the Main document. Notice how the Mail Merge toolbar is now displayed above the ruler. You use the buttons on this toolbar to set up the main document.

Creating the Main Document

16. Position the insertion point so there are two blank lines between it and the date line.

17. Click the **Insert Merge Field** button on the Mail Merge toolbar to display a list of the field names in the source file, then click the **Salutation** field name to select it and insert it into the document as <<*Salutation*>>.

18. Pressing ⎵Spacebar or ⏎Enter where necessary, repeat Step 17 to enter the rest of the merge fields and text shown in the figure "The Main Document." Be sure to enter the comma following the <<City>> merge field and the colon after <<LastName>> in the salutation.

«Salutation» «FirstName» «LastName»
«Company»
«Address1»
«City», «State» «PostalCode»

Dear «Salutation» «LastName»:

I am pleased to confirm your appointment at my office.

Sincerely yours,

your name

The Main Document

Entering Fill-In Fields

19. Pull down the **Tools** menu, click the **Options** command to display the Options dialog box, and on the **View** tab click the **Field Codes** check box to turn it on (⊠). Click the **OK** command button to return to the document.

20. With the insertion point between the word *office* and the period at the end of the sentence in the body paragraph press Spacebar, type **at**, press Spacebar again, then click the **Insert Word Field** command button to display a list of fields.

21. Click the **Fill-in** field name to display the Insert Word Field dialog box, then in the **Prompt** text box type **Enter the time** and click the **OK** command button to display a dialog box asking you to enter the time. Click the **OK** command button to close the dialog box without entering a time.

22. Press Spacebar and then type **on** and press Spacebar again. Click the **Insert Word Field** command button to display a list of fields and then repeat Step 21, this time entering **Enter the date** in the **Prompt** text box. Your document should now look like the one shown in the figure "The Finished Main Document."

The Finished Main Document

23. Click the **Save** button on the toolbar to save the finished document.

Previewing the Results

24. Pull down the **Tools** menu, click the **Options** command to display the Options dialog box, and on the **View** tab click the **Field Codes** check box to turn it off (☐). Click the **OK** command button to return to the document. Notice how the two Fill-in field codes are no longer displayed.

25. Click the **View Merged Data** button on the toolbar to display the first record in the main document. This command allows you to see how data from the data source will look when inserted into the document in place of the merge fields.

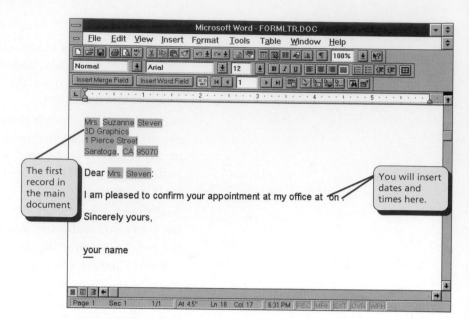

26. Click the **Next Record** button (▶) on the Mail Merge toolbar to scroll through the four records to preview how each will appear when merged.

Mail-Merging the Documents

27. Click the **Merge to New Document** button on the toolbar to merge the two documents. As they are merged, dialog boxes prompt you to enter the time and date for each of the four letters. Do so using the times and dates listed in the table "Appointment Times and Dates" on the next page (the number of the current record is always displayed on the status bar). After entering each time and date, click the **OK** command button to continue. After entering times and dates for the first merged document, the previous entry is displayed in the dialog box. Type the new time and date over it to replace it. When you click **OK** the last time, the merged letters appear on the screen.

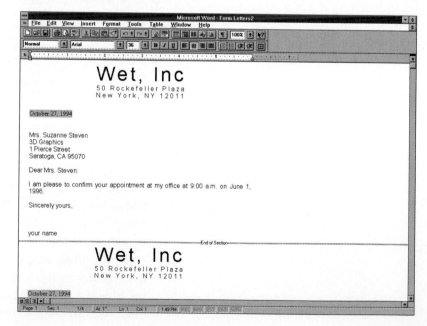

Appointment Times and Dates		
Letter	Time	Date
1	9:00 a.m.	June 1, 1996
2	2:00 p.m.	June 3, 1996
3	10:00 a.m.	June 4, 1996
4	1:00 p.m.	June 5, 1996

Finishing Up

28. Scroll through the letters and notice the following:

   ▶ The merge fields in each letter have been replaced with data from the corresponding fields in the data source.

   ▶ The Fill-in fields have been replaced with text you typed from the keyboard when prompted to enter times and dates.

   ▶ Although Debbie Star has no company address in the data source, there is no blank line in her letter.

29. Print the first page of the document.

30. Save the *formltr.doc* and *namelist.doc* documents but close the unnamed merged document (called *Form Letters2* or something similar) without saving it.

5-3. MAIL-MERGING LABELS

Once you have created a data source for form letters, you can also use it to print mailing labels or envelopes. To print labels, you create a main document by specifying the type of labels you want to print on and then enter merge fields that print the data you want to appear on the labels. When you then merge the main document, all of the labels are automatically filled in from the associated data source.

TUTORIAL

In this tutorial you use Word's Mail Merge Helper to create a main document to print mailing labels. The data source is a list of some of the leading companies on the Fortune 500 list. The names and addresses of the companies are already stored in a data source file on the disk.

Getting Started

1. Open the *fort500.doc* document stored in the *tutorial* directory of the *Word Student Resource Disk (Part1)*. This is the data source for the mailing labels you are about to create. It is formatted as a Word table, described in Section 6-5.

Creating the Main Document

2. Pull down the **Tools** menu and click the **Mail Merge** command to display the Mail Merge Helper dialog box.

3. Click the **Create** button under the section heading *1 Main Document* to display a list of main document types you can create.

4. Click the **Mailing Labels** command to display a dialog box asking if you want to use the document in the **Active Window** or a **New Main Document**.

5. Click the **New Main Document** button to open a new document and return to the Mail Merge Helper dialog box.

Creating the Data Source

6. Click the **Get Data** button under the section heading *2 Data Source* and then click the **Open Data Source** command to display the Open Data Source dialog box.

7. Select the *fort500.doc* file on the **File Name** list and click the **OK** command button. A dialog box tells you that Word needs to set up the main document.

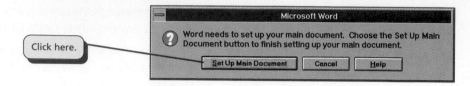

Click here.

Setting Up the Main Document

8. Click the **Set Up Main Document** button to display the Label Options dialog box.

9. Click the **Dot Matrix** or **Laser** option button to specify the type of printer you'll be using.

10. The label that you select depends on the printer type you specified.

   ▶ If you selected **Dot Matrix**, choose *4603-Address* from the **Product Number** list and then click the **OK** command button to display the Create Labels dialog box.

   ▶ If you selected **Laser**, choose *5160-Address* from the **Product Number** list and then click the **OK** command button to display the Create Labels dialog box.

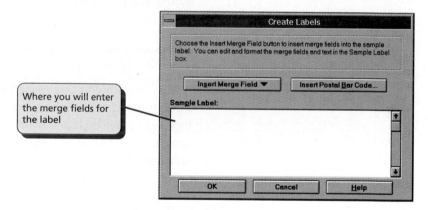

Where you will enter the merge fields for the label

«SAL» «FIRST» «LAST»
«COMPANY»
«STREET»
«CITY», «ST» «ZIP»

The Label Fields

11. Click the **Insert Merge Field** button in the dialog box to display a list of the fields in the attached data source, and click *SAL* to insert it into the **Sample Label** window. Using Spacebar and Enter↵ where necessary, continue inserting the merge fields needed to lay out the label so it matches the one shown in the figure "The Label Fields."

12. Click the Insert Postal Bar Code button to display the Insert Postal Bar code dialog box.

13. Click the **Merge Field with ZIP code** drop-down arrow (⬇) and click *ZIP* to select it.

14. Click the **Merge Field with Street Address** drop-down arrow (⬇) and click *STREET* to select it.

15. Click the **OK** command button twice, first to return to the Create Labels dialog box and then to return to the Mail Merge Helper dialog box.

16. Click the **Merge** command button to display the Merge dialog box. All of the default settings are acceptable.

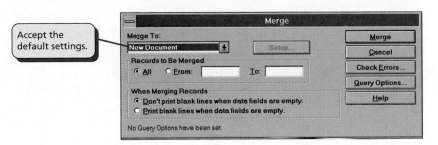

17. Click the **Merge** command button to merge the main document and the data source to a new document on the screen. Notice how the postal bar code is added above each label. These can be read by the Post Office's automatic mail-sorting equipment; under certain conditions using them entitles the sender to a lower postal rate.

Finishing Up

18. Click the **Print Preview** button to see the results and if they look right, print the document.

19. Save the main document (the one with the merge fields) as *labels.doc* in the *tutorial* directory of the *Word Student Resource Disk (Part 1)* and then close it. (You will have to pull down the **Window** menu and click its name (*Document1*, *Document2*, or some such name).

20. Close all other open documents without saving them.

5-4. SELECTING SPECIFIC RECORDS TO MERGE

There are times when you do not want to merge all of the records in the data source. You may want to merge letters just to people in New York, or to those that owe over $100. In these cases, you merge as you normally would but when the Mail Merge Helper dialog box is displayed, you click the **Query Options** command button and then specify conditions to filter or sort records to be merged. The choices you can make when querying a data source are described in the box "Understanding The Query Options Dialog Box."

UNDERSTANDING THE QUERY OPTIONS DIALOG BOX

When you click the **Query Options** command button in the Mail Merge Helper dialog box, the Query Options dialog box is displayed. You can then click the **Filter Records** or **Sort Records** tabs to make those the active page.

The Filter Records Page

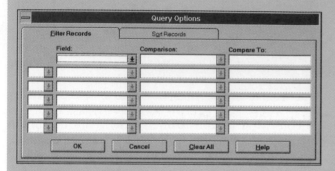

Field drop-down arrows (⬇) display the names of fields in the data source so you can select one.

Comparison drop-down arrows (⬇) displays a list of comparison operators that compare one value to another. For example, **Equal to** will print all records that match the entry in the **Compare** text box next to it. **Greater than** will print records with larger numbers or that appear alphabetically later.

Compare text boxes are where you enter what the field is being searched for. For example, if the **Field** is *State* and the **Comparison** is *Equal to*, entering **NY** here will merge only records with NY is the State field.

The Sort Records Page

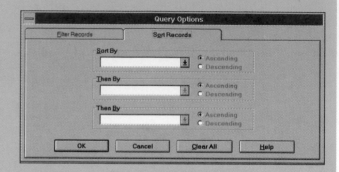

Sort By specifies the first field to sort by. Click the **Ascending** or **Descending** option button to specify the order of the sort.

Then By specifies the second field to sort by. This field will break any ties in the first sort by subsorting the list based on the contents of this field. Click the **Ascending** or **Descending** option button to specify the order of the sort.

Then By specifies the third field to sort by. Click the **Ascending** or **Descending** option button to specify the order of the sort.

TUTORIAL

In this tutorial you use the *labels.doc* main document that you created in Section 5-3 to merge just selected labels from the *fort500.doc* data source.

Getting Ready

1. Open the *labels.doc* document stored in the *tutorial* directory on the *Word Student Resource Disk (Part 1)*. When it opens, the Mail Merge toolbar is displayed.

2. Click the **Mail Merge Helper** button on the toolbar to display the Mail Merge Helper.

Merging Just New York Records

3. Click the **Query Options** command button under the section heading *3 Merge the Data with the Document* in the Mail Merge Helper dialog box to display the Query Options dialog box.

4. Click the **Field** drop-down arrow (⬇), and then click the *ST* field name to select it. Notice how the *Comparison* default is *Equal to*. That's the one we want to use.

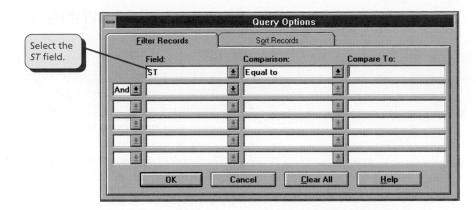

Select the *ST* field.

5. With the insertion point in the topmost *Compare To* text box, type **NY** and then click the **OK** command button to return to the Mail Merge Helper dialog box.

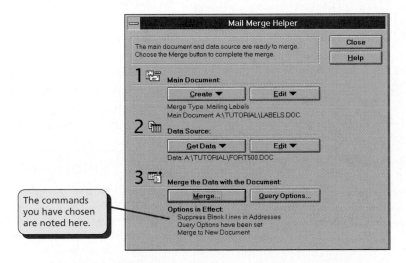

The commands you have chosen are noted here.

6. Click the **Merge** button under the heading *3 Merge the Data with the Document* to display the Merge dialog box.

7. Click the **Merge** command button to merge the document. Notice how labels are now merged only when they have NY in the ST field.

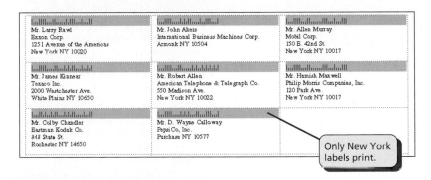

Only New York labels print.

Finishing Up

8. Print the document and then close all open documents without saving them.

5-5. AUTOMATING WITH MACROS

Since many of the tasks you perform while working at a computer are repetitive, you often find yourself pressing the same sequence of keys to format text or complete some other complex series of commands. Programs such as Word allow you to create macros that automate these repetitive tasks. Macros are simply a way to record keystrokes so that they can be played back later. Creating a macro is like making a piano into a player piano; the only difference is that the computer's keys do not move up and down—it is all done electronically.

There are two steps to using macros: recording them and then running them. You can record and then run any sequence of keystrokes, including entering text and executing commands. Doing so is easy and can save you a lot of time if you use the same long sequence of commands over and over again.

RECORDING MACROS

To create a macro, you turn on the program's record mode, enter the keystrokes you want to record, and then turn off record mode. In the process you can assign the macro to keys on the keyboard, a menu, or the toolbar so you can quickly execute it later. Keep in mind that a macro is not saved until you save the template in which it is stored. You will be prompted to save the template when you close the document or exit Word. You can also save it using the **Save All** command on the **File** menu.

QUICKSTEPS: RECORDING A MACRO

1. Pull down the **Tools** menu and click the **Macro** command to display the Macro dialog box.
2. Type a name for the macro in the **Macro Name** text box and then click the **Record** command button to display the Record Macro dialog box. If you plan to assign the macro to a menu or the toolbar, enter text in the **Description** text box that will be displayed on the status bar when you highlight the menu command or point to the button on the toolbar.
3. Click **OK** if you don't want to assign the macro and skip to 6 below, or click **Keyboard** in the *Assign Macro To* section (**Toolbars** and **Menus** are not covered in this text) to display the Customize dialog box. **Current Keys** lists the keys already assigned to macros during earlier sessions. **Commands** lists macros and a separator you can choose to add to a menu. The separator separates your command on the menu from others that might be listed.
4. With the insertion point in the **Press New Shortcut Key** text box, hold down [Alt], [Ctrl], or [⇧ Shift] and press the key you want to assign the macro to.
5. Click the **Close** command button to close the Customize dialog box. The mouse pointer has the recorder graphic added to it when in the text area to indicate that you are in record mode. Also, the Macro Record toolbar is displayed.
6. Type the text and/or execute the commands you want to record. (When recording a macro, you must use the keyboard to move the insertion point in the document. The mouse pointer has a recorder graphic attached to it when in the text area to indicate that you can't use it to position the insertion point although you can use it to select menu commands and click buttons on the toolbar.) The **Pause** button temporarily pauses it so you can enter commands you don't want recorded. Click the **Pause** button again to resume recording.
7. When finished, click the **Stop** button on the Macro Record toolbar.

**TIP:
UNDERSTANDING
TEMPLATES**

A *template* is like a plan for a particular type of document. It controls how text, graphics, and formatting are handled and stores specific styles, macros, AutoText entries, toolbar buttons, and customized menu and shortcut key settings. When you open a new document it uses the *Normal.dot* document template unless you specify otherwise. When you record a macro, you can specify which document template it is saved to using the **Save Changes In** drop-down list. Normally it is saved to the *Normal.dot* document template so it's available whenever you open a new document using that template.

RUNNING MACROS

Once you have recorded a macro, it is available in all existing and new documents that you create. The way you run it depends on whether or not you added it to a toolbar, menu, or keyboard.

QUICKSTEPS: RUNNING A MACRO

▶ If you did not add the macro to a toolbar, menu, or keyboard, pull down the **Tools** menu and click the **Macro** command to display the Macro dialog box. Click the name of the macro in the **Macro Name** text box and then click the **Run** command button to run the macro.

▶ If you assigned the macro to the keyboard, press the keys you assigned it to.

EDITING MACROS

Word allows you to edit macros so that you can correct mistakes or add procedures without having to rerecord the text or commands.

QUICKSTEPS: EDITING A MACRO

1. Pull down the **Tools** menu and click the **Macro** command to display the Macro dialog box.

2. Click the name of the macro in the **Macro Name** text box and then click the **Edit** command button to open the macro just as if it were a document.

3. Edit the macro and then save and close it as you'd save or close any document.

TUTORIAL

In this tutorial you are introduced to recording a macro and then running it to play back the text and commands it recorded.

Getting Started

1. Open the *macro.doc* document stored in the *tutorial* directory on the *Word Student Resource Disk (Part 1)* and enter your name.

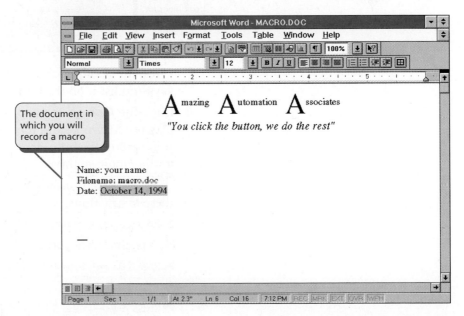

The document in which you will record a macro

2. Move the insertion point to a blank line below the date.

Recording the Macro

3. Pull down the **Tools** menu and click the **Macro** command to display the Macro dialog box.

4. Type **ltrclose** in the **Macro Name** text box and then click the **Record** command button to display the Record Macro dialog box.

The macro name

Click here to assign a keyboard shortcut.

5. Click the **Keyboard** button in the *Assign Macros To* section to display the Customize dialog box.

6. With the insertion point in the **Press New Shortcut Key** text box, press Alt+A; *Currently Assigned To* should read *[unassigned]*.

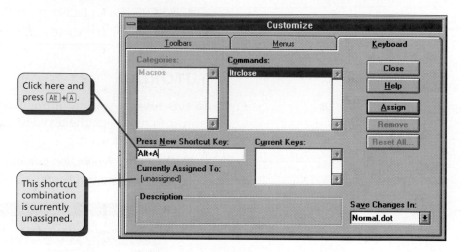

Click here and press Alt+A.

This shortcut combination is currently unassigned.

7. Click the **Assign** command button to assign the macro to those keys and list it on the **Current Keys** list.

8. Click the **Close** command button to close the dialog box and display the Macro Record toolbar. The toolbar has two buttons: one to stop recording and other to pause it. The recorder graphic is added to the mouse pointer.

9. With the insertion point on any blank line below the date, follow these instructions:

▶ Press Enter↵ twice.

▶ Type **Sincerely yours,**

▶ Press Enter↵ four times.

▶ Type your name.

▶ Press Enter↵.

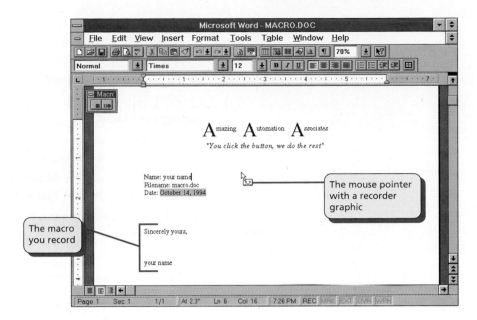

The mouse pointer with a recorder graphic

The macro you record

10. Click the **Stop** button on the Macro Record toolbar to turn off recording.

Running the Macro

11. Press `Alt`+`A` a few times to enter the letter close just as you typed it while recording.

Editing the Macro

12. Pull down the **Tools** menu and click the **Macro** command to display the Macro dialog box.

13. Click *ltrclose* in the **Macro Name** text box and then click the **Edit** command button to open the macro just as if it were a document. Notice that a Macro toolbar is displayed below the normal toolbars.

14. Move the insertion point into the space between your first and last names, and type in a middle initial (for example, P.) so it is spaced correctly in the name. (If you had entered your middle initial originally, then delete it now.)

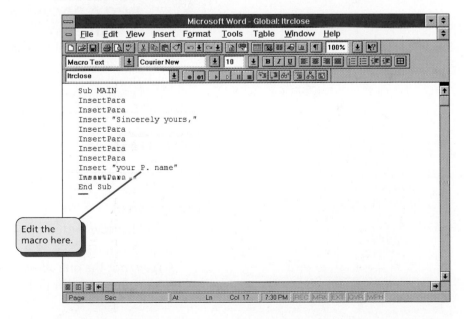

Edit the macro here.

15. Save and close the document just as you would any normal document. (On the File menu the command will read **Save Template**.) If asked if you want to save the changes to the macro, click **Yes**.

16. Press Alt+A to play the macro again, and notice how it now enters your middle initial.

Deleting the Macro

17. Pull down the **Tools** menu and click the **Macro** command to display the Macro dialog box.

18. Click *ltrclose* in the **Macro Name** text box and then click **Delete** command button. A dialog box asks you to confirm the deletion.

19. Click the **Yes** command button to delete the macro, then click the **Close** command button to close the Edit Macro dialog box.

Finishing Up

20. Print the document and then close it without saving your changes.

5-6. USING AUTOTEXT

When you find yourself entering the same text over and over again, you can store it as AutoText and enter it with a few clicks of the mouse. This is great not only for text, but also for symbols and special characters.

QUICKSTEPS: STORING AUTOTEXT

1. Select the text you want to store as AutoText, then click the AutoText button on the Standard toolbar, or pull down the **Edit** menu and click the **AutoText** command to display the AutoText dialog box.

2. Type the name you want to store the AutoText entry under into the **Name** text box and click the **Add** button.

QUICKSTEPS: INSERTING AUTOTEXT INTO A DOCUMENT

1. With the insertion point where you want to insert AutoText, pull down the **Edit** menu and click the **AutoText** command to display the AutoText dialog box.

2. Click the name of the AutoText you want to enter in the **Name** list, and click the **Insert** button.

TUTORIAL

In this tutorial you add an entry to AutoText and then copy it back into the document.

Getting Started

1. Click the **New** button on the toolbar to open a document.

2. Hold down Ctrl+Alt and press the minus key (-) *on the numeric keypad* (not the one above the letter keys—this will cause problems) to enter an em dash (—). Em dashes can be used in place of paren-

theses to set off phrases—or other elements—that you want to highlight in some way.

Adding Text to AutoText

3. Click the em dash to select it, pull down the **Edit** menu, and click the **AutoText** command to display the AutoText dialog box.

4. Type **em dash** in the **Name** text box and click the **Add** button.

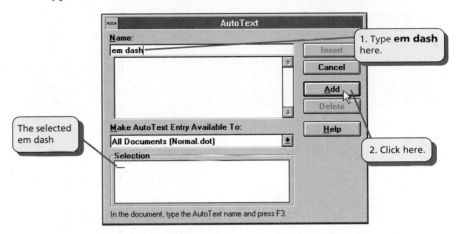

Entering AutoText in the Document

5. Click anywhere in the document, pull down the **Edit** menu, and click the **AutoText** command to display the AutoText dialog box.

6. Click *em dash* to enter it into the **Name** text box, and click the **Insert** button.

Deleting AutoText

7. Click anywhere in the document, pull down the **Edit** menu, and click the **AutoText** command to display the AutoText dialog box.

8. Click *em dash* to enter it into the **Name** text box, and click the **Delete** button.

Finishing Up

9. Close the document without saving it.

5-7. USING AUTOCORRECT

Word's AutoCorrect fixes typing mistakes as you make them. For example, it will automatically change *i* to *I*, *teh* to *the*, and *adn* to *and*. You can also have AutoCorrect convert quote marks and check capitalization. AutoCorrect is normally on and corrects a limited number of preassigned words. However, you can add words to correct or turn AutoCorrect off. You can even add words such as *asap* so they are automatically expanded into *as soon as possible* when you type them and press [Spacebar].

QUICKSTEPS: USING AUTOCORRECT OPTIONS

1. Pull down the **Tools** menu and click the **AutoCorrect** command to display the AutoCorrect dialog box.

2. Change any of the settings described in the box "Understanding the AutoCorrect Dialog Box" and then click the **OK** command button.

UNDERSTANDING THE AUTOCORRECT DIALOG BOX

When you pull down the **Tools** menu and click the **AutoCorrect** command the AutoCorrect dialog box is displayed. Here are the settings you can change.

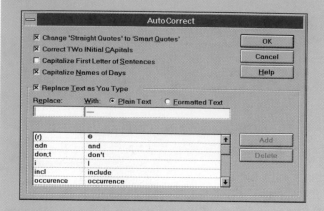

Change Straight Quotes to Smart Quotes check box changes quotation marks you enter on the keyboard (' and ") to typographic quote marks (' ' and " ")

Correct Two Initial Capitals check box changes the case of the second letter should you type two capital letters to begin a word.

Capitalize First Letter of Sentences check box corrects the case of the first character in a sentence.

Capitalize Names of Days check box corrects the first character in names of days.

Replace Text as You Type check box turns AutoCorrect on and off.

Replace and **With** text boxes are where you enter the text you type incorrectly and the text you want it changed to.

Add command button adds any entries currently in the **Replace** and **With** text boxes.

Delete command button deletes the highlighted entry in the **Replace** and **With** lists.

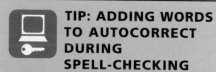

TIP: ADDING WORDS TO AUTOCORRECT DURING SPELL-CHECKING

When spell-checking a document, you can add word pairs to the **Replace** and **With** lists by clicking the **AutoCorrect** command button in the Spelling dialog box. Only click the button when the incorrectly spelled word is displayed in the **Not in Dictionary** text box and the correct spelling is displayed in the **Change To** text box.

TUTORIAL

In this tutorial you explore how AutoCorrect corrects certain entries as you type them.

Getting Started

1. Click the **New** button on the toolbar to open a document.

Using AutoCorrect

2. Pull down the **Tools** menu and click the **AutoCorrect** command to display the AutoCorrect dialog box.

3. Click on any check boxes that are off and look at the list in the bottom of the dialog box. It should list a set of words and how they will be changed should you enter them. Jot down in the table "AutoCorrect Word Pairs" the word pairs that you see listed.

AutoCorrect Word Pairs	
If You Enter	**It is Changed To**
_____	_____
_____	_____
_____	_____
_____	_____
_____	_____
_____	_____
_____	_____

4. Click the **OK** command to close the AutoCorrect dialog box, then type a sentence made up of the words you listed in the *If you Enter* column of the table "AutoCorrect Word Pairs." Notice how as you type each one and then press [Spacebar], it is immediately changed into the word listed in the *It is Changed To* column.

5. Type the sentence **"in january and FEbruary, our "wildest" months, we head south."** exactly as shown, including quotes and capitalization. Notice how all of the capitalizations are corrected and the quote marks change to SmartQuotes ("" instead of "").

Finishing Up

6. Save the document as *autofix.doc* in the *tutorial* directory of the *Word Student Resource Disk (Part 1)*, print it, and then close it.

PicTorial 5 Review Questions

 True-False

T F **1.** One of the most common uses of Mail Merge is the printing of form letters.

T F **2.** Names and addresses are stored in the main document.

T F **3.** The first row in a data source contains the fields.

T F **4.** All data merged into a main document has to come from the data source.

T F **5.** When performing a mail merge, you will always merge all of the records in the data source with the main document.

T F **6.** A macro is not saved until the template in which it is stored is saved.

T F **7.** When creating a macro, you cannot use the mouse to move the insertion point.

T F **8.** You cannot edit macros; only delete them and recreate them.

T F **9.** You can add words to the AutoCorrect feature.

T F **10.** The data source is used to personalize the information in the main document.

 Multiple Choice

1. With mail merges, the _____ document contains the data that is to appear in each copy.

a. Primary

b. Source

c. Original

d. Main

2. In a data source, the first row in the table is the _____.

a. Record

b. Fields

c. Headers

d. Titles

3. In a data source, the table's rows are _____.

a. Records

b. Fields

c. Header row

d. Title row

4. When you enter merge fields in a document, they are enclosed in
   _____.

   a. Quotation marks

   b. Asterisks

   c. Chevrons

   d. Parentheses

5. The _____ field prompts you to type data that is then merged
   into the document.

   a. Keyboard

   b. Fill-in

   c. Insert

   d. Enter

6. Macro shortcut keys can begin with _____.

   a. [Alt]

   b. [⇧ Shift]

   c. [Ctrl]

   d. Any of the above

7. To see how data from the data source will look when inserted into
   the document in place of merge fields, click the _____
   button.

   a. Next Record

   b. View Merged Data

   c. Merge to New Document

   d. Field Codes

8. The mailing label that you select depends on the _____ you
   specified.

   a. Font size

   b. Printer type

   c. Label size

   d. Document

9. When using the Query Options dialog box, you can specify up to
   _____ sort levels.

   a. 2

   b. 3

   c. 4

   d. 5

10. _____ are used to record keystrokes so that they can be played
    back later.

    a. Files

    b. Templates

    c. Macros

    d. Modules

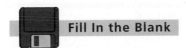

1. The _____ feature enters text that you have previously saved.
2. Mail merge combines two documents, a _____ document and a _____.
3. A data source contains three basic parts: records, fields, and _____.
4. In a data source, the table's columns are _____.
5. The part of a mail-merged document that stays the same from copy to copy is stored in the _____.
6. The main document contains codes, called _____.
7. The _____ option allows you to be selective in merging records.
8. There are two steps to using macros: _____ and _____.
9. When you find yourself entering the same text over and over again, you can store it as _____ and enter it with a few clicks of the mouse.
10. The _____ feature fixes mistakes as you make them.

PicTorial 5 Lab Activities

COMPUTER-BASED TUTORIALS

We suggest you complete the following computer-based lessons to learn more about the features discussed in this PicTorial. To do so, pull down the **Help** menu and click the **Examples and Demos** command, click the *Topic* listed in the table "Suggested Examples and Demos to Complete," and then click the *Subtopic* listed in that same table. (If you need more help on using the system, see the "Computer-Based Tutorials" section at the end of PicTorial 2.)

Suggested Examples and Demos to Complete		
Done	**Topic**	**Subtopic**
☐	Mail Merge	Overview of Mail Merge
☐	Mail Merge	Setting up and printing form letters
☐	Mail Merge	Setting up and printing mailing labels by using Mail Merge
☐	Automating Your Work	Assigning a command or macro
☐	Automating Your Work	Overview of Recording and Running Macros
☐	Automating Your Work	Recording a macro
☐	Automating Your Work	Running a macro
☐	Typing and Editing	Overview of AutoCorrect and AutoText: Reusing Text and Graphics
☐	Typing and Editing	Creating and Inserting an AutoText Entry

▶▶ QUICKSTEP DRILLS

5-1. Introduction to Mail Merge

Whenever you need to make multiple copies of the same document, Mail Merge is very useful. In this drill you use Word's Mail Merge Helper to merge a data source containing names, departments, and phone numbers with a main document formatted as a name tag.

1. Open the *mrgdata.doc* document stored in the *drill* directory on the *Word Student Resource Disk (Part 1)*. Notice how the data is organized in a table into rows and columns. (Tables are discussed in detail in PicTorial 6.) The first row contains the names of the columns (fields). Each of the following rows contains data. The data is divided into columns or fields.

2. Open the *mrgform.doc* document stored in the *drill* directory on the *Word Student Resource Disk (Part 1)* and enter your name, then click anywhere in the date and press F9 to update it. The file contains three merge fields that refer by name to fields in the data file: <<FirstName>>, <<LastName>>, and <<Department>>. When you open the document, the Mail Merge toolbar is displayed.

3. Click the Mail Merge Helper button on the Mail Merge toolbar to display the Mail Merge Helper. The *mrgform.doc* main document and *mrgdata.doc* data source are already listed in the dialog box so click the **Merge** button to display the Merge dialog box. Click the **Merge** button to merge to a new document.

    When the merge is completed, each of the merge fields in the main document is replaced with data from the *mrgdata.doc* data source. Page through the document and you'll see that since that data source contained three records, three copies of the main document have been printed—each containing the data from a single record.

4. Print any single page of the merged document and then close all of the documents without saving them.

5-2A. Mail-Merging Form Letters

The most common application of Mail Merge is the printing of form letters. In this drill you use Word's Mail Merge Helper to create a very simple data source and main document and then merge them.

1. Click the **New** button on the Standard toolbar to open a new document.

2. Use the **Tools**, **Mail Merge** command to display the Mail Merge Helper.

3. Click the **Create** button under the *Main Document* heading, then specify first **Form Letters** and then **Active Window**.

4. Click the **Get Data** button under the *Data Source* heading and then click **Create Data Source** to display the Create Data Source dialog box. Create a data source containing the three field names *FirstName*, *JobTitle*, and *WorkPhone* by removing all other field

names. Save the document as *stafdata.doc* in the *drill* directory on the *Word Student Resource Disk (Part 1)*. Then click the **Edit Data Source** button and enter the three records shown in the table "Staff Data." When finished, the main document appears.

Staff Data		
FirstName	**JobTitle**	**WorkPhone**
Betty	Accounting	1002
Bob	Manufacturing	1005
Jose	Sales	1008

5. Edit the main document. Enter the text and use the **Insert Merge Field** button on the Mail Merge toolbar to enter the three merge fields shown in the figure "The Staff Main Document." Save the main document as *stafform.doc* in the *drill* directory on the *Word Student Resource Disk (Part 1)*.

6. Click the **Merge to New Document** button on the Mail Merge toolbar to merge the *stafform.doc* main document and the *stafdata.doc* data source.

7. Print the first page of the merged document and then close the merged document without saving it. However, save *stafform.doc* and *stafdata.doc* if prompted to do so.

5-2B. Using Operator Input

Data that changes frequently should not be stored in a data source because that file would have to be frequently updated. Instead, it can be typed in from the keyboard during merging. In this drill you create a main document with three fields that prompt you to enter data when the file is being merged.

1. Open the *students.doc* document stored in the *drill* directory on the *Word Student Resource Disk (Part 1)*. This document is a data source organized as a table.

2. Open the *award.doc* document stored in the *drill* directory on the *Word Student Resource Disk (Part 1)*. This document is a partially completed main document. It contains three merge fields that refer to the data source for the student's name and course.

3. With the insertion point to the left of the dash in front of *Teacher*, use the **Insert Word Field** button on the Mail Merge toolbar to enter a **Fill-in** field. When a dialog box asks you to enter the prompt, type **Enter the name of the teacher** and click the next two **OK** command buttons. (The field code is not displayed unless you use the **Tools**, **Options** command and click the **Field Codes** check box on the **View** tab to turn it on.)

4. With the insertion point to the left of the dash in front of *Dean of Instruction*, use the **Insert Word Field** button on the Mail Merge toolbar to enter a **Fill-in** field. When a dialog box asks you to enter the prompt, type **Enter the name of the Dean of Instruction** and click the next two **OK** command buttons. (If you displayed field codes, use the **Tools**, **Options** command and click the **Field Codes** check box on the **View** tab to turn it off.)

Your Name

Name: <<FirstName>>
Department: <<JobTitle>>
Extension: <<WorkPhone>>

The Staff Main Document

5. Save your changes to the main document. Then click the **Merge to New Document** button on the Mail Merge toolbar.

  ▶ The first time the prompt reads *Enter the name of the teacher*, type **Ms. Mary Lewis** and click **OK**.

  ▶ The first time the prompt reads *Enter the name of the Dean of Instruction*, type **Mr. Roger Stuart** and click **OK**.

  ▶ The next two times you are asked to enter the name of the teacher or dean, just click **OK** to accept the same names you entered for the first document

6. Scroll through the document to see how the student names and curriculums are taken from the data source but the teacher's and dean's names have been entered from the keyboard.

7. Print the first page of the merged document. (Note that this page can take a long time to print since it has a picture. Don't print it if you have little time left. If a number of you share a printer, only one of you should print the document or you'll tie the printer up for others.)

8. Close the merged document without saving it. However, save *award.doc* and *students.doc* if prompted to do so.

5-3. Mail-Merging Labels

Printing labels is one of the leading applications of mail merge. In this drill you create a main document that prints labels using an existing data source already on the *Word Student Resource Disk*.

1. Click the **New** button on the Standard toolbar to open a new document.

2. Use the **Tools**, **Mail Merge** command to display the Mail Merge Helper.

3. Click the **Create** button under the *Main Document* heading, then specify first **Mailing Labels** and then **Active Window**.

4. Click the **Get Data** button under the *Data Source* heading, then click the **Open Data Source** button, and select the *publist.doc* data source stored in the *drill* directory on the *Word Student Resource Disk (Part 1)*. When a dialog box appears, click the **Set Up Main Document** button to display the Label Options dialog box.

5. Select a label for the printer type you are using:

  ▶ If you are using a dot matrix printer, click the **Dot Matrix** option button, choose *4603-Address* from the **Product Number** list, and then click the **OK** command button to display the Create Labels dialog box.

  ▶ If you are using a laser printer, click the **Laser** options button, choose *5160-Address* from the **Product Number** list, and then click the **OK** command button to display the Create Labels dialog box.

6. Type your name in the **Sample Label** window, and then use the **Insert Merge Field** button in the dialog box to enter the merge fields shown in the figure "Sample Label." When finished, click the **OK** command button to return to the Mail Merge Helper dialog box.

Your Name
<<COMPANY>>
<<STREET>>
<<CITY>>, <<ST>> <<ZIP>>

Sample Label

7. Click the **Merge** button in the Mail Merge Helper dialog box and the **Merge** button in the Merge dialog box to merge to a new document.

8. Print the first page of the merged document and then close the merged document without saving it.

9. Save the new main document with the merge fields as *labels.doc* in the *drill* directory on the *Word Student Resource Disk (Part 1)* and then close it.

5-4. Selecting Specific Records to Merge

As you have seen, it isn't necessary to merge all of the names in a data source. In this drill you merge only those records with Massachusetts addresses.

1. Open the *publtr.doc* document stored in the *drill* directory on the *Word Student Resource Disk (Part 1)*. Enter your name and address at the top of the document and your name at the bottom where indicated by the placeholders. Save the document with these changes.

2. Use the **Tools**, **Mail Merge** command to merge the *publtr.doc* main document and *publist.doc* data source stored in the *drill* directory on the *Word Student Resource Disk (Part 1)*. Use the Mail Merge Helper's **Query Options** button to specify that only records with *MA* in the *ST* field be printed.

3. Print the first page of the merged documents and then close the merged document without saving your changes, but save *publtr.doc* and then close it.

5-5. Automating with Macros

Macros can take much of the repetition out of word processing. In this drill you record a macro that automatically enters a heading for memos into a document.

1. Click the **New** button on the Standard toolbar to open a new document.

2. Use the **Tools**, **Macro** command to record a macro named MEMO-HEAD. When the Record Macro dialog box appears, just click the **OK** command button. (Don't assign the macro to a toolbar, menu, or keyboard.)

3. Type the document shown in the figure "Recorded Memo Heading" on the next page. When you do so, boldface and center the *INTEROFFICE MEMORANDUM* heading and insert today's date where it reads *Date*.

4. Click the **Stop** button on the Macro Record toolbar to turn off record mode and close the document on the screen without saving it.

5. Click the **New** button on the Standard toolbar to open a new document and use the **Tools**, **Macro** command to run the macro and insert the memo heading in the new document.

6. Print the new document and then save it as *memohead.doc* in the *drill* directory of the *Word Student Resource Disk* (you'll need the document in the next exercise).

7. Use the **Tools**, **Macro** command to delete the macro named MEMO-HEAD.

INTEROFFICE MEMORANDUM

Date

TO:

FROM:

SUBJECT:

Recorded Memo Heading

5-6. Using AutoText

Using a macro to store text isn't the only way to automate that procedure. You can also use Word's AutoText command to store any amount of text and then insert it into any document you choose. In this drill you store the memo heading you created in Drill 5-5 as AutoText and then insert it into a new document.

1. Open the *memohead.doc* document stored in the *drill* directory on the *Word Student Resource Disk (Part 1)*.

2. Select the entire memo heading and then use the **Edit**, **AutoText** command to add it to AutoText using the name *Memo Heading*.

3. Close the *memohead.doc* document without saving it.

4. Open a new document and use the **Edit**, **AutoText** command to insert the AutoText named *Memo Heading*.

5. Print the document.

6. Use the **Edit**, **AutoText** command to delete the AutoText named *Memo Heading*.

7. Close the new document without saving it.

5-7. Using AutoCorrect

Word's AutoCorrect will automatically correct a number of common mistypings and provide other services for you as you type. In this drill you explore how this command works.

1. Open a new document.

2. Use the **Tools**, **AutoCorrect** command to display the AutoCorrect dialog box. Make sure the first five check boxes are all on (⊠) and then click the **OK** command button.

3. Type the document in the figure "The AutoCorrect Document" on the next page exactly as shown (but enter your own name in place of *your name*) and then compare the way it appears on the screen against the figure. (The "mistakes" are underlined in the figure.)

4. Print the document and then close it without saving it.

<u>w</u>ord's AutoCorrect command automatically fixes a lower-case letter beginning a sentence and corrects misspellings such as "<u>teh</u>" and "<u>adn</u>" as soon as you press the spacebar. It also corrects two initial capital letters in a word such as <u>MA</u>ine and changes the quotation marks entered from the keyboard into <u>"</u>typographic<u>"</u> quotation marks. Finally, it will automatically uppercase the first letter in days of the week such as <u>m</u>onday, <u>t</u>uesday, and so on.
your name

The AutoCorrect Document

▶▶ SKILL-BUILDING EXERCISES

5-1. Merge-Printing a Form Letter to Computer Companies

In this exercise you use Word's Mail Merge Helper to create a form letter main document and a data source containing names and addresses. You then merge the two files to create letters requesting catalogs from leading computer mail order businesses. Finally, you create a new main document to print mailing labels for the envelopes used to mail the letters.

1. Open a new document and use the **Tools**, **Mail Merge** command to display the Mail Merge Helper.

2. Click the **Create** button under the *Main Document* heading, then specify first **Form Letters** and then **Active Window**.

3. Click the **Get Data** button under the *Data Source* heading and then click **Create Data Source** to display the Create Data Source dialog box. Create a data source containing the five field names *Company, Address1, City, State,* and *PostalCode* by removing all other field names. Save the document as *complist.doc* in the *exercise* directory on the *Word Student Resource Disk (Part 2)*. Then click the **Edit Data Source** button and enter the four records shown in the table " Computer Companies." When finished, the main document appears.

Computer Companies				
Company	**Address1**	**City**	**State**	**PostalCode**
PC Connection	6 Mill Street	Marlow	NH	03456
Gateway 2000	610 Gateway Drive	North Sioux City	SD	57049
Dell Computer Corporation	9505 Arboretum Blvd.	Austin	TX	78759
Zeos International, Ltd.	530 5th Avenue N.W.	St. Paul	MN	55112

5. Enter the text shown in the figure "Form Letter to Computer Companies" on the next page and use the **Insert Merge Field** button on the Mail Merge toolbar to enter the merge fields shown. Save the main document as *compltr.doc* in the *exercise* directory on the *Word Student Resource Disk (Part 2)*.

```
                        Your Name
                        Your Street
                     Your City, State ZIP

Today's date

Catalog Department
<<Company>>
<<Address1>>
<<City>>, <<State>>  <<PostalCode>>

Dear Sir or Madam:

Please send me a catalog of your current computer offerings.

Sincerely yours,


Your name
```

Form Letter to Computer Companies

6. Click the **Merge to New Document** button on the Mail Merge tool-bar to merge the *complist.doc* main document and the *compltr.doc* data source.

7. Print the first page of the merged document and then close the merged document without saving it. Save *compltr.doc* and then close it.

5-2. Merge-Printing Mailing Labels to Computer Companies

In this exercise you use Word's Mail Merge Helper to create mailing labels for the envelopes used to mail the letters to computer companies.

1. Click the **New** button on the Standard toolbar to open a new document.

2. Use the **Tools**, **Mail Merge** command to display the Mail Merge Helper.

3. Click the **Create** button under the *Main Document* heading, then specify first **Mailing Labels** and then **Active Window**.

4. Click the **Get Data** button under the *Data Source* heading, then click the **Open Data Source** button and select the *complist.doc* data source stored in the *exercise* directory on the *Word Student Resource Disk (Part 2)*. When a dialog box appears, click the **Set Up Main Document** button to display the Label Options dialog box.

5. Select a label for the printer type you are using:

   ▶ If you are using a dot matrix printer, click the **Dot Matrix** option button, choose *4603-Address* from the **Product Number** list, and then click the **OK** command button to display the Create Labels dialog box.

   ▶ If you are using a laser printer, click the **Laser** options button, choose *5160-Address* from the **Product Number** list, and then click the **OK** command button to display the Create Labels dialog box.

6. Type **Catalog Department** in the **Sample Label** window, and then use the **Insert Merge Field** button in the dialog box to enter the merge fields shown in the figure "Labels to Computer Companies." When finished, click the **OK** command button to return to the Mail Merge Helper dialog box.

7. Click the **Merge** button in the Mail Merge Helper dialog box and the **Merge** button in the Merge dialog box to merge to a new document.

8. Print the first page of the merged document and then close the merged document without saving it.

9. Save the new main document with the merge fields as *complbl.doc* in the *exercise* directory on the *Word Student Resource Disk (Part 2)* and then close it.

Catalog Department
<<Company>>
<<Address1>>
<<City>>, <<State>> <<PostalCode>>

Labels to Computer Companies

5-3. **Keyboarding Data into the Letter to Computer Companies**

In this exercise you revise the main document requesting a catalog from computer companies so you can type in information specific to each company during the merge.

1. Open the *complist.doc* document stored in the *exercise* directory on the *Word Student Resource Disk (Part 2)*. This document is the data source you are going to use.

2. Open the *compltr.doc* document stored in the *exercise* directory on the *Word Student Resource Disk (Part 2)*. This document is the partially completed main document you are going to use. It contains five merge fields that refer to the data source for the company's name and address.

3. With the insertion point to the left of the period at the end of the body paragraph, type **, especially those** (including the comma at the beginning and the space at the end) and then use the **Insert Word Field** button on the Mail Merge toolbar to enter a **Fill-in** field. When a dialog box asks you to enter the prompt, type **Enter the type of computer that most interests you** and click the next two **OK** command buttons. (To see or hide the field, use the **Tools, Options** command and click the **Field Codes** check box on the **View** tab to turn it on or off.)

5. Click the **Save** button on the Standard toolbar to save your changes to the main document. Then click the **Merge to New Document** button on the Mail Merge toolbar. When prompted *Enter the type of computer that most interests you* type one of the following for each letter:

▶ **featuring complete multimedia capability** and click **OK**.

▶ **with the most recent Intel microprocessors** and click **OK**.

▶ **that are low priced** and click **OK**.

▶ **that have only recently been introduced** and click **OK**.

6. Scroll through the document to see how the company names and addresses are taken from the data source but the last phrases in the body paragraphs have been entered from the keyboard.

7. Print the first page of the merged document and then close the merged document and *complist.doc* without saving them. However, save *compltr.doc* and then close it.

5-4. Creating Macros to Enter Fractions

One way to enter symbols you use frequently is with a macro. In this exercise you record a series of macros that enter fractions into a document.

1. Open the *macros.doc* document stored in the *exercise* directory on the *Word Student Resource Disk (Part 2)* and enter your name, then click anywhere in the date and press [F9] to update it.

2. Position the insertion point in the column that reads *Record Here* on any row of the table in the top half of the screen, then:
   - ▶ Use the **Tools**, **Macro** command to display the Macro dialog box.
   - ▶ In the **Macro Name** text box, enter the name given in the *Macro Name* column on the same row of the table. Then click the **Record** command button to display the Record Macro dialog box and click its **OK** command button to begin recording.
   - ▶ Press [NumLock] to turn it on, hold down [Alt] and type the numbers shown in the *Shortcut Keys* column on the same row of the table. You must type them using the numeric keypad.
   - ▶ Press [NumLock] to turn it off, then click the **Stop** button on the Record Macro toolbar to end recording.
   - ▶ Repeat this procedure for each of the other characters described in the top half of the screen.

3. Position the insertion point in the column that reads *Play Here* on any row of the table in the lower half of the screen, then use the **Tools**, **Macro** command to run the macro named on the same row of the table.

4. Save the document and print it.

5. Use the **Tools**, **Macro** command to delete all of the macros that you created.

6. Close the document.

 ▶▶ **REAL-WORLD PROJECTS**

5-1. Mail-Merging the Cover Letter

When you hear stories about people sending out 10,000 résumés to find a job, you hope they are using some form of automation. In this project you convert your cover letter to a main document and then use the *fort500.doc* list of company names to mail-merge copies.

1. Open the *coverltr.doc* document that you are created and saved in the *project* directory on the *Word Student Resource Disk (Part 2)*.

2. Display Mail Merge Helper and use *coverltr.doc* as the main document and *fort500.doc* in the *tutorial* directory on the *Word Student Resource Disk (Part 1)* as the data source.

3. Edit *coverltr.doc* to replace the inside address with field names from the *fort500.doc* data source and save the changes.

4. Merge the two documents then print out one or two pages of the merged document.

PicTorial 6

Desktop Publishing

After completing this PicTorial, you will be able to:

▸ Add borders and shading to paragraphs

▸ Generate tables of contents

▸ Print in two or more columns

▸ Insert pictures into your documents

▸ Create and format tables

No course is long enough to introduce you to all of the features of a program as powerful as Word. What you have learned so far are the basic and most frequently used features of the program. In this PicTorial we introduce you to a few of the features used in desktop publishing—preparing documents that look as if they had been printed by a professional printer. Special programs exist for desktop publishing, but today many desktop publishing features have been added to word processing programs such as Word. In this PicTorial you learn about those features including borders and shading, tables of contents, columns, pictures, and tables.

6-1. ADDING PARAGRAPH BORDERS AND SHADING

You can add borders and shading to paragraphs to set them off from other elements or to make them look more attractive. You can do so from the toolbar or with menu commands.

You can add borders and shading to paragraphs to set them off.	You can add borders and shading to paragraphs to set them off.
You can add borders and shading to paragraphs to set them off.	You can add borders and shading to paragraphs to set them off.

QUICKSTEPS: ADDING PARAGRAPH BORDERS AND SHADING WITH THE TOOLBAR

1. Select the paragraphs you want to add a border to, then click the **Borders** button on the Formatting toolbar to display the Border toolbar.

2. Click the **Line Style** drop-down arrow (⬇) and select a line style for the border, then click one of the **Border** buttons to specify where the border is to be positioned.

3. Click the **Shading** drop-down arrow (⬇) to select a shading.

4. Click the **Borders** button on the toolbar to close the Border toolbar.

UNDERSTANDING THE PARAGRAPH BORDERS AND SHADING DIALOG BOX

When you pull down the **Format** menu and click the **Borders and Shading** command, the Paragraph Borders and Shading dialog box is displayed. Here are the choices.

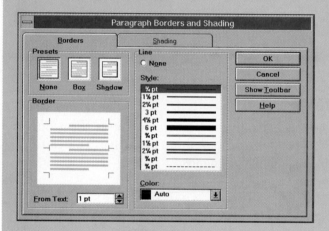

Borders Tab

Presets section lets you click a graphic to select a pre-designed **Box** or **Shadow** border, or click **None** to remove any border you previously applied.

From Text spin buttons (⬍) specify the distance between a border and the text within it.

Line section lets you click a line **Style** to select its width or type, and click the **Color** drop-down arrow (⬇) to

select a line color. Click the **None** option button off to remove any lines.

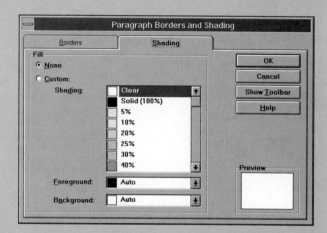

Shading Tab

None turns off any previously applied shading.

Custom allows you to then specify a color or pattern:

▶ **Shading** adds a gray shading or any color selected in the **Background** box in densities between 5 and 90 percent. **Clear** applies the color shown in the **Background** box and **Solid (100%)** applies the color shown in the **Foreground** box.

▶ **Foreground** specifies the colors used for the dots and lines in the selected pattern. **Auto** usually displays as black.

▶ **Background** specifies the background color used for shading. **Auto** usually displays as white.

TIP: PRINTING COLORS

Most printers don't print colors even though you can use colors in the document. When you print a document with colors, each of them prints in its own shade of gray.

TUTORIAL

In this tutorial you explore adding borders and shading to set off the heading in the *educom.doc* document.

Getting Started

1. Open the *educom.doc* document stored in the *tutorial* directory on the *Word Student Resource Disk (Part 1)*.

Selecting a Paragraph Border Style

2. Select the 4-line heading at the top of the document, including the line with your name on it.

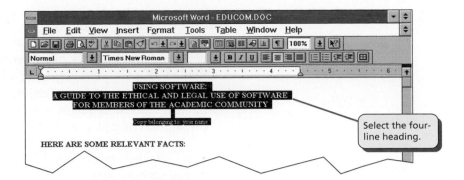

3. Pull down the **Format** menu and click the **Borders and Shading** command to display the Paragraph Borders and Shading dialog box.

4. On the **Borders** tab, click the **Shadow** button under the *Presets* heading and the **3 pt** line under the *Style* heading. The results are previewed for you in the **Border** window.

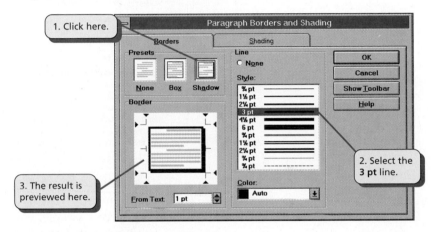

Selecting a Shading Style

5. On the **Shading** tab, click the **Background** drop-down arrow to display a list of colors, and click **Cyan** to select it. A sample of the border is displayed in the *Preview* box to the right.

6. Click the **OK** command button to apply the styles to the heading. Click anywhere to remove the highlight from the heading to see your results.

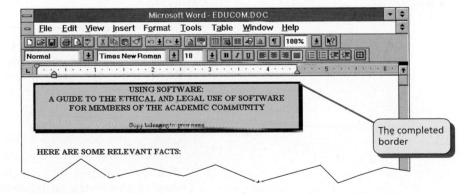

Finishing Up

7. Save the document, print the first page, and then close the document.

6-2. GENERATING A TABLE OF CONTENTS

When working on a long document with many headings, you often need to prepare a table of contents to help readers find the information they need. Manually preparing a table of contents takes a great deal of time; moreover, if any revisions are made in the document, all page number references might have to be changed. Word has automated the preparation of tables of contents to make it easy for you.

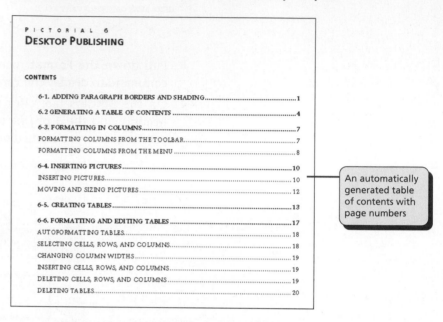

PICTORIAL 6
DESKTOP PUBLISHING

CONTENTS

6-1. ADDING PARAGRAPH BORDERS AND SHADING..1

6.2 GENERATING A TABLE OF CONTENTS 4

6-3. FORMATTING IN COLUMNS..7
FORMATTING COLUMNS FROM THE TOOLBAR 7
FORMATTING COLUMNS FROM THE MENU 8

6-4. INSERTING PICTURES..10
INSERTING PICTURES..10
MOVING AND SIZING PICTURES..12

6-5. CREATING TABLES..13

6-6. FORMATTING AND EDITING TABLES..17
AUTOFORMATTING TABLES..18
SELECTING CELLS, ROWS, AND COLUMNS..18
CHANGING COLUMN WIDTHS..19
INSERTING CELLS, ROWS, AND COLUMNS..19
DELETING CELLS, ROWS, AND COLUMNS..19
DELETING TABLES..20

An automatically generated table of contents with page numbers

To insert a table of contents the first step is to format the entries you want to appear in it with styles. Styles are formats that have been saved for later use. For example, you can create and save a style that formats a main heading (called *Heading 1*) so that it is printed in bold, 14 point type, with more space above it than below it. When you then save this format as a style, you can apply it to any heading just by selecting its name *Heading 1* from a drop-down list on the toolbar. However, to use styles you needn't know how to create them. Word has a number of them already defined for you. To use them you just select the paragraph you want to apply them to and select them from the **Style** drop-down list on the toolbar. It is these predefined styles you use to create a table of contents.

QUICKSTEPS: APPLYING HEADING STYLES FOR TABLE OF CONTENTS ENTRIES

1. Click in each heading that you want listed in the table of contents, click the **Style** drop-down arrow (⬇) on the toolbar, and click *Heading 1* through *Heading 3* depending on the level of the entry.

2. Click in the document where you want the table of contents to appear—usually on a line by itself.

3. Pull down the **Insert** menu, click the **Index and Tables** command to display the Index and Tables dialog box, and on the **Table of Contents** tab make any of the settings described in the box "Understanding The Table Of Contents Tab."

4. Click the **OK** command button to insert the table of contents.

UNDERSTANDING THE TABLE OF CONTENTS TAB

When you display the **Table of Contents** tab on the Index and Tables dialog box, you use the options to specify the design of your table of contents. The results of the current settings are displayed in the **Preview** box.

Formats allows you to choose one of six predefined formats, or choose **Custom** and design your own. As you click each format name, its appearance is displayed in the **Preview** box.

Show Page Numbers check box, when on (⊠), adds page numbers to each entry in the table of contents.

Right Align Page Numbers check box, when on (⊠), aligns page numbers in the table of contents with the right margin.

Show Levels spin buttons (🗘) set the number of levels to appear in the table of contents. You don't have to list all of the heading levels that you applied styles to.

Tab Leader drop-down arrow (🔽) adds leaders of your choice between the entries and the page numbers in the table of contents.

TUTORIAL

In this tutorial you apply heading styles to the *educom.doc* document and then use those headings to generate a table of contents.

Getting Started

1. Open the *educom.doc* document stored in the *tutorial* directory on the *Word Student Resource Disk (Part 1)*.

Formatting Headings with Styles

2. Click in the heading *HERE ARE SOME RELEVANT FACTS*, click the **Style** drop-down arrow (🔽) on the toolbar to display a list of styles, and click *Heading 1*. The heading immediately is formatted based on the definition of the *Heading 1* style.

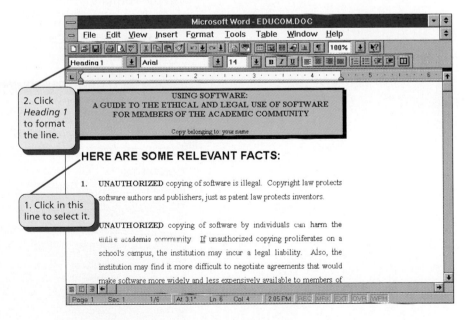

3. Repeat Step 2 for each of the other all-cap headings shown here.

SOFTWARE AND INTELLECTUAL RIGHTS
QUESTIONS YOU MAY HAVE ABOUT USING SOFTWARE

ALTERNATIVES TO EXPLORE
A FINAL NOTE

4. Repeats Step 2 for each of the subheadings under the *ALTERNA-TIVES TO EXPLORE* heading (shown below) but select *Heading 2* from the **Style** drop-down list.

Site-Licensed and Bulk-Purchased Software
Shareware
Public Domain Software

Inserting the Table of Contents

5. Insert a blank line above the heading *HERE ARE SOME RELE-VANT FACTS*, enter the title **CONTENTS**, and then press Enter ↵.

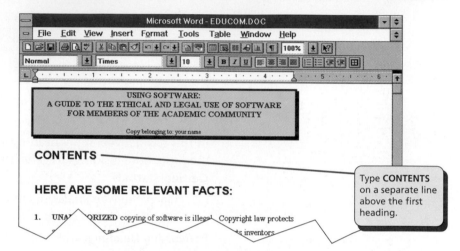

6. Pull down the **Insert** menu, and click the **Index and Tables** command to display the Index and Tables dialog box.

7. On the **Table of Contents** tab, click each of the format names listed in the **Formats** window to see how they look in the **Preview** box.

8. Click the **Formal** format name in the **Formats** window to select it, and then click the **OK** command button to insert the table of contents in the document.

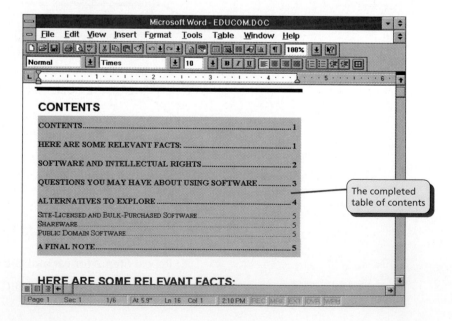

9. Save the document and print the first page.

Finishing Up

10. Close the document without saving your changes.

6-3. FORMATTING IN COLUMNS

Word makes it easy to format a document in columns. Commonly called n*ewspaper-style columns* or *snaking columns*, they are just like those you see in newspapers, newsletters, and books. As you enter text, it gradually fills the first column. When that column is full, text flows into the next column. When the last column on the page is full, text starts to fill the first column on the next page. If you add text to or delete text from any of the columns, the following text moves down or up in the columns.

FORMATTING COLUMNS FROM THE TOOLBAR

You can format the entire document in columns using the **Columns** button on the toolbar. However, if you select text first and then use the **Columns** button, only the selected section is affected. Word automatically puts section breaks above and below the formatted text.

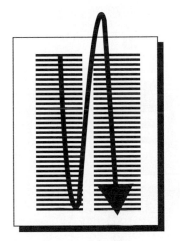

Text flow in newspaper columns

QUICKSTEPS: FORMATTING IN COLUMNS USING THE TOOLBAR

1. Leave the insertion point anywhere in the document to format it all, or select the text you want to be in columns.
2. Click the **Columns** button on the toolbar, point to the first column in the drop-down column window, hold down the left mouse button, and drag to highlight the number of columns you want to use. When you do so and then release the mouse button, the document is immediately formatted in the specified number of columns.
3. Click the **Page Layout View** button to see the columns side by side on the screen. (In Normal View they are shown as a long narrow column.)

FORMATTING COLUMNS FROM THE MENU

When you want more control over how your columns look, you use menu commands and specify options in the Columns dialog box. Using the menu allows you to format the entire document, a selected area of the document, or all of the document from the insertion point forward. This last choice is ideal when you want everything in two or three columns but the heading.

QUICKSTEPS: FORMATTING IN COLUMNS USING THE MENU

1. Move the insertion point to where columns are to begin, or select the text you want to be in columns.

2. Pull down the **Format** menu and click the **Columns** command to display the Columns dialog box.

3. Enter any of the settings described in the box "Understanding the Columns Dialog Box."

4. Click the **OK** command button.

5. Click the **Page Layout View** button to see the columns side by side on the screen.

UNDERSTANDING THE COLUMNS DIALOG BOX

When you use the **Format**, **Columns** command, the Columns dialog box appears. You use the settings in this box to define the way you want your columns laid out on the page. A preview of the current settings is always displayed in the Preview box.

Presets section provides you with five column formats from which to choose.

Number of Columns spin buttons (⬍) specify the number of columns and makes them all equal width with equal spacing between them.

Line Between check box, when on (⊠) , prints a vertical line between columns.

Width and Spacing section displays settings for predefined columns, but you can also enter your own Width and Spacing for each.

Equal Column Width check box, when on (⊠), sets all columns to the same width.

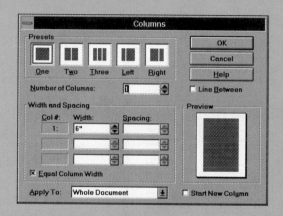

Apply To drop-down arrow (⬇) lets you specify if the columns apply to the whole document, selected text, selected sections, or from the insertion point forward.

Start New Column check box, when on (⊠), starts a new column at the insertion point.

TIP: COLUMN BREAKS

To start a new column when another isn't full, press Ctrl+⇧Shift+Enter↵ or pull down the **Insert** menu, click the **Break** command to display the Break menu, click the **Column Break** option button to turn it on, and then click the **OK** command button.

TIP: COLUMNS AND THE RULER BAR

With the insertion point in text formatted in columns, the horizontal ruler looks different than it normally looks. It works the same way it does in normal text, but there is a set of margin borders for each of the columns. This allows you to adjust margins for each column separately.

TUTORIAL

In this tutorial, you format all or part of the *overview.doc* document in two and three columns using both the toolbar and the menu.

Getting Started

1. Open the *overview.doc* document stored in the *tutorial* directory on the *Word Student Resource Disk (Part 1)*.

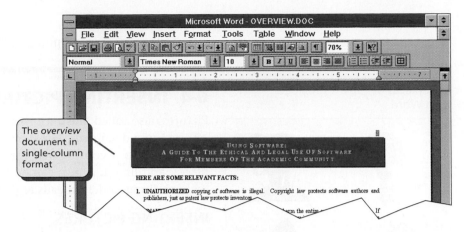

The *overview* document in single-column format

Formatting in Columns Using the Toolbar

2. Click the **Columns** button on the toolbar to display a series of columns, and click the second column from the left. The entire document is immediately formatted in two columns. (Click the **Page Layout View** button to see the columns side by side on the screen.)

3. Click the **Columns** button on the toolbar to display a series of columns, and click the leftmost column. The entire document immediately returns to a single column.

Formatting in Columns Using the Menu

4. Click in the heading that reads HERE ARE SOME RELEVANT FACTS, then pull down the **Format** menu and click the **Columns** command to display the Columns dialog box.

5. Click the **Three** box in the *Presets* section.

6. Click the **Line Between** check box to turn it on.

7. Click the **Apply To** drop-down arrow (⬇), and click **This Point Forward** to select it.

8. Click the **OK** command button, and the document is immediately formatted in three columns separated by vertical lines. The heading remains in a single column because you didn't apply columns to the entire document.

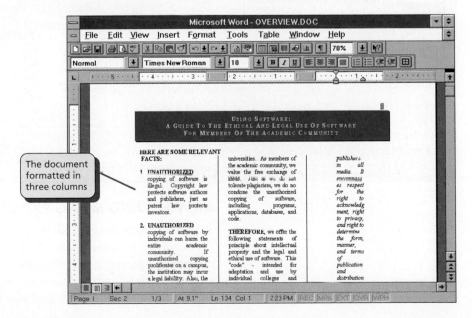

The document formatted in three columns

9. Save the document, print the first page, and then close the document.

Four pieces of clip art provided with Word

6-4. INSERTING PICTURES

Pictures (also called illustrations or graphics) can add greatly to the interest level of a document. For example, charts, maps, and graphs can provide detail in a compressed form, photographs can show people or places, and line drawings can add decoration. You can also use pictures for such things as letterheads and facsimile signatures.

INSERTING PICTURES

Word allows you to insert pictures directly into your document and to move and change their size once they are there. Word also includes many pictures, called clip art, that you can insert into a document. The images are stored in files with the extension *.wmf* in the directory *c:\winword\clipart* (see the examples in the margin).

TIP: PICTURES SLOWING DOWN YOUR SYSTEM?

Displaying pictures on the screen can bring some systems to a crawl. To hide pictures on the screen (but not the printout) to speed things up, pull down the **Tools** menu, click the **Options** command to display the Options dialog box, and on the **View** tab turn on the **Picture Placeholders** check box. This will display boxes on the screen where the pictures will print.

QUICKSTEPS: INSERTING A PICTURE IN A DOCUMENT

1. Position the insertion point where you want the picture to appear—usually on a line by itself.
2. Pull down the **Insert** menu and click the **Picture** command to display the Insert Picture dialog box. The *c:\winword\clipart* directory is opened, and its files are displayed in the **File Name** list.
3. Click the name of the figure you want to insert on the **File Name** list to select it.
4. Use any of the options described in the box "Understanding the Insert Picture Dialog Box."
5. Click the **OK** command button to insert the picture in the document.

UNDERSTANDING THE INSERT PICTURE DIALOG BOX

When you use the **Insert**, **Picture** command, the Insert Picture dialog box is displayed. In addition to selecting the picture file you want to insert in the document, you also have the following options.

Link to File check box links the file to the document.

Preview File check box, when on (⊠), displays a preview of the picture in the Preview box.

Save Picture in Document check box is on only when **Link to File** is also. When on (⊠), a copy of the picture file is saved in the document.

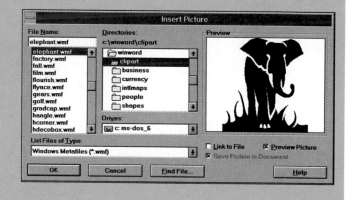

MOVING AND SIZING PICTURES

When a picture is selected, it has small black squares, called handles, on each corner and each side. You can drag any one of these handles to change the picture's size. To select a picture, click it (to unselect a picture click anywhere in the document outside of it.) When selected, you can format the picture, drag it, and size it with the handles.

QUICKSTEPS: MOVING, SIZING, AND FORMATTING PICTURES

▶ To move a selected picture, point to it anywhere but the handles, hold down the left mouse button, and drag it to where you want it. This works best in Page Layout View.

▶ To size a selected picture, point to any of its handles and drag them. Dragging the corner handles changes both the width and height at the same time and retains the picture's proportions.

▶ To format a selected picture, use alignment buttons on the toolbar or add borders to the picture.

TUTORIAL

In this tutorial, you insert a picture into one of your documents, then move and size it.

Getting Ready

1. Open the *macro.doc* document stored in the *tutorial* directory on the *Word Student Resource Disk (Part 1)*. Click anywhere in the date and press F9 to update it.

Inserting a Picture

2. With the insertion point on the line below the centered heading, pull down the **Insert** menu and click the **Picture** command to display the Insert Picture dialog box. The *c:\winword\clipart* directory is opened, and its files are displayed in the **File Name** list.

3. Click the name of any figure on the **File Name** list to select it and display it in the Preview box. If it isn't displayed there, click the **Preview File** check box to turn it on (⊠).

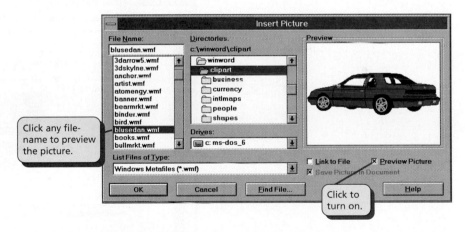

4. Press ↑ and ↓ to select other pictures and see them displayed in the Preview box.

5. After exploring the pictures, click *computer.wmf* to select it, click the **OK** command button to insert the picture in the document.

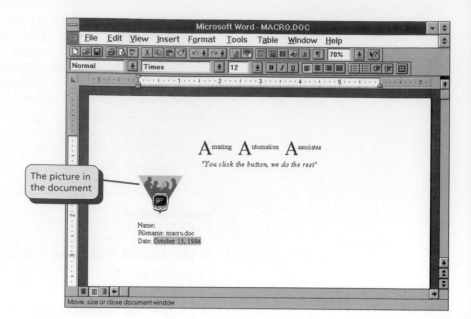

The picture in the document

6. Click the picture to select it, then click the **Center** button on the toolbar to center it under the heading.

Resizing the Picture

7. Point to one of the picture's corner handles, and the mouse pointer will turn into a diagonal arrow. When it does, hold down the left mouse button and drag the figure so its the same width as the line of text above it. When it is, release the mouse button. This may take a few attempts.

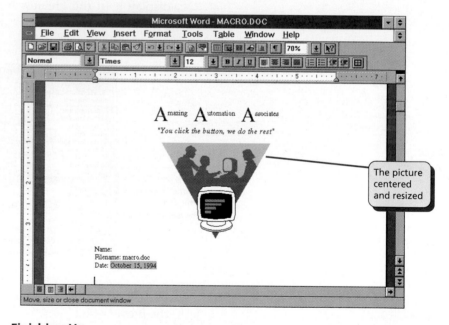

The picture centered and resized

Finishing Up

8. Save the document, print the first page (if your lab instructor approves—it can take what seems forever on some systems), and then close the document.

6-5. CREATING TABLES

Tables are made up of rows that run horizontally and columns that run vertically. These elements are indicated by dotted gridlines on the screen. The intersections of rows and columns are called cells, and cells are where you enter data into the table. As you type data into a cell, text will wrap when it hits the margin, and the depth of the cell will adjust automatically.

You can either create a table from scratch and enter data into it or you can convert a table with tabbed columns to a Word table. When you create a table from scratch, you specify how many rows and columns it should have, and then Word divides the screen so each column is of equal width. When you select a table with tabbed columns and create a table, the tab stops in the table determine the width of columns in the new table.

Word's Table Wizard makes it easy to create tables of data. Table Wizard guides you through the process of creating the table by asking you questions about column and row headers, cell formats, and other elements. As you answer the questions, it builds and formats the table for you.

When entering data in a table, you can press Tab↹ to move the insertion point from cell to cell. If you press Tab↹ with the insertion point in the last cell on the last row, you will add a new row to the table. To insert a tab character in a cell, press Ctrl+Tab↹.

QUICKSTEPS: CREATING A NEW TABLE USING THE TOOLBAR

1. Position the insertion point where you want a new table.

2. Click the **Insert Table** button on the toolbar to display a grid of cells.

3. Drag with the mouse to highlight the number of rows and columns you want in your table and then release the mouse button to create the table. (The grid will expand if you drag against its borders.)

QUICKSTEPS: CREATING A NEW TABLE USING THE MENU

1. Position the insertion point where you want a new table.

2. Pull down the **Table** menu and click the **Insert Table** command to display the Insert Table dialog box.

3. Enter the number of columns for the table in the **Number of Columns** text box and the number of rows in the **Number of Rows** text box. If you don't want their widths set automatically, enter a width in the **Column Width** text box.

4. Do one of the following:

▶ Click the **OK** command button to create the table.

▶ Click the **Wizard** command button to be led step by step through the rest of the process. To advance to the next step, click the **Next** button, and click the **Finish** button when done.

▶ Click the **AutoFormat** button to select a table for the format. (AutoFormat is discussed in Section 6-6.)

TUTORIAL

In this tutorial, you use Word's table feature to create a résumé, a document that is usually very difficult to format.

Getting Started

1. Open the *resume.doc* document stored in the *tutorial* directory on the *Word Student Resource Disk (Part 1)* and enter your name in place of the *Your Name* heading.

Creating a Table

2. With the insertion point on the second line below the centered address, pull down the **Table** menu and click the **Insert Table** command to display the Insert Table dialog box.

3. Change the number of **Rows** to **1** and then click the **OK** command button. A table with two cells—formed from two columns and one row—appears at the insertion point. If dotted gridlines are not displayed around each cell, pull down the **View** menu and click the **Table Gridlines** command to turn them on.

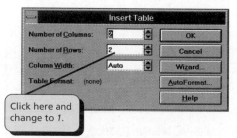

The Insert Table dialog box

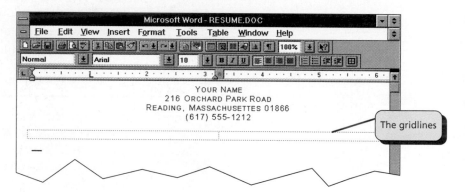

4. Enter the résumé shown in the figure "The Résumé" on the next page, following these procedures:

   ▶ Press Tab↹ to move the insertion point to the next cell (where shown with Tab↹ symbols in the figure). When you press Tab↹ with the insertion point at the end of any text in a cell in the lower-right column, a new row is added to the table.

   ▶ Don't press Enter↵ within a cell when typing a paragraph. The paragraph will automatically wrap within the cell and the cell will expand to accommodate it.

   ▶ Press Enter↵ within a cell to start a new line (where shown with Enter↵ symbols in the figure). The cell will expand for the new line.

▶ To enter the bullets, pull down the **Insert** menu and click the **Symbol** command to display the Symbol dialog box. Select *Wingdings* from the **Font** drop-down list, click the 6th character from the right on the 3rd row, and then click the **Insert** button. Click the **Close** button to close the Symbol dialog box. (You may want to insert one symbol this way and then copy and paste the rest.)

YOUR NAME 216 ORCHARD PARK ROAD READING, MASSACHUSETTS 01866 (617) 555-1212	
Objective [Tab↹]	To obtain a teaching position in an Early Childhood Special Needs setting [Tab↹]
Education [Tab↹]	Westfield State College (Westfield, MA) [Enter↵] Young Children with Special Needs major (BED) [Enter↵] Expected graduation date, May 1996 [Tab↹]
Teacher Training Experience [Tab↹]	■ Brightwood Elementary School, Springfield, MA [Enter↵] Student teacher in an integrated preschool [Enter↵] ■ Woodland Elementary School, Southwick, MA [Enter↵] Practicum in an integrated preschool [Enter↵] ■ Juniper Park Campus Elementary School, Westfield MA [Enter↵] Pre-practicum in first grade [Tab↹]
Work Experience [Tab↹]	■ Cradle Beach Camp, Angola, NY [Enter↵] Summer camp counselor for children who were physically disabled, mentally disabled, and/or disadvantaged [Enter↵] ■ Reading, MA: part-time jobs while in school, at retail stores, food markets, and a nursing home [Tab↹]
Certifications and Memberships [Tab↹]	■ Massachusetts Certification in Young Children with Special Needs (Ages 3-7), May 1995 [Enter↵] ■ Member, Association of Adults with Learning Disabilities

The résumé

Finishing Up

5. Save, print, and close the document.

6-6. FORMATTING AND EDITING TABLES

Once you have created a table, you can easily edit or format it so it looks exactly as you want it to look.

AUTOFORMATTING TABLES

Once you have created a table, you can quickly format it using Word's Table AutoFormat command. You can also format part or all of the table using the **Format** menu's **Borders and Shading** command just as you would format regular paragraphs.

QUICKSTEPS: AUTOFORMATTING A TABLE

1. Click anywhere in the table, pull down the **Table** menu and click the **Table AutoFormat** command to display the Table AutoFormat dialog box.

2. Click any format on the **Formats** list to select it and display a preview in the Preview box.

3. Click any check boxes in the *Formats to Apply* or *Apply Special Formats To* sections to turn them on or off. (Click the dialog box's **Help** button for a description of these options.)

4. Click the **OK** command button to format the table.

SELECTING CELLS, ROWS, AND COLUMNS

When editing and formatting tables, you usually begin by selecting the cells, rows, or columns you want to format. You can select cells by putting the insertion point in one of the cells and then holding down the left button as you drag the highlight. You can also click in one cell and then hold down ⇧Shift while you click in another to select all cells between the two. Finally, you can select cells using commands on the **Table** menu or by clicking, as shown in the table "Selecting Cells, Rows, and Columns."

Selecting Cells, Rows, and Columns	
To Select	**Click**
Cell	Click the cell's selection bar—the narrow area just to the right of the cell's left border.
Row	Click the row's selection bar—the area to the left of the table.
Column	Click the top gridline or border.
Table	Triple-click on a row selection bar.

CHANGING COLUMN WIDTHS

To change a column's width, point to its right boundary gridline, and the mouse pointer turns into a two-headed arrow. With the mouse pointer in this form, hold down the left mouse button and drag the column wider or narrower. As you do so, the other columns to its right change size proportionally and the overall table width remains unchanged. To have the column widths displayed on the ruler, hold down Alt as you drag the boundary.

INSERTING CELLS, ROWS, AND COLUMNS

To insert rows or columns in a table, begin by selecting the same number of rows or columns that you want to insert. For example, to insert two new rows, select two rows in the table. New rows will be inserted above the rows you select, and new columns will be inserted to the left of the columns you select.

TIPS: CHANGING TABLE COLUMN WIDTHS

When dragging table column boundaries to change column widths, there are options you can use.

▶ To move just the boundary you are pointing to (and change the width of the columns to the left and right), hold down ⇧Shift while dragging.

▶ To change the width of the column to the left of the gridline you point to and leave all other columns the same width, hold down Ctrl+⇧Shift while dragging. This changes the overall size of the table.

Once you have selected rows or columns, use commands on the **Table** menu to make the insertion, or click the **Insert Table** button on the toolbar. The name of the button changes to **Insert Rows**, **Insert Cells**, or **Insert Columns** depending on what you have selected.

To insert a row at the bottom of the table, position the insertion point in the lower-right cell and press Tab⇆. To insert a column on the right side of the table, click to the right of the table and click the **Insert Columns** button on the toolbar.

DELETING CELLS, ROWS, AND COLUMNS

You can easily delete cells, rows, or columns. To do so, select the section of the table you want to delete, pull down the **Table** menu and click the **Delete Rows**, **Delete Columns**, or **Delete Cells** command (The command's name changes depending on what you have selected.) If you delete cells but not entire rows or columns, the Delete Cells dialog box asks you how you want the remaining cells to shift.

DELETING TABLES

When you no longer need a table, you can delete its structure, its content, or both.

▶ To delete the structure but not the contents, select the entire table, pull down the **Table** menu and click the **Convert Table to Text** command. You can then specify if you want the cell contents separated by paragraph marks, tabs, commas, or other character of your choice.

▶ To delete the contents but not the structure, select all or part of the table and press Del.

▶ To delete both structure and contents, select the table, pull down the **Table** menu and select the **Delete Rows** command. You can also select the table and one paragraph mark outside of it and press Del.

TUTORIAL

Getting Started

1. Open the *resume.doc* document stored in the *tutorial* directory on the *Word Student Resource Disk (Part 1)*. If dotted gridlines are not displayed around each cell, pull down the **View** menu and click the **Table Gridlines** command to turn them on.

Inserting a New Row

2. Click in the row selection bar to select the row that reads *Certifications and Memberships*, pull down the **Table** menu, and click the **Insert Rows** command to insert a single row.

3. On that blank row, enter the new text shown in bold in the figure "The Edited Résumé" on the next page. Press Tab⇆ and Enter↵ only where indicated.

WORK EXPERIENCE `Tab⇆`	■ *Cradle Beach Camp*, Angola, NY `Enter⏎` Summer camp counselor for children who were physically disabled, mentally disabled, and/or disadvantaged `Enter⏎` ■ Reading, MA: part-time jobs while in school, at retail stores, food markets, and a nursing home `Tab⇆`
VOLUNTEER EXPERIENCE `Tab⇆`	■ **Spinning Wheels, Reading, MA** `Enter⏎` ■ **Coach for Special Olympics Track and Field for mentally and physically disabled young adults** `Enter⏎` ■ **Co-leader for weekend recreational activities for mentally and physically disabled young adults**
CERTIFICATIONS AND MEMBERSHIPS `Tab⇆`	■ Massachusetts Certification in Young Children with Special Needs (Ages 3-7), May 1995 `Enter⏎` ■ Member, Association of Adults with Learning Disabilities

The edited résumé

Formatting a Column

4. Click anywhere in the left column, pull down the **Table** menu, and click the **Select Column** command to select the entire column.

5. Pull down the **Format** menu, click the **Font** command to display the Font dialog box, click the **Small Caps** check box to turn it on, then click the **OK** command button. All of the headings in the left column are now formatted as small caps.

6. Italicize each of the institutional names as shown in the figure "The Final Résumé."

Adjusting Column Widths

7. Click anywhere in the table, point to the column border on the gridline between the two columns, and the mouse pointer turns into a two-headed split arrow. Hold down `Alt` and drag this border to the left until the left column is as close to 2.25" as you can get. Then release the mouse button and the `Alt` key in that order. When finished, your résumé should look like the figure "The Final Résumé."

	YOUR NAME 216 ORCHARD PARK ROAD READING, MASSACHUSETTS 01866 (617) 555-1212
OBJECTIVE	To obtain a teaching position in an Early Childhood Special Needs setting
EDUCATION	*Westfield State College* (Westfield, MA) Young Children with Special Needs major (BED) Expected graduation date, May 1996
TEACHER TRAINING EXPERIENCE	■ *Brightwood Elementary School*, Springfield, MA Student teacher in an integrated preschool ■ *Woodland Elementary School*, Southwick, MA Practicum in an integrated preschool ■ *Juniper Park Campus Elementary School*, Westfield MA Pre-practicum in first grade
WORK EXPERIENCE	■ *Cradle Beach Camp*, Angola, NY Summer camp counselor for children who were physically disabled, mentally disabled, and/or disadvantaged ■ Reading, MA: part-time jobs while in school, at retail stores, food markets, and a nursing home
VOLUNTEER EXPERIENCE	■ Spinning Wheels, Reading, MA ■ Coach for Special Olympics Track and Field for mentally and physically disabled young adults ■ Co-leader for weekend recreational activities for mentally and physically disabled young adults
CERTIFICATIONS AND MEMBERSHIPS	■ Massachusetts Certification in Young Children with Special Needs (Ages 3-7), May 1995 ■ Member, Association of Adults with Learning Disabilities

The final résumé

Changing Line Spacing

8. Triple-click in a row selection bar to select the entire table, pull down the **Format** menu, and click the **Paragraph** command to display the Paragraph menu. On the **Indents and Spacing** tab, click the **Line Spacing** drop-down arrow (⬇), click the **1.5 Lines** option to select it, and then click the **OK** command button. All table text now has more line spacing.

9. Click the **Page Layout View** button to display the document in that view.

Finishing Up

10. Save, print, and close the document.

PicTorial 6 Review Questions

 **True-False**

T F **1.** You can add borders to sentences.

T F **2.** You can format an entire document or selected text into columns.

T F **3.** When the insertion point is in columns of text, the horizontal ruler looks different than it normally looks.

T F **4.** When pictures are hidden on the screen, they will not print.

T F **5.** To move a selected picture, point to any of its handles and drag them.

T F **6.** To size a selected picture, point to anywhere but the handles, hold down the left mouse button, and drag to change the width and height of the picture.

T F **7.** When working with columns of text, there is a set of margins for each column.

T F **8.** If you press Tab⇆ with the insertion point in the last cell on the last row, you will add a new column to the table.

T F **9.** When tabbed text is converted to a table, the width of all columns in the table, except the last, will be determined by the tab stops you have entered.

T F **10.** To use styles, you do not have to know how to create them.

 Multiple Choice

1. The clip art that comes with Word has the extension _____.

  a. *wpg*

  b. *wmf*

  c. *wcp*

  d. *pic*

2. To select a picture, _____ it.

  a. Double-click

  b. Click

  c. Triple-click

  d. Press Ctrl and click

3. The intersection of a row and a column is called a _____.

  a. Range

  b. Lock

  c. Block

  d. Cell

4. To move the insertion point from cell to cell in a table, press _____.

  a. Tab⇆

  b. ⇧Shift + Tab⇆

c. [Alt]+[Tab]

d. [Ctrl]+[Tab]

5. To insert a tab character in a table cell, press _____.

a. [Tab]

b. [Shift]+[Tab]

c. [Alt]+[Tab]

d. [Ctrl]+[Tab]

6. To select an entire table, _____.

a. Click the narrow area just to the right of the cell's border

b. Click the top gridline or border

c. Triple-click on a row selection bar

d. Click the area to the left of the table

7. When changing a column's width, the mouse pointer turns into a(n) _____.

a. Two-headed arrow

b. I-beam

c. Left-pointing arrow

d. Right-pointing arrow

8. When changing column widths, to have column widths displayed on the ruler, hold down _____ as you drag the boundary.

a. [Ctrl]

b. [Shift]

c. [Alt]

d. [Tab]

9. To select an entire row in a table, _____.

a. Click the narrow area just to the right of the cell's border

b. Click the top gridline or border

c. Triple-click on a row selection bar

d. Click the area to the left of the table

10. To create a table of contents, pull down the _____ menu.

a. **Format**

b. **Edit**

c. **Insert**

d. **Style**

Fill In the Blank

1. Another name for newspaper-style columns is _____ columns.

2. Pictures are also called _____ or _____.

3. Tables are made up of _____ and _____.

4. Columns run _____.

5. If a tabbed table already exists, you can select it and then click the _____ button to convert it to a Word table.

6. To delete the table structure but not the contents, pull down the **Ta̲ble** menu and click the _____ command.

7. When a picture is selected, it has _____, called handles, on each corner and on each side.

8. Rows run _____.

9. To delete the table contents but not the structure, select all or part of the table and press _____.

10. The first step to perform when creating a table of contents is to _____.

 ▶▶ **COMPUTER-BASED TUTORIALS**

We suggest you complete the following computer-based lessons to learn more about the features discussed in this PicTorial. To do so, pull down the **Help** menu and click the **Examples and Demos** command, click the _Topic_ listed in the table "Suggested Examples and Demos to Complete," and then click the _Subtopic_ listed in that same table. (If you need more help on using the system, see the "Computer-Based Tutorials" section at the end of PicTorial 2.)

Suggested Examples and Demos to Complete		
Done	Topic	Subtopic
☐	Formatting Paragraphs	Applying or removing borders
☐	Formatting Paragraphs	Applying shading
☐	Working with Tables	Overview of Working with Tables
☐	Working with Tables	Creating a table
☐	Working with Tables	Converting text to a table or a table to text
☐	Working with Tables	Automatically formatting a table
☐	Working with Tables	Adding rows and columns to a table
☐	Working with Tables	Deleting rows and columns
☐	Working with Tables	Applying or removing borders
☐	Working with Tables	Applying shading
☐	Page Design and Layout	Working with newspaper-style columns
☐	Page Design and Layout	Creating columns of equal width
☐	Page Design and Layout	Changing column width and the space between columns
☐	Page Design and Layout	Starting a new column
☐	Graphics and Frames	Overview of Importing and Creating Graphics
☐	Graphics and Frames	Importing an entire graphics file
☐	Graphics and Frames	Resizing or cropping and imported graphic
☐	Graphics and Frames	Creating a drawing object
☐	Graphics and Frames	Specifying the line and fill for a drawing object
☐	Graphics and Frames	Overview of Positioning Text and Graphics with Frames
☐	Graphics and Frames	Inserting a frame around selected items
☐	Graphics and Frames	Positioning a frame by dragging

6-1. Adding Borders Around Paragraphs

Adding borders around paragraphs is a great way to make them stand out from the rest of the document. In this drill you copy a key phrase from the document and enclose it in a border. This kind of box, used in newspaper and magazine articles, is called a "pull quote." It is designed to catch your interest as you browse so you will then read the entire article.

1. Open the *borders.doc* document stored in the *drill* directory on the *Word Student Resource Disk (Part 1)* and enter your name, then click anywhere in the date and press ⌐F9⌐ to update it.

2. Copy the paragraph that begins "Pull-quotes..." right below the existing paragraph and be sure there is a blank line above and below it.

3. Use the **F**o**rmat**, **B**orders and Shading command to add a **Bo**x border and 10% shading to the copied paragraph.

4. Select the paragraph that begins *When using rules...* and the three bulleted paragraphs that follow. Use the **F**o**rmat**, **B**orders and **Shading** command to add a **Sh**a**dow** border and 10% shading to the selected paragraphs.

5. Save, print, and close the document.

6-2. Generating a Table of Contents

Almost all long documents benefit from a table of contents because it makes it easier for the reader to grasp the document's contents and to locate items of interest. In this drill you insert a table of contents for the document on clouds.

1. Open the *clouds.doc* document stored in the *tutorial* (not the *drill*) directory of the *Word Student Resource Disk (Part 1)*.

2. Click anywhere in the first uppercase heading shown in the figure "Table of Contents Headings," click the **Style** drop-down arrow (⬇) on the toolbar, and select *Heading 1*. Immediately click in each of the other uppercase headings and press ⌐F4⌐ to repeat the format.

3. Click anywhere in the first heading with an initial cap (*Cirrus*) shown in the figure "Table of Contents Headings," click the **Style** drop-down arrow (⬇) on the toolbar, and select *Heading 2*. Immediately click in each of the other headings with initial caps and press ⌐F4⌐ to repeat the format.

4. In the tutorial for Section 4-8, you entered section breaks in this document. There should be a section break and a new page following the *CLOUDS* title. Now you will insert another section in this spot, to make room for a table of contents.

   With the insertion point at the end of the section containing the title *Clouds* (page 1 in Section 1—check the status bar for your position), use the **Insert**, **B**reak command to insert a **N**ext Page section break. You should now have two end-of-section markers, and the insertion point should between them. Press ⌐Enter ↵⌐ twice to insert blank lines.

IDENTIFICATION
HIGH CLOUDS
    Cirrus
    Cirrocumulus
    Cirrostratus
MIDDLE CLOUDS
    Altocumulus
    Altostratus
    Altocumulus Castellanus
    Standing Lenticular
       Altocumulus Clouds
    Nimbostratus
LOW CLOUDS
    Stratus
    Stratocumulus
    Cumulus
    Towering Cumulus
    Cumulonimbus
CLOUDS WITH EXTENSIVE
    VERTICAL
    DEVELOPMENT

Table of Contents Headings

5. In the new empty section center the heading CONTENTS.

6. On the blank line below the new heading, use the **Insert**, **Inde_x_ and Tables** command and on the **Table of _C_ontents** tab select _Fancy_ from the **Forma_t_s** list and click the **OK** command button to insert the table of contents.

7. Repeat Step 6 to select other styles from the **Forma_t_s** list. When you find one you particularly like, make a printout.

8. Save the document, print the page with the table of contents, then close the document.

6-3. Formatting in Columns

Long documents can often be shortened somewhat and made easier to read by formatting them in multiple columns. In this drill you format the document on clouds in first two and then three columns.

1. Open the _clouds.doc_ document stored in the _tutorial_ directory of the _Word Student Resource Disk (Part 1)._

2. Display the document in Page Layout view to see the results of the following commands.

3. With the insertion point anywhere in the first page below the table of contents, use the **Columns** button on the Standard toolbar to format the document in two columns.

4. With the insertion point anywhere in the first page below the table of contents, use the **Columns** button on the Standard toolbar to format the document in three columns.

5. With the insertion point anywhere in the first page below the table of contents, use the **Columns** button on the Standard toolbar to format the document in one column.

6. With the insertion point anywhere in the first page below the table of contents, use the **F_o_rmat**, **_C_olumns** command to format the section in three columns with a line between them. (Be sure **Apply to** is set to **This Section**).

7. Save the document, print the first page of the three-column section, and close the document.

6-4. Inserting Pictures

Pictures make documents more attractive and inviting. In this drill you add a picture to the document on clouds.

1. Open the _clouds.doc_ document stored in the _tutorial_ directory of the _Word Student Resource Disk (Part 1)._

2. With the insertion point on the blank line below the word _Clouds_ on the first page, use the **Insert**, **_P_icture** command to insert the figure _flyace.wmf._

3. Size the picture so it fills the space between the margins.

4. Save the document, print the first page, and then close the document. (Note that this page can take a long time to print since it has a picture. Don't print it if you have little time left. If a number of you share a printer, only one of you should print the document or you'll tie the printer up for others.)

6-5. Creating Tables

One of the most useful features of tables created with Word's **T**able command is the way text entries will wrap in a cell. When working with tabbed columns, this doesn't happen. In this drill you convert a table laid out in tabbed columns to a Word table.

1. Open the *bugs.doc* document stored in the *drill* directory on the *Word Student Resource Disk (Part 1)*.

2. Delete all of the entries following *Baseball Bugs* near the bottom of the first page.

3. Select all remaining entries (including the column headings) and use the **T**able, **Con**v**ert Text to Table** command to create a table from tabular columns. The default entries in the dialog box are all correct, so just click the **OK** command button.

4. Use the **F**ile, **Save** **A**s command to save the document under the new name *bugs2.doc* in the *drill* directory on the *Word Student Resource Disk (Part 1)*.

5. Close the document.

6-6. Editing and Formatting Tables

Tables are not only easy to create, they are easy to format. All you have to do is select one or more rows or columns and then use formatting commands to format all of the entries identically. In this drill you format the table you created listing films in which Bugs Bunny is the star.

1. Open the *bugs2.doc* document stored in the *drill* directory on the *Word Student Resource Disk (Part 1)* and enter your name, then click anywhere in the date and press `F9` to update it.

2. Select the entire table and use the **T**able, **Table Auto**F**ormat** command to display the Table AutoFormat dialog box. In the **Formats** list, click the *Simple 1* format and then click the **OK** command button. Click anywhere to remove the highlight to see your results. To hide gridlines if they are displayed, use the **T**able, **Grid**l**ines** command.

3. Repeat Step 2, selecting other formats to see how they affect the table's appearance. When you find a format you particularly like, print the document.

4. Save and then close the document.

▶▶ SKILL-BUILDING EXERCISES

6-1. Formatting the Job-Guide Document

In this exercise you desktop-publish the *jobs.doc* document by adding paragraph borders, formatting it in two columns with a line between them, and adding a picture to the first page.

1. Open the *jobs.doc* document stored in the *exercise* directory on the *Word Student Resource Disk (Part 2)* and display it in Page Layout View.

2. Use the **Format**, **Borders and Shading** command to add a border to each of headings *The Cover Letter*, *The Resume*, and *The Followup Letter* that prints a thin line above and below the heading. (On the **Border** graphic in the dialog box, you have to click on the top and bottom borders to add two separate borders. If you make a mistake, click the **None** icon and try again.)

3. Starting with the first body paragraph, use the **Format**, **Columns** command to format the document in two columns with a line between them.

4. On a blank line above the heading *The Cover Letter*, use the **Insert**, **Picture** command to insert the *mail.wmf* picture.

5. Save the document and print the first page.

6-2. Formatting the Bill of Rights Document

In this exercise you desktop-publish the Bill of Rights document by adding borders, formatting it in two columns with a line between them, adding a table of contents, and inserting a picture.

1. Open the *rights.doc* document stored in the *exercise* directory on the *Word Student Resource Disk (Part 2)* and display it in Page Layout View.

2. Use the **Format**, **Borders and Shading** command to add a border and shading of your choice around the heading *The Bill of Rights* at the top of the document.

3. Use the **Style** drop-down arrow (⬇) on the Formatting toolbar to format each of the amendment numbers (but not the titles) as *Heading 1*.

4. On a blank line below the *Bill of Rights* heading, use the **Insert**, **Index and Tables** command to insert an *Elegant* table of contents.

5. On a blank line above the heading for the first amendment, use the **Insert**, **Picture** command to insert the *scales.wmf* picture.

6. Save the document, print the first page, and then close the document.

6-3. Formatting the Newsletter Document

In this exercise you desktop-publish the newsletter document by adding paragraph borders, formatting it in two columns with a line between them, and adding a table of contents.

1. Open the *newsltr.doc* document stored in the *exercise* directory on the *Word Student Resource Disk (Part 2)* and display it in Page Layout View.

2. Use the **Format**, **Borders and Shading** command to add a border and shading of your choice around the *Staff* heading and the four lines of names that follow it.

3. Use the **Format**, **Borders and Shading** command to add a border of your choice around the two headings that begin *Checklist* and the bulleted items that follow each heading.

4. Just below the *Volume 1 Number 1* line, use the **Format**, **Columns** command to format the document into two columns with a line between them from that point forward.

5. Use the **Style** drop-down arrow (⬇) on the Formatting toolbar to format each of the four all-caps headings as *Heading 1*. (Remember you can use F4 to repeat a format.)

6. Add the boldfaced heading **CONTENTS** so there is a blank line between it and the box listing the staff above it.

7. With the insertion point on a blank line below the *CONTENTS* heading, use the **Insert**, **Index and Tables** command to insert a *Formal* table of contents.

8. Save the document, print the first page, and then close the document.

6-4. Adding Tables to the Sexism Guidelines Document

It's easy to have your writing subtly affect the way others think about themselves. Writing that offends others because of race, sex, or religion should be avoided. In this exercise, you create a table listing examples of biased and unbiased references to women.

1. Open the *sexism.doc* document stored in the *exercise* directory on the *Word Student Resource Disk (Part 2)*.

2. With the insertion point on a blank line under the paragraph of body text in the section headed *Omission*, use the **Table**, **Insert Table** command to insert a table with 2 columns and 4 rows.

3. Enter the table shown in the figure "The Omission Table."

Biased	Unbiased
The pioneers crossed the desert with their women, children, and possessions.	Pioneer families crossed the desert carrying all their possessions.
Radium was discovered by a woman, Marie Curie.	Marie Curie discovered radium.
When setting up his experiment, the researcher must always check his sample for error.	When setting up an experiment, a researcher must always check for sampling error.

The Omission Table

4. With the insertion point on a blank line under the paragraph of body text in the section headed *Equal Treatment*, use the **Table**, **Insert Table** command to insert a table with 2 columns and 4 rows.

5. Enter the table shown in the figure "The Equal Treatment Table."

Biased	Unbiased
Though a woman, she ran the business effectively.	She ran the business effectively.
The little girls played with the boys.	The girls played with the boys; the children played; the little girls played with the little boys.
The line manager was angry, and his secretary told him she was upset too.	The line manager and his secretary were both upset by the mistake.

The Equal Treatment Table

6. Save the document, print the page(s) with the tables, and then close the document.

▸▸ REAL-WORLD PROJECTS

6-1. Desktop-Publishing a Booklet

In this project you desktop-publish the document describing your rights as an airline passenger. To do so, you'll format the document in four columns, in landscape orientation, and insert a table of contents and a picture.

1. Open the *flyright.doc* document stored in the *project* directory on the *Word Student Resource Disk (Part 2)*.

2. Format the document in four columns, with landscape orientation. Insert the picture *jet.wmf* after the title, and follow it with a one-level table of contents. (See the figure "The Fly-Right Document.")

3. Go through the document and use what you have learned about formatting to make it look professional. Change paragraph spacing and indents, bullets, headers and footers, and anything else you like. Look for other pictures to insert at appropriate spots.

4. When you have finished, save the document, print at least the first page, and then close the document.

FLY-RIGHTS

INTRODUCTION 1

AIR FARES 1

RESERVATIONS AND TICKETS 1

DELAYED AND CANCELED FLIGHTS 2

OVERBOOKING 3

BAGGAGE 4

SMOKING 5

NOTICE OF CONTRACT TERMS 5

AIRLINE SAFETY 6

COMPLAINING 7

Introduction

Deregulating the airlines was a statement of faith by the government in the free marketplace.

The elimination of government regulation has resulted in lower air fares for the American public and a wide variety of price/service options. The spectrum of air service available to consumers has ranged from super premium coast-to-coast service where a limousine picks you up at your door, to no-frills, low-cost shuttle service where passengers carry their bags on board.

In this new commercial environment, consumers have had to take a more active role in choosing their air service by learning to ask a number of questions.

- Am I more concerned with price or scheduling? Am I willing to fly at an odd hour if it means saving $25.?
- Will the airline penalize me for changing my reservation?
- What will the airline do for me if it cancels my flight?

This booklet is designed to explain your rights and responsibilities as an air traveler. We hope it helps you become a resourceful consumer.

Air Fares

Because of the emphasis on price competition, airlines don't all charge the same fares anymore. Some of them are trying a "back to basics" approach-offering plane rides at bargain basement prices with few if any extras.

For fare information, you can contact a travel agent, other ticket marketer or an airline serving the places you want to visit. Ask them to tell you the names of all airlines flying there. Then you can call

and any special low fares they may offer. You can also watch the newspapers where airlines advertise many of their discount plans. Finally, be alert to new companies serving the market. They may offer lower fares or different services than older established airlines.

Here are some tips to help you decide among air fares:

- Be flexible in your travel plans in order to get the lowest fare. Often there are complicated conditions you must meet to qualify for a discount.
- Plan as far ahead as you can. Some airlines set aside only a few seats on each flight at the lower rates. The real bargains often sell out very quickly.
- Some airlines may have discounts that others don't offer. In a large metropolitan area, the fare could depend on which airport you use.
- Does the air fare include types of service that airlines have traditionally provided, such as meals or free baggage handling? If you are stranded, will the ticket be good on another airline at no extra charge? Will the first airline pay for meals or hotel rooms during the wait? Find out what will happen if you decide to switch flights. Will you lose the benefit of your discount fare? Are there any cancellation fees? Is there a cut-off date for making and changing reservations without paying more money?
- Some airlines will not increase the fare after the ticket is issued and paid for. (Simply holding a reservation without a ticket does not guarantee the fare). Other airlines reserve the right to collect more money if the fare goes up before departure time. Find out from the airline before you buy your ticket

increases after the ticket is purchased.

- Differences in airfare can be substantial. Careful comparison shopping among airlines does take time, but it can lead to real savings.

Reservations and Tickets

Once you decide when and where you want to go, and which airline you want to use, getting reservations and tickets is a fairly simple process. You can make all of your arrangements by telephone, at the airline's ticket office, or through a travel agent or other ticket marketer. There are a few potential pitfalls, however, and these pointers should help you avoid them.

- If your travel plans fall into a busy period, call for reservations early. Flights for holidays may sell out weeks-sometimes months- ahead of time.
- When you make a reservation, be sure the airline records the information accurately. Before you hang up or leave the ticket office, review all of the essential information with the agent- the spelling of your name, the flight numbers and travel dates, and the cities you are traveling between. If there is more than one airport at either city, be sure you check which one you'll be using. It's also important to give the airline your home and work telephone numbers so they can let you know if there is any change in their schedule.
- Your ticket will show the flight numbers and departure times and dates and the status of your reservation for each leg of your itinerary. The "status" box is important. "OK" 1

The Fly-Right document

INDEX

Addresses, indenting, 123
Aligning text, 106-7
  spaces for, 42
  with tab stops, 114-15
Antonyms, 70-72
Application icons, 2
Application programs, 1
Application window, 3-6
Arrow keys, directional, 18
AutoCorrect, 213-15
AutoFormatting tables, 242
Automating procedures, 189-226
AutoText, 212-13

Bar tab stop, 115
Borders, paragraph, 227-29
Box(es). *See also* Dialog box(es)
  check, 9, 69
  Control-menu, 8
  list, 9
  Reveal Styles, 98
  scroll, 15, 17
  text, 9
Bullets, 123-25
Button(s)
  Bold, 25
  Bullets, 24
  Center, 25
  command, 9
  Cut, 62
  Format Painter, 151
  Italic, 25, 96
  Multiple Pages, 54
  One Page, 55
  option, 9
  Page Layout View, 15
  Paste, 63
  Print, 26
  Print Preview, 54
  Replace All, 69
  Save, 12, 26
  Show/Hide , 42, 47
  spin, 9
  Tab Alignment, 147
  Undo, 43

CapsLock key, 42
Cells, 242-43
Centered tab stop, 115, 116
Centered text, 106, 107
Character formatting, 95, 103
Check boxes, 9
  Match Case, 69
Clipboard, 59-63, 69
Closing documents, 7-8, 10
Colons, spaces following, 42
Colors, printing, 228
Column breaks, 234
Columns
  changing widths of, 242, 244
  deleting, 243
  formatting, 233-36
  inserting, 242-43
  ruler bar and, 234
  selecting, 242
  tabbed, 116, 240
Column tabs, 118-19
Command(s). *See also* Button(s)
  AutoFormat, 97
  50%, 26
  Find, 68
  Go To, 19
  Page Width, 26
  Repeat, 97
Copying
  of formats, 151-52
  of text, 59-68
Correcting mistakes, 43

Cutting and pasting, 59-63

Dashes, en and em, 138
Data source, 189, 190, 194-95, 198-200, 204
Date fields, updating, 44
Decimal tab stop, 115, 116
Deleting
  AutoText, 213
  cells, rows, and columns, 243
  macros, 212
  paragraph marks, 97
  tables, 243
  text, 19, 20-21
Desktop publishing, 227-43
Dialog box(es), 9
  AutoCorrect, 214
  Break, 169
  Columns, 234
  displaying, 148
  Font, 103
  Insert Picture, 236
  Note Options, 163
  Page Numbers, 159
  Paragraph, 113, 120
  Paragraph Borders and Shading, 228
  Print, 53
  Query Options, 206
  Save As, 13-14
  Sort Text, 174
  Summary Information, 13
  Tab Set, 116
  Thesaurus, 71
Directional arrow keys, 18
Display elements, 4
.DOC extension, 7
Document(s). *See also* Text
  closing, 7-8, 10
  editing, 19-22
  entering, 11-12, 44-45
  mail-merge, 189, 191, 192-93, 197-98, 200, 204-5
  missing, 6
  navigating around, 15-19
  opening, 6-7, 10
  previewing, 52
  printing, 52-55
  saving, 12-15, 30
  scrolling the, 15-18
  searching part of, 68
  sorting, 173-76
  unsaved, 8
Dot leaders, 115
Double indent, 119
Down scroll arrow, 15
Drag and drop feature, 57, 64-68
Dragging text, 57
Drop-down arrow, 25, 108
Drop-down list box, 9
Duplicate filenames, 14

Editing, 4
  footnotes and endnotes, 162
  macros, 209, 211-12
  tables, 241-44
  text and documents, 19-22, 45-50
Edit menu, selecting text with, 57
Em and en dashes, 138
Endnotes, 161-65
End-of-document mark, 4
Entering text, 41-45
Exiting Word for Windows, 29-30

Field(s)
  date, 44
  fill-in, 201
  merge, 191

Field(s) *(continued)*
  sorting by, 173
Filenames, 12, 14
Fill-in fields, 201
Finding, 68. *See also* Searching
  formats, 153-55
  repeating previous Find command, 68
  special characters, 154-55
  specific font and size, 154
First line indent, 119
Floppy disks, removing too soon, 14
Fonts, font sizes, and font styles, 101-5
Footers, 155-58
Footnotes, 161-65
Formatting, 4, 23-25, 95-188
  aligning text, 42, 106-7, 114-15
  applied to existing text, 96-97, 98-99
  applied to new text, 96, 99
  of characters, 95, 103
  in columns, 233-36
  copying formats, 151-52
  finding and replacing, 153-55
  fonts, font sizes, and font styles, 101-5
  footnotes and endnotes, 161-65
  headers and footers, 155-58
  identifying, 98, 100-101
  line spacing, 107-8, 109, 245
  numbered and bulleted lists, 123-25
  page breaks, 43, 111-14
    hard, 112, 113
    protecting paragraph from, 114
    soft, 111
  page numbering, 158-61
  page setup, 165-68
    margins, 165-66
    page size and orientation, 166-68
  of paragraphs, 95-96, 99-100
    indenting, 119-23, 149-51
    spacing, 108, 109-11
  of pictures, 237
  removing, 97, 101
  from ruler, 145-51
    indents, 146-47
    margins, 146
    tab stops, 147-51
  of section, 96
  section breaks, 168-73
    headers in, 171-72
    inserting, 169-70
    moving between, 170-71
    printing pages, 172-73
  with shortcut keys, 102
  sorting documents, 173-76
  of tables, 241-44
  tab stops, 114-19
    aligning text with, 114-15
    changing, 115-19
    column tabs, 118-19
    setting, 117-18
    types of, 115-16
Formatting toolbar, 4, 22
Form letters, 196

Gridlines, 240
Group icons, 2
Group windows, 2
Gutter margins, 166

Hanging indents, 119, 120-22, 150-51
Hard page breaks, 112, 113
Hard returns, 41-42, 63-64

Headers, 155-58
  in section breaks, 171-72
Heading styles, 230
Help, on-line, 26-29
Horizontal ruler, 4, 5
Horizontal scroll bars, 4, 15

Icons, 2
Indent(s), 119-23
  changing from ruler, 146-47
  types of, 119-23
    hanging indents, 119, 120-22, 150-51
    left-indent, 122-23
Insertion point, 4, 11
  moving, 15-19
Insert mode, 45-46

Justified text, 106

Keyboard
  navigating document with, 18-19
  selecting text with, 59

Labels, 203-5
Landscape orientation, 167-68
Left-aligned tab stop, 115, 116
Left aligned text, 106
Left-indents, 119, 122-23
Legal characters for filenames, 12
Letters, form, 196
Line spacing, 107-8, 109, 245
Line Spacing drop-down arrow, 108
List boxes, 9
Lists
  numbered and bulleted, 123-25
  sorting, 175-76

Macros, 208-12
  deleting, 212
  editing, 209, 211-12
  recording, 208, 210-11
  running, 209, 211
Mail merging, 189-207
  data source for, 189, 190, 194-95, 198-200, 204
  fill-in fields, 201
  form letters, 196
  of labels, 203-5
  Mail Merge Helper, 191-92
  main document for, 189, 191, 192-93, 197-98, 200, 204-5
  merge-printing, 190, 191
  previewing results, 201-2
  selecting specific records to merge, 205-7
Margins
  changing from ruler, 146
  in page setup, 165-66
Menu(s)
  changing font styles with, 105
  column formatting from, 233-34, 235
  opening documents using, 10
  tables using, 239
Merge fields, 191
Merge-printing, 190, 191
Mirror margins, 166
Mistakes, correcting, 43
Mouse
  navigating documents using, 15-18
  selecting text using, 55-58
Mouse pointer, 4, 5-6
Moving text
  with Clipboard, 59-63
  by dragging and dropping, 64-68

Navigation elements, 4
Newspaper-style columns, 233
Nonprinting characters, displaying, 46
Normal template, 7
Numbered lists, 123-25
Numbers, entering, 42
NumLock key, 42

Object linking and embedding (OLE), 45
On-line help, 26-29
Opening documents, 6-7, 10
Orientation, page, 166-68
Orphans, 112, 113
Overtype mode, 45-46
OVR indicator, 5, 6

Page breaks, 43, 111-14
    hard, 112, 113
    protecting paragraph from, 114
    soft, 111
Page numbering, 158-61
    choices in, 113
    printing, 172-73
Page setup, 165-68
    margins, 165-66
    page size and orientation, 166-68
Paragraph(s). *See also* Text
    borders and shading for, 227-29
    bulleting, 124
    copying, 63, 66
    formatting, 95-96, 99-100
        indenting, 119-23, 149-51
        spacing, 108, 109-11
    joining, 47-50
    moving, 62-63, 65-66
    numbering, 124
    protecting from page breaks, 114
    sorting, 173, 174-75
    splitting, 46-47, 48-49
Paragraph marks (), 42
    deleting, 97
    selecting, 63
Periods, spaces following, 42
Phrases, moving, 61
Pictures, inserting, 236-38
Pointer, mouse, 4, 5-6
Points, 109
Portrait orientation, 167-68
Previewing documents, 52
Printing
    colors, 228
    documents, 52-55
    merge-printing, 190, 191
    pages, 172-73

Printouts, previewing, 52
Program Manager, 2
Publishing, desktop. *See* Desktop publishing

Quicksteps boxes, 2

Records to merge, selecting, 205-7
Replacing
    formats, 153-55
    text, 21, 55, 69-70
Returns
    fixing, 63-64
    hard, 41-42, 63-64
    soft, 41-42
Reveal Styles box, 98
Right-aligned tab stop, 115, 116
Right aligned text, 106
Right indent, 119
Rows
    deleting, 243
    inserting, 242-43
    selecting, 242
Ruler, 4, 5
    displaying, 145
    formatting from, 145-51
        indents, 146-47
        margins, 146
        tab stops, 147-51
Ruler bar, columns and, 234

Sans serif fonts, 101
Saving documents, 12-15, 30
Scroll arrow, 15, 16
Scroll bars, 15, 16
Scroll box, 15, 17
Scrolling, 15-18, 43
Searching. *See also* Finding
    for help, 27
    part of a document, 68
Section breaks, 168-73
    headers in, 171-72
    inserting, 169-70
    moving between, 170-71
    printing pages, 172-73
Section formatting, 96
Selecting
    cells, rows, and columns, 242
    paragraph marks, 63
    records, 205-7
    text, 19-20, 55-59
        with Edit menu, 57
        with keyboard, 59
        with mouse, 55-58
Selection bar, 55
Serif fonts, 101

Shading, paragraph, 227-29
Shift key, 42
Snaking columns, 233
Soft page breaks, 43, 111
Soft returns, 41-42
Sorting
    documents, 173-76
    lists, 175-76
    paragraphs, 174-75
Spaces, 42
Spacing
    character, 103
    line, 107-8, 109, 245
    paragraph, 108, 109-11
Special characters, finding, 154-55
Spell-checking, 50-51
    adding words to AutoCorrect during, 214
Standard toolbar, 4, 22
Starting Word for Windows, 2-3
Status bar, 4, 5, 6
Status elements, 4
Styles, 98
    heading, 230
Symbols, 42, 136
Synonyms, 70-72

Tabbed columns, converting into tables, 240
Table of contents, 230-33
Tables, 239-45
    converting tabbed columns into, 240
    deleting, 243
    formatting and editing, 241-44
    using menu, 239
    using toolbar, 239
Table Wizard, 239
Tabs (in dialog boxes), 9
Tab stops, 114-19
    aligning text with, 114-15
    changing, 115-19, 147-51
    column tabs, 118-19
    types of, 115-16
Templates, 7, 209
Text. *See also* Document(s); Paragraph(s)
    aligning, 106-7
        spaces for, 42
        with tab stops, 114-15
    copying and moving, 59-68
        with Clipboard, 59-63
        by dragging and dropping, 64-68
    deleting, 20-21
    dragging, 57

Text. *(Continued)*
    editing, 45-50
    entering, 41-45
    finding, 154
    formatting, 23-25
    inserting, 20, 46
    keeping together, 112
    replacing, 21, 55, 69-70
    selecting, 19-20, 55-59
        with Edit menu, 57
        with keyboard, 59
        with mouse, 55-58
Text boxes, 9
Text formatting, 96-99
Thesaurus, 70-72
Tip of the Day window, 2
Title bar, 4
Toolbar(s), 4, 5, 6, 22-26
    changing font sizes from, 105
    changing font styles from, 104-5
    column formatting from, 233, 235
    Formatting, 98
    Header and Footer, 156
    Mail Merge, 196-97
    Print Preview, 52
    tables using, 239
ToolTip, 6
Typeface, 101
Typing area, 4

Undoing mistakes, 43
Up scroll arrow, 15

Vertical ruler, 4
Vertical scroll bars, 4, 15, 16
View buttons display, 4

Widows, 112, 113
Wildcards, 7
Word for Windows
    application window, 3-6
    exiting, 29-30
    starting, 2-3
Words, finding, 68
Word wrap, 41
Workplace, 3
WYSIWYG, 95

Zoom Control drop-down arrow, 25

APPENDIX

INTRODUCING WINDOWS 3.1

After completing this PicTorial, you will be able to:

▶ Start your computer system and load Windows

▶ Name and describe the parts of a window

▶ Point with the mouse

▶ Click, double-click, and drag with the mouse

▶ Minimize, maximize, and restore windows

▶ Exit Windows and turn off your equipment

The microcomputer is a versatile machine. With it you can calculate a budget for this year's educational expenses, plot a graph of the results, and, finding that you won't have enough money, write a letter to your boss asking for a raise. To perform each of these tasks on the computer, you load an *application program* specific to it. For example, WordPerfect® and Microsoft® Word are word processing application programs used to enter, edit, and format memos, letters, reports, and other documents. Excel and Lotus® 1-2-3® are spreadsheet application programs used to work with numbers and make calculations.

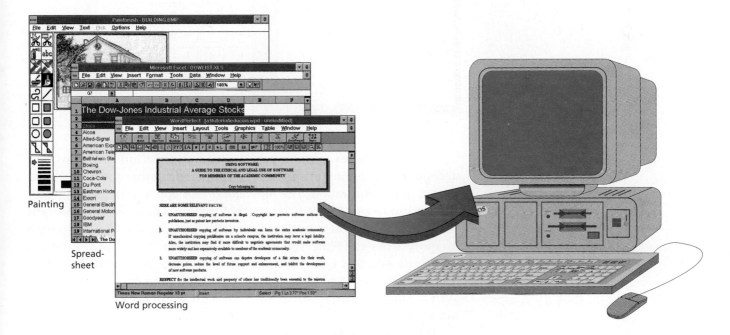

Painting

Spread-sheet

Word processing

To change from one application to another you switch from one application program to another. In this sense, the computer is like an actor, and the application programs are like scripts. When the actor changes scripts, he or she can perform a different role. By changing application programs, you can make your computer perform different applications. Being *computer literate* means that you understand how to use application programs to perform useful work.

Windows is designed to make it easy to work with application programs. Unlike earlier systems where the screen displayed just a command prompt (such as C:\>) and where you had to type all of the commands, Windows' *Graphical User Interface* (also called a GUI—pronounced "goo-ee") allows you to choose commands from pull-down menus and run more than one application program at a time, each in its own window. Using Windows you can run a spreadsheet in one window and a word processor in another. Windows also gives a common look to most programs that are developed to take advantage of its features. Standard commands are used to load programs; call up help; save, retrieve, and print files; enter and edit data; and quit applications. This makes it easier to learn new programs because many of your existing skills are transferable.

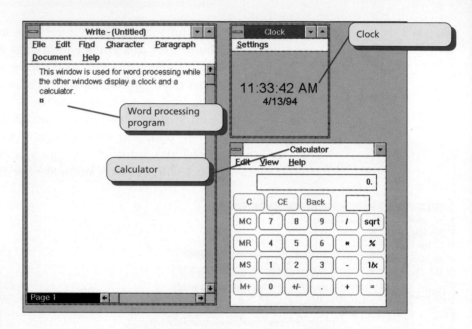

Windows comes with several built-in application programs and accessories, including a word processor, a calculator, and a clock—as shown in the illustration. The most important application program built into Windows is *Program Manager*. Program Manager is important because, unlike most other applications, it remains in the computer's memory from the time you load Windows until you quit. Program Manager's sole task is to start or *launch* all other Windows application programs such as word processors, spreadsheets, and database managers. When you exit an application that you launched from Program Manager, you always return to Program Manager.

This PicTorial gives you enough information about Program Manager to enable you to manipulate the screen and start your application programs. To learn more about Windows 3.1, you might like to read a companion volume in this series, *Windows 3.1 by PicTorial*.

A-1. LOADING WINDOWS

Before you can use Windows, you must load the computer's disk operating system, referred to as *DOS*. This is called *booting the system*. (The term *booting* comes from the expression "pulling yourself up by your bootstraps.") You boot the system by turning on your computer.

COMMON WRONG TURNS: ANXIETY

If you don't have lots of computer experience, now's the time to *relax*. New computer users often have anxieties about things that might go wrong. These fears, all of which are unjustified, include the fear they will somehow cause damage to the computer. There is nothing you can do to blow up the computer or otherwise hurt the system, so there is no reason to be anxious. Also, don't be intimidated by others who seem to grasp the procedures more quickly than you do. They may have had previous experience with computers or just have a knack at these things. These differences among users tend to level out after a few weeks when everyone feels comfortable.

TUTORIAL

1. Before you turn on your computer, check to see whether there is a disk in floppy drive A. If there is, eject it or open the drive door. (Ask how to do this if you don't know.) When you turn on a computer, it looks to the *startup drive* for the operating system files that it needs to start up. On a hard disk system like the one you are using, the startup drive is hard drive C, but the computer still looks to floppy drive A first. If there is a disk in that drive when you turn on the computer, you could have a problem loading Windows.

2. Now boot the system by turning on the computer and the display monitor. If you can't find the on/off switches, ask someone where they are.

   When you turn on the computer, it may seem to be inactive for a few moments. In fact, it is running a diagnostic program to be sure the system is operating correctly. What then happens and what you do next depends on how your system is set up. Windows may load automatically, or one of the other outcomes illustrated in the figure "Things That Can Happen When You Boot a System" may occur.

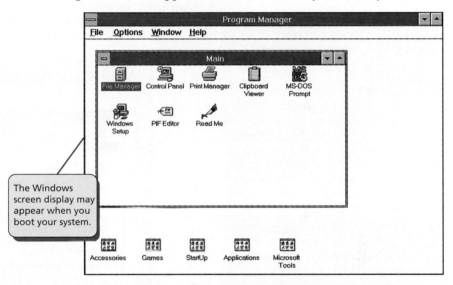

The Windows screen display may appear when you boot your system.

THINGS THAT CAN HAPPEN WHEN YOU BOOT A SYSTEM

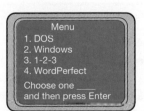

A menu designed specifically for your computer lab may appear. If it does, you can usually type a number and press Enter ⏎ to load Windows.

The screen may be blank. If it is, turn on the display monitor or adjust its brightness and contrast.

The DOS command prompt may appear. If this happens, type WIN and press Enter ⏎.

An error message may read "Non-System disk or disk error." Remove the disk in drive A and follow the instructions on the screen.

3. If Windows does not load automatically, follow the directions that apply to the result you get.

TIP: ARE WE TIMING EGGS HERE, OR WHAT?

When you first load Windows, and at other times when you are using it, an hourglass will appear on the screen. This is Windows' way of telling you it's busy and that you should wait before expecting it to do anything else.

A-2. EXPLORING THE WINDOWS SCREEN

When Windows is first installed on a computer system, it is set to open with a screen that looks like the illustration shown here. But Windows can be customized, and your screen may not look like this. To follow the discussion on the next few pages, you may need to make some adjustments in your screen. Ask someone how to do this for you, or do it yourself following the instructions in the Tip box "Setting the Windows Opening Screen."

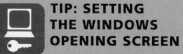

TIP: SETTING THE WINDOWS OPENING SCREEN

▶ If the area labeled "Program Manager window" in the illustration fills your whole screen, hold down [Alt] and press [Spacebar]. Release both keys and then press [R]. The Program Manager window should become smaller, revealing the area labeled "Desktop" in the illustration.

▶ If the area labeled "Main window" in the illustration does not appear on your screen, look for the word **Main** in the Program Manager window. Hold down [Ctrl] and repeatedly press [Tab] until a highlight appears over the word **Main**. Now release [Ctrl] and press [Enter]. The Main window should appear.

Now your screen should resemble the one in the illustration.

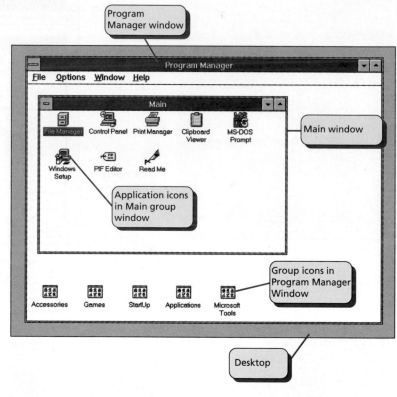

First, notice the boxlike area with a title bar at its top labeled *Program Manager*. This is a *window*. Inside this first window is another window with a title bar labeled *Main*. When working with Windows, it's common to see one window inside another.

Inside the Main window are graphical symbols called *icons*. Each icon has a descriptive label, and its design also gives you a visual clue to what it does. In fact, the term *icon* means "a picture, image, or other representation." Well-designed icons accurately represent their assigned function and are easy to remember. For example, the File Manager icon looks like a file cabinet because you use this application to manage the files on your disks.

Below the Main window are a series of small labeled boxes, also called icons. Your screen may display icons in this area that are labeled *Accessories*, *Games*, *StartUp*, and *Applications* and perhaps *Microsoft Tools*.

Notice that the windows and icons occupy only part of the screen. Around them (and beneath them) is an area called the *desktop*. This desktop is simply the space on the screen available for the display of Windows' various elements. You can add items to this electronic desktop, move items about on it, or take them away from it just as you can on the top of a real desk. In fact, some systems may display one or more icons on the desktop (and not in other windows) when you start Windows. For example, you may see an icon labeled *Vsafe Manager*. This application continually scans the system for signs of viruses that may damage data. If your desktop displays icons, you might ask what they are for.

TIP: DIFFERENT KINDS OF WINDOWS

As you work with Windows, you will find that there are different kinds of windows and icons. They all work the same, but they are referred to by different names. For example, since Program Manager is an application, its window and icon are referred to as an *application window* and an *application icon*. When Program Manager is displayed as a window, it may contain other windows that are called *group windows* because they contain groups of application icons. When you close one of these group windows to an icon, it is called a *group icon*. Group windows are simply a way to keep related application icons together so the desktop is organized.

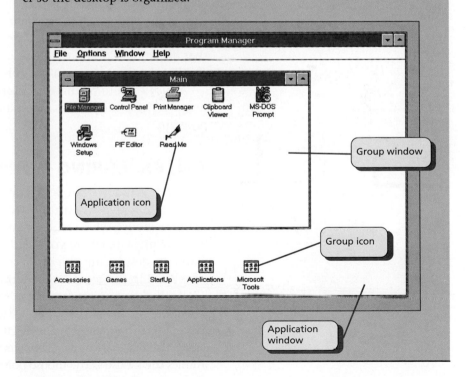

A-3. EXPLORING PROGRAM MANAGER

Windows gets its name because it displays application programs and documents in boxes called windows. All of these windows have many of the same features.

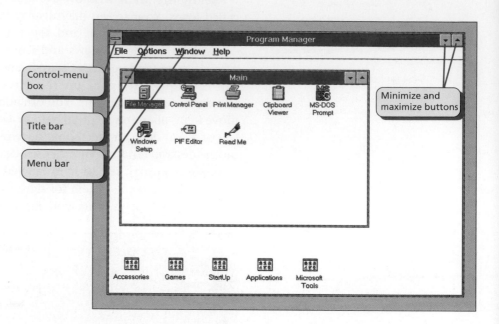

At the top of each window is a *title bar* that lists the name of the application program running in the window or otherwise describes the window's contents.

Every window displays up- and down-pointing arrowheads to the right of the title bar. These are called the Minimize ([▼]) and Maximize ([▲]) buttons. As you'll soon see, they are used to change the size of the window.

The upper-left corner of every window displays a *Control-menu box* that displays a Control menu when you click it with the mouse. We shall see that the Control-menu box can also be used to close an open window.

A *menu bar* immediately below the title bar displays the names of menus. These menus list commands that you execute to operate your program.

A-4. EXPLORING YOUR MOUSE

Although Windows can be operated from the keyboard, it is designed to be most effective when used with a pointing device such as a *mouse*. Using a mouse, you can execute commands, specify options, display help, or indicate where you want to type in data. Mice can vary considerably in design, but the most common mouse has two buttons and is connected to the computer by a thin cable.

Turn your mouse over and you may see part of a ball protruding through its bottom (not all mice use balls). Moving the mouse across the table surface makes this ball rotate and send electrical signals to the computer through the cable. These signals move the *mouse pointer* on the screen so its movement mimics the mouse's. The mouse pointer changes shape depending on what it is pointing to and what function it is ready to perform (see the upper margin

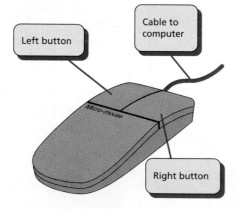

Mouse Pointer Shapes

Normal

Pointing to left or right window border

Pointing to window corner

Pointing to top or bottom window border

Rest your index finger on the left button.

Grip the sides of the mouse with your thumb and ring finger.

illustration). For example, when it is a single-headed arrow, you can click menu names, commands, icons, or buttons. When it is a two-headed arrow, you can drag a window's border to make the window wider or deeper.

TUTORIAL

1. With the mouse cable facing away from you, grip the mouse with your thumb and ring finger (see the lower margin illustration).

2. Move the mouse about the desk and watch the mouse pointer move about the screen. This is called *pointing*. If you haven't used a mouse before, you'll see that you need practice to make the mouse pointer move in a predictable fashion. If you run out of room on the desk or mouse pad when moving the mouse, lift it and place it in a new position and then continue moving it. When you lift the mouse off the desk or mouse pad, the mouse pointer remains fixed on the screen.

COMMON WRONG TURNS: MOVING THE MOUSE POINTER

When first using a mouse, most people cannot control the mouse pointer on the screen. It seems to move in unpredictable directions. To gain control, hold the mouse exactly perpendicular to the front of the screen. Now when you move it left or right, the pointer on the screen moves left or right on the screen. When you move the mouse forward or backward, the pointer moves up or down on the screen. If you hold the mouse at an angle other than perpendicular to the front of the screen, it's harder to predict the direction in which the pointer will move.

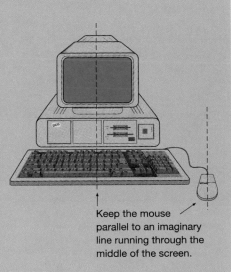

Keep the mouse parallel to an imaginary line running through the middle of the screen.

3. Point to each side of the Program Manager window, and you'll see the pointer change shape.

4. Point to each corner of the Program Manager window, and you'll see the pointer take other shapes.

PAUSING FOR PRACTICE

Moving the mouse pointer is one of the most fundamental skills you must master. Pause at this point to practice. At first, it seems hard to point to just the right place. Don't be discouraged; it just takes some practice. Pick out an object on the screen, perhaps one of the letters in an icon's title, and then quickly move the mouse pointer to it. Point to window borders and corners until you can accurately make the pointer change shape. Continue practicing until you can move it to any point you want on the first try.

A-5. CLICKING, DOUBLE-CLICKING, AND DRAGGING

Moving the mouse pointer around the screen isn't enough to operate Windows. You must also know how and when to click the mouse buttons. Depending on the situation, you either click once or you click twice in quick succession—called double-clicking. The first question a new user always asks is "When do I click and when do I double-click?" Generally, you click once to select an item and double-click to execute an action. In other words, clicking an item tells Windows you want to use it. Double-clicking starts an application or executes a command.

The Windows desktop can display more than one window at a time, and sometimes one window can hide another one. You therefore need to know how to drag a window or icon around the screen with the mouse, to reveal the window you are interested in.

> ### QUICKSTEPS: CLICKING, DOUBLE-CLICKING, AND DRAGGING
>
> ▶ *Clicking* is quickly pressing and then releasing a mouse button—usually the left one. The finger action is similar to that of typing a character on the keyboard. (Windows has a command that swaps the functions of the left and right buttons on the mouse. If you are left-handed and having trouble, ask for help.)
>
> ▶ *Double-clicking* is quickly pressing a button twice in succession. Double-clicking takes practice.
>
> ▶ *Dragging* is pointing to an object, holding down the left mouse button, and moving the mouse to position the object. When you have dragged it to where you want it, you release the mouse button. To cancel a move once you have begun it, you press ⌜Esc⌝ before releasing the mouse button.

TUTORIAL

Clicking and Double-Clicking

1. With the mouse cable facing away from you, grip the mouse with your thumb and ring finger so that your index finger rests on the left mouse button (see the upper margin illustration).

2. Look closely at the title bar labeled *Main* (the smaller of the two windows on the screen), and you'll see two arrowheads, called buttons, to the right of the title (see the lower margin illustration). The Minimize button (▾) points down and the Maximize button (▴) points up. Move the mouse until the mouse pointer is pointing to the Main window's Minimize button (▾).

3. Click (the left button) once, and the Main window changes to an icon. It now looks just like the other icons at the bottom of the Program Manager window, but it is labeled *Main* just as the window was.

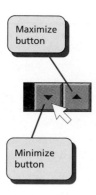

Maximize button

Minimize button

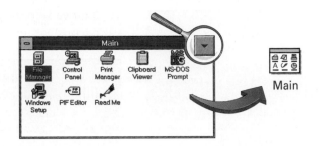

4. Double-click the Main icon to open it up into a window. (If you have problems doing this, see the box "Common Wrong Turns: Double-Clicking.")

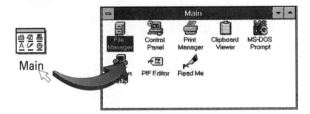

Dragging Windows and Icons

5. Point to Program Manager's title bar.

6. Hold down the left mouse button.

7. Drag the window to where you want it. As you are dragging the window, its outline is displayed.

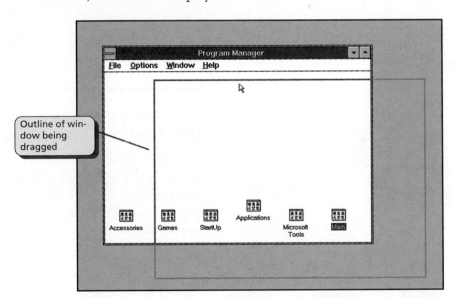

Outline of window being dragged

8. Release the left button.

9. If the Main group window is open, click its Minimize button to reduce it to an icon. Now point to the Main icon and hold down the left mouse button.

10. Drag the icon to where you want it and then release the mouse button.

11. Point to the Main icon again, hold down the left mouse button, and drag the icon to a new position but press [Esc] to cancel the

move before you release the mouse button. (This works with group icons but not with application icons.)

TIP: USING THE WINDOWS TUTORIAL TO LEARN ABOUT YOUR MOUSE

You can use Windows' built-in tutorial to learn more about using the mouse.

1. Point to the word **Help** on Program Manager's menu bar and click. A menu is pulled down.
2. Point to the **Windows Tutorial** command on the menu and click to execute the command.

This Tutorial has two lessons.

- If you want to learn how to use the mouse, or if you need to brush up on your mouse skills, type M to begin the Mouse lesson.

- If you are already a skilled mouse user, type W to begin the Windows Basics lesson.

Or, if you want to run the Tutorial at another time:

- Press the ESC key to exit the Tutorial.

Program Manager
File   Options   Window   Help

Press the ESC key to exit the Tutorial.

3. Press M to begin the mouse lesson.
4. Press Enter↵ to continue, and then follow the instructions that appear on the screen. You can press Esc at any point to end the tutorial.

A-6. MINIMIZING, MAXIMIZING, AND RESTORING WINDOWS

A window can be any one of three sizes: maximized so it fills the entire screen or the window that contains it, minimized to an icon, or restored to its original size to occupy only a part of the screen. To change sizes, you use the Maximize, Minimize, and Restore buttons located in the upper-right corner of each window (see the margin illustration).

▸ Clicking the Minimize button (▾) minimizes the window to an icon. (Double-clicking an icon opens it up into a window of the same size it was before it was minimized.)

▸ Clicking the Maximize button (▴) expands the window to fill the screen or the window that contains it. Once you have clicked the Maximize button, it is replaced by the *Restore button*, which has both an up and a down arrowhead.

▸ Clicking the Restore button (⬍) returns the window to its original size.

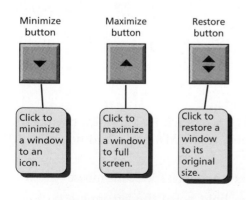

Minimize button — Click to minimize a window to an icon.

Maximize button — Click to maximize a window to full screen.

Restore button — Click to restore a window to its original size.

1. Click Program Manager's Maximize button to enlarge the window to full screen.

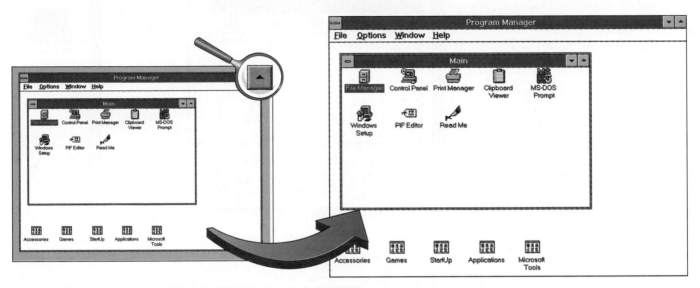

2. Click Program Manager's Restore button to restore the window to its original size.

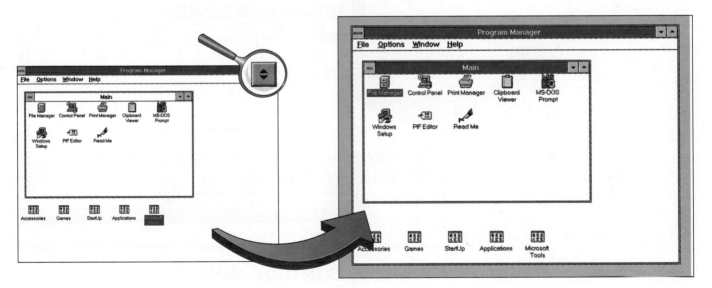

3. Click Program Manager's Minimize button to reduce the window to an icon.

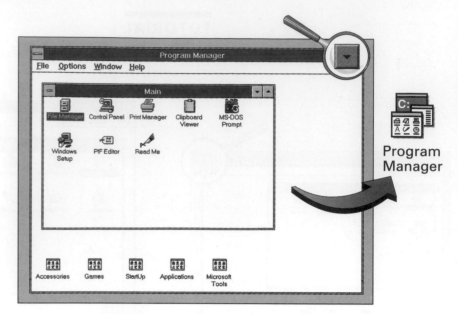

4. Double-click Program Manager's icon to open it back up into a window.

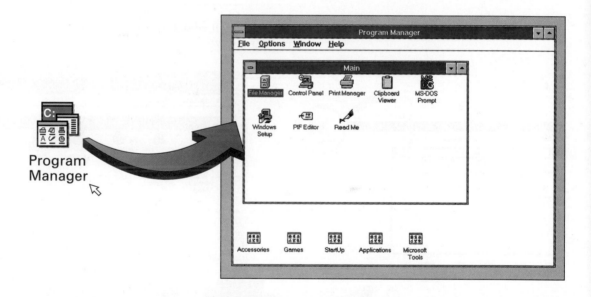

A-7. USING CONTROL MENUS

Every window has a Control-menu box in its upper-left corner. You can click this box to display a menu that performs such procedures as minimizing, maximizing, and restoring windows. (You display an icon's Control menu by clicking the icon.)

Double-clicking the Control-menu box also provides you with a shortcut to closing an open window. This procedure has different results depending on where you use it. For example, if you double-click Program Manager's Control-menu box, it ends your Windows session. If you double-click an application's Control-menu box, it closes the application. If you double-click a group window's Control-menu box, it minimizes it to an icon.

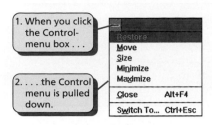

1. When you click the Control-menu box . . .

2. . . . the Control menu is pulled down.

The Control menu

TUTORIAL

1. Click Program Manager's Control-menu box located in the upper-left corner of its window to pull down the Control menu (see the upper margin illustration).

2. Click the **Minimize** command on the Control menu to reduce Program Manager to an icon.

3. Click Program Manager's icon to display its Control menu.

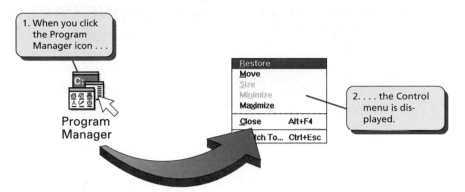

1. When you click the Program Manager icon . . .

Program Manager

2. . . . the Control menu is displayed.

4. Click the Control menu's **Restore** command to restore Program Manager to its original size.

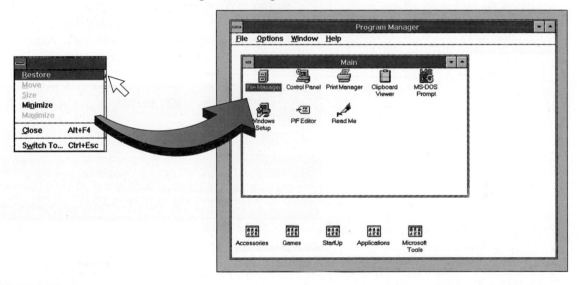

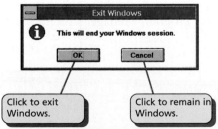

Exit Windows

This will end your Windows session.

OK   Cancel

Click to exit Windows.

Click to remain in Windows.

The Exit Windows dialog box

5. Double-click Program Manager's Control-menu box to display a dialog box warning you that this will end your Windows session (see the lower margin illustration).

6. Click the **Cancel** command button to cancel the command. If you had clicked the **OK** command button, you would have exited the Windows program.

A-8. EXITING WINDOWS

When you have finished for the day, you should always exit Windows to return to the operating system. Windows frequently creates temporary files on the disk. When you exit correctly, these files are closed and all data is stored where it should be.

After exiting Windows, always do the following:

1. Remove any disks from the floppy disk drives. This will prevent their loss, increase security, and ensure that no one mistakenly erases them. (It also prevents the disk drives' read/write heads from leaving indentations in the disks' surfaces.) Make sure you take your own disks with you.

2. Turn off the computer or use the display monitor's controls to dim the screen so that an image will not be burned into its phosphor surface. (Windows has a built-in *screen saver* that you can turn on to prevent the screen from being damaged when the computer is left on for long periods of time with Windows running, but it is not available after you have exited Windows.)

QUICKSTEPS: EXIT-ING WINDOWS
Fastest

▶ Double-click Program Manager's Control-menu box, then click the **OK** command button.

▶ Press [Alt]+[F4], then click the **OK** command button.

Menus

1. Click the **File** menu to pull it down, then click the **Exit Windows** command to display a dialog box.

2. Click the **OK** command button to exit or the **Cancel** command button to return to where you were.

TIP: EXITING WHEN YOU HAVEN'T SAVED YOUR WORK

If you try to exit Windows without first saving your work in an open application, you are prompted to save it and are offered the choices **Yes**, **No**, and **Cancel**. Click the **Yes** command button to save the file and the **No** command button to abandon it. To cancel the exit command and return to where you were, click the **Cancel** command button.

TUTORIAL

1. If Program Manager is displayed as an icon, double-click it to open it up into a window. Click **File** on Program Manager's menu bar to pull down the menu (see the margin illustration).

Point to the **File** menu name and click to pull down the menu.

File	Options	Window	H
New...			
Open	Enter		
Move...	F7		
Copy...	F8		
Delete	Del		
Properties...	Alt+Enter		
Run...			
E**x**it Windows...			

The File menu

COMMON WRONG TURNS: CLICKING COM-MANDS

Many first-time users have trouble choosing commands because they don't point to the right place before clicking. The point of the mouse pointer must be over one of the letters in the command when you click. If it is above or below a letter, even by a little bit, you may execute the wrong command or the menu may disappear.

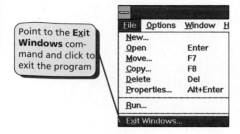

Point to the **Exit Windows** command and click to exit the program

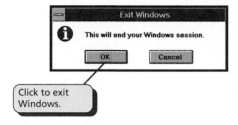

Click to exit Windows.

2. Click the **Exit Windows** command on the menu (see the top margin illustration). A dialog box appears telling you that this will end your Windows session (see the bottom margin illustration).

3. Click the **OK** command button to exit or click the **Cancel** button to return to where you were if you want to continue working.

TIP: USING THE WINDOWS TUTORIAL TO LEARN MORE ABOUT WINDOWS

You can use Windows' built-in tutorial to learn more about using Windows. You run this tutorial from Windows Program Manager.

1. Point to Program Manager's **Help** menu and click to pull down the menu.

2. Point to the **Windows Tutorial** command and click to execute the command.

3. Press W to begin the Windows Basics lesson.

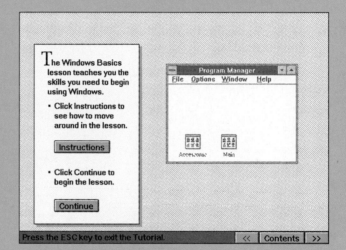

4. Follow the instructions that appear on the screen. Click the **Instructions** command button for advice on how to use the tutorial.

5. You can press Esc at any point to end the tutorial. To resume later, or to jump to another topic, click the **Contents** command button at the bottom of the screen. Then click the button in front of the topic you want to learn about.